Forgotten Books

The Writings of Samuel Adams Collected An Edited

By

Harry Alonzo Cushing

Published by Forgotten Books 2012

Originally Published 1907

PIBN 1000543683

THE WRITINGS

OF

SAMUEL ADAMS

VOLUME III.

1773–1777

THIS LETTER-PRESS EDITION

'ES HAVE BEEN PRINTED FOR SALE

No.

G. P. Putnam's S

THE WRITINGS

OF

SAMUEL ADAMS

COLLECTED AND EDITED

BY

HARRY ALONZO CUSHING

VOLUME III

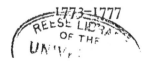
G. P. PUTNAM'S SONS

NEW YORK   LONDON

27 WEST TWENTY-THIRD STREET   24 BEDFORD STREET, STRAND

The Knickerbocker Press

1907

The Knickerbocker Press, New York

CONTENTS OF VOLUME III.

1773.

1775.

THE WRITINGS OF
SAMUEL ADAMS.

TO JAMES OTIS.

[MS., copy in Samuel Adams Papers, Lenox Library.]

BOSTON, March 19th 1773

SIR

I have the honor of joining with my brethren the Committee of Correspondence for the town in a letter to you, which the bearer of this is chargd with & will deliver to you.

The occasion is somewhat singular. Our Brother Mr William Molineux, a few days ago receiv'd an *anonymous* letter dated Barnstable &.c, in which mention is made of some rude Aspersions cast upon the characters of himself and several others of our Committee by your Representative Mr Bacon in a public meeting of your Town. As the intelligence was thus uncertain the Committee would fain hope that it was impossible for one of Mr Bacon's station in life to act so unjustifiable a part; especially after the handsome things which he had the credit of saying of every one of Committee upon a late occasion in the House of Representatives. Admitting however, that this might be the case, they thought it prudent to address you,

as the Moderator of your meeting, and it is their de
sire, if you judge there is a proper foundation for this
letter *and not otherwise*, to obtain the consent of the
Town that it should be openly read in the meeting at
the ensuing adjournment. This the Committee refer to
your known discretion, as they cannot place a full de
pendence upon an anonymous letter, although there are
some circumstances that may seem to corroborate it.

As there is no measure which tends more to discon
cert the Designs of the enemies of the public liberty,
than the raising Committees of Correspondence in
the several towns throughout the Province, it is not to
be wondered at that the whole strength of their oppo
sition is aim'd against it. Whether Mr B. is of this
character is a question in which his Constituents ought
certainly to satisfy themselves beyond a reasonable
doubt. A man's professions may be as he pleases ;
but I honestly confess I cannot easily believe him to
be a sincere friend to his Country, who can upon any
consideration be prevail'd upon to associate with so
detestable an enemy to it as I take a *Boston born* (I
cannot say educated) Commissioner of Customs to be.

I am with great regard for your family and con
nexions in B[arnstable.]

Sir your assured Friend
& most humble servant

P. S. If there is not foundation for what is asserted
in the anonymous letter, we desire that you will not
only not read our letter in your meeting but also not
let the original or a copy of it go out of your hands,
but return it by the first opportunity.

ut supra

REPORT TO THE TOWN OF BOSTON, MARCH 23, 1773.

[MS., Boston Public Library; the text, with slight variations, was printed in the *Boston Gazette*, March 29, 1773, in the *Massachusetts Spy*, March 25, 1773, and in *Boston Record Commissioner's Report*, vol. xviii., pp. 120–125.]

At a legal Meeting of the Freeholders and other Inhabitants of the Town of Boston, at Faneuil-Hall on Monday the 8th of March 1773, and continued by Adjournment to the 23d instant.

Mr. Samuel Adams acquainted the Moderator, that he was directed by a Committee (of which he was Chairman) to make a report; and the same was read as follows, viz.[1]

The Committee appointed "to consider what is proper to be done, to vindicate the Town from the gross Misrepresentations & groundless Charges in his Excellencys Message to both Houses" of the General Assembly "respecting the Proceedings of the Town at their last Meeting", beg Leave to report.

That having carefully looked over the several Speeches of the Governor of the Province, to the Council and House of Representatives, in the last Session of the General Assembly, they find that his Excellency has plainly insinuated;

First, that the said Meeting of the Town was illegal in itself.

Secondly, that the Points therein determind were such, as the Law gives the Inhabitants of Towns in their Corporate Capacity no Power to act upon; and therefore that the Proceedings of said Meeting were against Law. And,

Thirdly, that the Inhabitants thus assembled ad-

---

[1] The preceding portion is in the *Gazette*, but not in the manuscript draft.

vanced and afterwards publishd to the World, such
Principles as have a direct Tendency to alienate the
Affections of the People from their Sovereign : And
he plainly asserts, that they "denied in the most ex
press terms the Supremacy of Parliament, and invited
every other Town & District in the Province to adopt
the same Principles."

We have therefore thought it necessary to recur to
the Methods taken for calling said Meeting. And
they find that three Petitions were prefer'd to the
Select Men, signd by 198 respectable Freeholders
and Inhabitants, making Mention of a Report that
then prevaild, & which since appears to have been
well grounded, that Salaries were allowd to be paid
to the Justices of the Superior Court of the Province
by Order of the Crown ; whereby they were to be
made totally independent of the General Assembly
and absolutely dependent on the Crown ; and setting
forth their Apprehensions that such an Establishment
would give a finishing Stroke to the System of Tyr
anny already begun, and compleat the Ruin of the
Liberties of the People. And therefore earnestly re
questing the Selectmen to call a Meeting, that this
Matter might be duly considerd by the Town, and
such Measures taken as the Necessity and Importance
thereof required. Whereupon the Selectmen issued
a Warrant for calling a Meeting accordingly. All
which was strictly agreable to the Laws of this Prov
ince, and the Practice of this and other Towns from
the earliest times.

By an Act of this Province made in the fourth year
of William & Mary it is enacted, that "when and so

often as there shall be Occasion of a Town Meeting for any Business of publick Concernment to the Town there to be done, the Constable or Constables of such Town, by Order of the Selectmen or major Part of them, or of the Town Clerk by their Order in each respective Town within this Province shall warn a Meeting of such Town" &c.[1] And by another Act made in the 2 Geo. I. it is enacted that "When and so often as ten or more of the Freeholders of any Town shall signify under their hands to the Selectmen their desire to have any Matter or thing inserted into a Warrant for calling a Town Meeting, the Selectmen are hereby required to insert the same in the next Warrant they shall issue for the Calling a Town Meeting."[2]

But were there no such Laws of the Province or should our Enemies pervert these & other Laws made for the same Purpose, from their plain and obvious Intent and Meaning, still there is the great and perpetual Law of Self preservation to which every natural Person or corporate Body hath an inherent Right to recur. This being the Law of the Creator, no human Law can be of force against it : And indeed it is an Absurdity to suppose that any such Law could be made by Common Consent, which alone gives validity to human Laws. If then the "*Matter or Thing*" viz the fixing Salaries to the Offices of the Judges of the Superior Court as aforesaid, was such as threatned the Lives, Liberties and Properties of the People, which we have the Authority of the greatest Assembly

---

[1] *Acts and Resolves of the Province of Massachusetts Bay*, vol. i., pp. 64, 68.
[2] *Ibid.*, vol. ii., p. 30.

of the Province to affirm, The Inhabitants of this
or any other Town had certainly an uncontrovertable
right to meet together, either in the Manner the Law
has prescribed, or in any other orderly Manner, joyntly
to consult the necessary Means of their own Preserva
tion and Safety. The Petitioners wisely chose the
Rule of the province Law, by applying to the Select
men for a Meeting ; and they, as it was their Duty to
do, followed the same Rule and called a Meeting
accordingly. We are therefore not a little surprizd,
that his Excellency, speaking of this and other prin
cipal Towns, should descend to such an artful Use of
Words, that a "*Number* of Inhabitants have assembled
together, and having *assumed* the Name of legal
Town Meetings" &c. Thereby appearing to have a
Design to lead an inattentive Reader to believe, that
no Regard was had to the Laws of the Province in
calling these Meetings, and consequently to consider
them as illegal & disorderly.

The Inhabitants being met, and for the Purpose
aforesaid, the Points determind, his Excellency says,
"were such as the Law gives the Inhabitants of Towns
in their *corporate* Capacity no Power to act upon."
It would be a sufficient Justification of the Town to
say, that no Law *forbids* the Inhabitants of Towns in
their corporate Capacity to determine such Points as
were then determined. And if there was no positive
legal Restraint upon their Conduct, it was doing them
an essential injury, to represent it to the World as
illegal. Where the Law makes no special Provision
for the common Safety, the People have a Right to
consult their own Preservation ; and the necessary

Means to withstand a most dangerous attack of arbitrary Power.[1]   At such a time, it is but a pitiful Objection to their thus doing, that the Law has not expressly given them a Power to act upon such Points. This is the very language of Tyranny: And when such Objections are offerd, to prevent the Peoples meeting together in a Time of publick Danger, it affords of it self just Grounds of Jealousy that a Plan is laid for their Slavery.

The Town enterd upon an Inquiry into the Grounds of a Report, in which the common Safety was very greatly interested.   They made their Application to the Governor, a fellow Citizen as well as the first Magistrate of the Province; but they were informd by his Excellency, that "it was by no means proper for him" "to acquaint them whether he had or had not receivd any Advices relating to the publick Affairs of the Government of the Province."   Their next Determination was, to petition the Governor, that the General Assembly might be allowd to meet at the time to which it then stood prorogud: But his Excellency refused to grant this Request, lest it should be "encouraging the Inhabitants of other Towns to assemble" "to consider of the Necessity or Expediency of a Session of the General Assembly."   Hitherto the Town had determind upon no Point but only that of petitioning the Governor.   And will his Excellency or any one else affirm, that the Inhabitants of this or any other Town, have not a Right in their corporate Capacity to petition for a Session of the General As-

---

[1] At this point the draft originally included the words: "when they see it approaching them with hasty Strides."

sembly, merely because the Law of this Province, that authorizes Towns to assemble, does not expressly make that the Business of a Town Meeting? It is the Declaration of the Bill of Rights, founded in[1] Reason, that it is the Right of the Subjects to petition the King: But it is apparent in his Excellencys Answer, that the Inhabitants of this Town were in Effect, denied, in one Instance at least, the Right of petitioning his Majestys Representative. Which was the more grievous to them, because the Prayer of their Petition was nothing more, than that the General Assembly might have the Opportunity of enquiring of the Governor into the Grounds of the Report of an intollerable Grievance, which his Excellency had before strongly intimated to them, it was not in his Power to inform *them* of, "consistent with Fidelity to the Trust which his Majesty had reposed in him."

We have been the more particular in reciting the Transactions of that Meeting thus far, in order that the Propriety and Necessity of the further proceedings of the same Meeting may appear in a true Point of Light.

His Excellency having thus frownd upon the reasonable Petitions of the Town; And they, having the strongest Apprehensions, that in Addition to, or rather in Consequence of other Grievances not redressd, a mortal Wound would very soon be given to the civil Constitution of the province; and no Assurance of the timely Interposition of the General Assembly, to whose Wisdom they were earnestly sollicitous to refer the whole Matter, The Town thought it ex-

---

[1] At this point the draft originally included the words: "Nature and."

pedient to state as far as they were able the Rights of
the Colonists & of this Province; to enumerate the
Infringements on those Rights, & in a circular Letter
to each of the Towns & Districts in the province, to
submit the same to their Consideration : That the
Subject might be weighd as its Importance required,
& the collected Wisdom of the whole people as far as
possible obtaind.   At the same [time], *not* "calling
upon" those Towns & Districts "to adopt their Prin
ciples" as his Excellency in one of his Speeches
affirms, but only informing them that "a free Com
munication of *their* Sentiments to this Town of our
common Danger was earnestly sollicited & would be
gratefully receivd.   We may justly affirm that the
Town had a Right at that Meeting, to communicate
their Sentiments of Matters which so nearly concernd
the publick Liberty & consequently their own Preser
vation.   They were matters of "publick Concernment" to this & every other Town & even Individual
in the province.   Any Attempt therefore to obstruct
the Channel of publick Intelligence in this way, argues
in our opinion, a Design to keep the people in Ignor
ance of their Danger that they may be the more
easily & speedily enslaved.   It is notorious to all the
World, that the Liberties of this Continent & espe
cially of this province, have been systematically &
successfully invaded from Step to Step; Is it not
then, to say the least justifiable, in any Town as *part
of the great whole*, when the last Effort of Tyranny is
about to be made, to spread the earliest Notice of it
far & wide, & hold up the *iniquitous System* in full
View.   It is a great Satisfaction to us, that so many

of the respectable Towns in the province, and we may
add Gentlemen of figure in other Colonies, have expressd, & continue to express themselves much pleasd
with the Measure ; and we encourage ourselves from
the *manifest Discovery* of an Union of Sentiments in
this province, which has been one happy fruit of the
Measure, there will be the united Efforts of *the whole*
in all constitutional & proper Methods to prevent the
entire ruin of our Liberties.

His Excellency is pleasd to say in one of his
Speeches, that the Town have " denied in the most
express Terms the Supremacy of Parliament." It
is fortunate for the town that they made Choice of
the very Mode of Expression, which the present
House of Representatives in their Wisdom made use
of in stating the Matter of Controversy between the
Governor & them : And after what they have ad
vanced upon the Subject, it appears to us impossible
to be shown that the Parliament of Great Britain can
exercise " the Powers of Legislation for the Colonists
in all Cases whatever " consistently with the Rights
which belong to the Colonists as Men as Christians
& as Subjects, or without destroying the foundation
of their own Constitution.—If the Assertion that the
Parliament hath no right to exercise a Power in cases
where it is plain they have no right, hath a direct
Tendency to alienate the Affections of the People
from their Sovereign, because He is a constituent
part of that parliament, as seems to be his Excellencys Manner of reasoning, it follows as we conceive,
that there must never be a complaint of any assump
tion of power in the Parliam', or petition for the repeal

of any Law made repugnant to the Constitution, lest
it should tend to alienate the Affections of the people
from their Sovereign ; but we have a better Opinion
of our fellow Subjects than to concede to such Con
clusions.   We are assured they can clearly see, that a
Mistake in Principle may consist with Integrity of
Heart ; And for our parts we shall ever be inclined to
attribute the Grievances of various Kinds which his
Majestys American Subjects have so long sufferd, to
the Weakness or Wickedness of his Ministers & Ser
vants, and not to any Disposition in *Him* to injure
them.   And we yet perswade our selves that could
the Petitions of his much aggrievd Subjects be trans
mitted to his Majesty thro the Hands of an honest
impartial Minister, we should not fail of ample redress.

His Excellencys Argument seems to us to be rather
straind, when he is attempting to show, that we have
"invited every other Town & District to adopt our
Principles". It is this. The Town says If it should be
the general Voice of the Province that the Rights as
stated do not belong [to] them, trusting however that
this cannot be the Case, they shall lament the Ex
tinction of Ardor for civil & religious Liberty ; *There
fore* says his Excellency The Town invited them to
adopt their principles.   Could it possibly be supposd
that when his Excy had declared to the whole Pro
vince that we had invited every other Town and Dis
trict in the province to adopt the same Principles he
intended to avail himself of such an Explanation !
Much the same Way of reasoning follows, (though it
would not be to the Reputation of the other Towns
if it should have any Weight).   That because *their*

consequent Doings were similar to those of this Town *therefore* they understood that they were in vited to *adopt* the same Principles, & therefore they were thus invited to adopt them.

Upon the whole, There can be no room to doubt but that every Town which has thought it expedient to correspond with this on the Occasion have acted their own Judgment & expressd their own principles : It is an unspeakeable Satisfaction to us that their Sentiments so nearly accord with ours, and it adds a Dignity to our Proceedings, that when the House of Representatives were called upon by the Governor to bear their Testimony against them, as " of a dan gerous Nature & Tendency," they saw reason to de clare that " they had not discoverd that the Principles advanced by the Town of Boston were unwarrantable by the Constitution."[1]

The foregoing Report was accepted in the Meet ing, Nemine Contradicente, and ordered to be re corded in the Town's Book, as the Sense of the Inhabitants of this Town.

It was also Voted, That said Report be printed in the several News-Papers, and that the Committee of Correspondence be directed to transmit a printed Copy thereof to such Towns and Districts as they have or may correspond with.

Attest.   WILLIAM COOPER, Town-Clerk.

---

[1] The following portion, from the *Gazette*, is not in the autograph draft by Adams.

TO JOHN DICKINSON.

[MS., Samuel Adams Papers, Lenox Library.]

BOSTON March 27 1773.

SIR,

I take the Liberty of inclosing an Oration deliv ered by D[r] Benjamin Church on the Anniversary of the 5th of March 1770, which I beg the favor of you to accept.

The Proceedings of our General Assembly at their last Session, you may perhaps have seen in the News papers. Our Governor in a manner forcd the Assembly to express their Sentiments of so delicate though important a Subject as the supreme Authority of the Parliament of Great Britain over the Colonies. The Silence of the other Assemblies of late upon every Subject that concerns the joynt Interest of the Colonies, renderd it somewhat difficult to determine what to say with Propriety. As the Sense of the Colonies might possibly be drawn from what might be advanced by this Province, you will easily conceive, that the Assembly would rather have chosen to have been silent till the Sentiments of at least Gentlemen of Eminence out of this province could be known ; at the same time that Silence would have been construed as the Acknowledgment of the Governor's Principles and a Submission to the fatal Effects of them. What will be the Consequence of this Controversy. Time must determine. If the Governor enterd into it of his own Motion, as I am apt to believe he did, he may not have the Approbation of the Ministry for counteracting what appears to me to have been for two years past their favorite Design, to keep the

Americans quiet & lull them into Security.   Could
your Health or Leisure admit of it, a publication of
your Sentiments on this & other Matters of the most
interresting Importance would be of substantial Ad
vantage to your Country.   Your Candor will excuse
the freedom I take in this repeated Request.   An
Individual has some Right, in behalf of the publick,
still to urge the Assistance of those who have hereto
fore approvd themselves its ablest advocates.

   I shall take it as a favor if you will present the
other inclosed Oration to Mr Reed, whom I once had
the pleasure of conversing with in this place, & to
whom I would have wrote by this unexpected Oppor
tunity, but am prevented by the Hurry of the Bearer.
             I am Sir with sincere Regards
                   Your most humble serv^t

M^r J[osiah] Q[uincy] a young Gent^l but eminent
here in the profession of the law is soon expected to
arrive at Philadelphia from South Carolina.   Could
he be introducd into the Company of Mr Dickinson
& Mr Reed he would esteem himself honord and his
Conversation m^t not be unentertaining even to them.

THE COMMITTEE OF CORRESPONDENCE OF BOSTON TO THE COMMITTEE OF CORRESPONDENCE OF LITTLETON.[1]

[MS., Committee of Correspondence Papers, Lenox Library.]

                                   BOSTON March 31 1773

GENTLEMEN

   The Committee of Correspondence of the Town
of Boston gratefully acknowledge your Letter of the

---

[1] Addressed "To Deacon Oliver Hoar Cap Jonathan Reed & Mr Aaron
Savit a Com^e of Correspondence of the Town of Littleton."

2 Instant accompanied with the declared Sentiments of the Town of Littleton at a legal meeting on the first of February.

The Sense which that Town has expressd of the Excellency of the British Constitution of Govern ment, which appears eminently to have its founda tion in nature, and of the Rights which are secured to the Inhabitants of this province by the Charter, is an evident token of their readiness "always to joyn in every regular & constitutional method to preserve the common Liberty."

We are perswaded that the Town whom we have the Honor to serve, although calumniated by the virulent Enemies of the province and of America, have nothing in view but to assist in "endeavoring to preserve our happy civil Constitution free from Innovation & maintain it inviolate" and we esteem our selves happy that the Town has receivd the Ap probation of so many of their respectable Brethren in the Country, & particularly the Inhabitants of Littleton. The agreable manner in which you have communicated to us their Sentiments lays [us] under great obligation. We heartily joyn with you in wishing that Peace & Unity may be established in America, upon the permanent Foundations of Liberty & Truth.

THE COMMITTEE OF CORRESPONDENCE OF BOSTON TO NATHAN SPARHAWK.[1]

[MS., Committee of Correspondence Papers, Lenox Library.]

BOSTON March 31 1773

SIR

Your attested Copy of the proceedings of Rutland District has been receivd and read by the Com⁰ of Correspondence for the Town of Boston. It affords us an unspeakeable Satisfaction to find so great a Number of the Towns & Districts in the province ex pressing a just Resentment at the repeated Attacks that have been made on the publick Liberty by a corrupt Administration and their wretched Tools & Dependents. Your District, in the Opinion of this Committee has very justly held up the publick Griev ances of America in one short but full View; first the power assumed by the British parliament (in which we cannot be represented) to tax us at pleas ure; and then their appropriating such taxes, to ren der the executive power of the province independent of the Legislative, or more properly speaking abso lutely dependent on the Crown. It was impossible for the Conspirators against our invalueable Rights, with all their Art & Assiduity, to prevent our sensible Brethren in the Country from seeing the fatal Ten dency of so dangerous an Innovation: And in a Virtuous Country it requires only a Sight of such daring Incroachments, to produce a manly & effectual Opposition to them. We applaud the patriotick De termination of the District of Rutland "that it is of the utmost Importance that the Inhabitants of this

---

[1] Clerk of the District of Rutland, Worcester County.

province stand firm as one man to support & maintain all their just Rights & Privileges." Such a resolution when general among the people can seldom
fail to reduce the most haughty Invaders of the com
mon Rights to a Submission to Reason.

THE COMMITTEE OF CORRESPONDENCE OF BOSTON TO
THOMAS MIGHILL.[1]

[MS., Committee of Correspondence Papers, Lenox Library.]

BOSTON April 7 1773

SIR

We the Committee of Correspondence for the
Town of Boston, acknowledge the very obliging
Letter to said town, signd by yourself & transmitted
to us by order of the Town of Rowley.

It gives us great pleasure to find that the proceed
ings of the Town we have the Honor to serve, have
been so acceptable to our worthy & much esteemed
Brethren of Rowley. This cannot fail to animate the
Metropolis in every laudable Exertion for the com
mon Cause of Liberty. The ardent Zeal of your
Town for that all interresting Cause, expressd in their
Letter and their judicious Instructions to their Rep
resentative which accompany it, afford us a very strong
Assurance of the high Esteem they have of our
invalueable Rights & their deep Sense of the Griev
ances we labour under. We joyn with them in sup
plicating Almighty God for his Direction Assistance

[1] Addressed as " late Moderator of a Meeting of the Freeholders & other In
habitants of the Town of Rowley held by Adjournment the third of February
1773."

& Blessing in every laudable Effort that may be made for the securing to our Selves & posterity the free & full Enjoyment of those precious Rights & privileges for which our renowned forefathers expended so much Treasure & Blood.

TO ARTHUR LEE.

[MS., Samuel Adams Papers, Lenox Library ; a text with modifications is in R. H. Lee, *Life of Arthur Lee*, vol. ii., pp. 197-203 ; printed also in the *Boston Gazette*, May 23, 1774.]

BOSTON 9 April 1773.

MY DEAR SIR

I must by no means omit to request you to present my most respectful Complim^ts to the Society of the Bill of Rights and return them my hearty Thanks for the great Honor they have done me in admitting me one of their Members. The Gentlemen may be assured that this unexpected mark of their Respect adds to the Obligation which I have ever held myself under, to employ the small Share of Ability which God has given me, in vindicating the Rights of my Country & of Mankind.

I can now assure you, that the Efforts of this Town at their Meeting in November last, have had Effects which are extremely mortifying to our petty Tyrants. Every Art & every Instrument was made use of to prevent the Meetings of the Towns in the Country but to no purpose. It is no Wonder that a Measure calculated to promote a Correspondence and a free Communication among the people, should awaken Apprehensions ; for they well know that it must de-

tect their Falshood in asserting that the people of this
Country were satisfied with the Measures of the
British parliament and the Administration of Govern
ment. ⁄Our Governor has in my Opinion merited
greatly of the Ministry by his constant Endeavors,
though in vain, to sooth & quiet the people & perswade them to think there were no Grievances that
might "be seen felt or understood.'⁄ And when the
House of Representatives in the last May Session, by
almost a unanimous Vote remonstrated against his
Independency, he, without the least Foundation in
Truth, & for no other Reason that I can conceive
but to give Countenance to his Patron Hillsborough,
or to establish himself in his Governm' which he
rec^d with so great *Reluctance*, did not scruple in his
Speech at the Close of that Session, to insinuate that
the House was under the Influence of a few factious
members. No Speech of Bernards ever gave greater
Disgust to the People, nor with more reason. ⁄

There has been another Session of the Genl As
sembly, wch began unexpectedly on the 6th of Jan^y
last. It is my Opinion that it would have been post
poned, as usual of late, till near the Close of our
political Year, had it not been for the Boston Town
Meeting ; I mean to prevent the designd Effects of
it, by giving an occasion to the small Jobbers in the
Country to say, that "however expedient it might
have been for them to have had their meetings be
fore, it now becomes unnecessary & improper since
their representatives are soon to meet in Genl As
sembly." This had an Influence in some Towns ; and
his *Excellency*, I suppose judgd it more probable that

he should be able to mannage the Members of the House and prevail upon them "to joyn with him in bearing Testimony against the *unwarrantable* Pro ceedings of Boston," if they came together without having the explicit Sentiments of their Constituents.

At the Meeting of the Assembly, he thought proper to open a Controversy with the two Houses, for which I think Hillsbro would not thank him; for he has thereby defeated the favorite Design of the Ministry, which was to lull the people into Security, and for the effecting of which Design, he had before thought himself, or endeavord to make Administration believe he was entitled to so great a Share of Merit. It has been publishd in most of the Newspapers in the Con tinent & engages much of the Attention of the other Colonies. This, together with ye proceedings of a *contemptible* Town meeting, has awakned the Jeal ousy of all, & has particularly raised ye Spirit of the most ancient & patriotick Colony of Virginia. Their manly Resolves have been transmitted to the Speaker of the House of Representatives in a printed Sheet of their Journals; and our Com^e of Correspondence have circulated Copies of them into every Town & District through the Province.[1]

I wish I could hear more of Lord D. to qualify him for his high office, than merely that he is a *good* Man. Goodness I confess is an essential, tho too rare a Qualification of a Minister of State. Possibly I may not have been informd of the whole of his Lordships Character. Without a Greatness of Mind

---

[1] An original print of this circular letter, dated April 9, 1773, is in the Lenox Library.

adequate to the Importance of his Station, I fear he
may find himself embarrassd with his present Con
nections. It can easily be conceivd what principle
induced Lord North to recommend to that Depart
ment a Nobleman characterizd in America for Piety;
but what could prevail on his Lordship to joyn with
such Connections, unless he had a Consciousness that
his own Abilities were sufficient to defeat the plans
of a corrupt Administration, I am not able to con
ceive. It might be well for his Lordship to be assured, that there is now a fairer prospect than ever of
an Union among the Colonies, which his predecessor
did & had reason to dread, tho he affected to de
spise it. Should the Correspondence proposd by Vir
ginia produce a Congress ; and that an *Assembly of
States*, it would require the Head of a very able
Minister to treat with so respectable a Body. This
perhaps is a mere fiction in the Mind of a political
Enthusiast. Ministers of State are not to be disturbd with Dreams.

I must now acknowledge your agreeable Letter of
the 24 of Dec^r.[1] I cannot wonder that you almost
despair of the British Nation. Can that people be
saved from Ruin, who carry their Liberties to market
& sell them to the highest Bidder ? But America.
" shall rise full plumed and glorious from her Mothers\
Ashes."

Our House of Representatives have sent a Letter
to Lord Dartmouth. This must without Question
be a wise measure, though I must own I was not
in it. I feard it would lead the people to a false

---

[1] R. H. Lee, *Life of Arthur Lee*, vol. i., pp. 224–226.

Dependence; I mean upon a Minister of State, when it ought to be placed, with Gods Assistance, upon *them selves*. You cannot better prepare him for the rep resentations of the House, than as you propose, by giving him a proper Idea of Hutchinson. I am much obligd to you for your Intention to hold up to the publick the Generosity of my esteemed friend Mr. Otis. I wish I could assure you that he is perfectly recoverd.

April 12.

This day I have the pleasure of receiving yours of the 25 of Jan^y.[1] Your putting me in mind of the Honor done me by the Society of the Bill of Rights is very kind. I ought sooner to have acknowledgd it. My omitting it was owing to being in a Hurry when I last wrote to you. I am sensible I am not one of the most regular Correspondents; perhaps not so as I should be. I duly rec^d tho I think not by Mr Storey, the Letter which inclosed the Answer to the Resolution of the Govr & Council against Junius Americanus, which I immediately publishd in the Boston Gazette. It was read with great Satisfaction by Men of Sense & Virtue. I am heartily glad to find that the proceedings of this Town are so pleas-ing to you. I have heard that Ld Dartmouth rec^d one of our pamphlets with Coolness & expressd his Concern that the Town had come into such Measures. His Lordship probably will be much surprizd to find a very great Number of the Towns in this province (& the Number is daily increasing) concurring fully in Sentiments with this Metropolis; expressing Loy-

---

[1] R. H. Lee, *Life of Arthur Lee*, vol. i., pp. 226–228.

alty to the King & Affection to the Mother Country
but at the same time a firm Resolution to maintain
their constitutional Rights & Liberties.   I send you
the proceedings of one town, which if you think
proper you may publish as a Specimen of the whole,
for the Inspection of an Administration either misinformd & credulous to the greatest Degree of human
Weakness, or Obstinate in wilfull Error.   They have
lately employd Eight Regiments of British Troops to
bring an handful of unfortunate Carribs to a Treaty
dishonorable to the Nation.   How many Regiments
will be thought necessary to penetrate the Heart of a
populous Country & subdue a sensible enlightned &
brave people to the ignominious Terms of Slavery?
Or will his Lordships superior Wisdom direct to more
salutary Measures, and by establishing Freedom in
every part of the Kings extensive Dominions, restore
that mutual Harmony & Affection which alone is
wanting to build up the greatest Empire the World
has ever yet seen.

Mr. Wilkes was certainly misinformd when he was
told that Mr H. had deserted the Cause of Liberty.
Great pains had been taken to have it thought to
be so ; and by a scurvy Trick of lying the Adversaries
effected a Coolness between that Gent^n & some others
who were zealous in that Cause.   But it was of short
Continuance, for their falshood was soon detected.
Lord Hillsbro I suppose was early informd of this
imaginary Conquest ; for I have it upon such Grounds
as I can rely upon, that he wrote to the Govr telling
him that he had it in Command from the *highest Au
thority* to enjoyn him to promote Mr H. upon every

Occasion. Accordingly, tho he had been before frownd upon & often negativd both by Bernard & Hutchinson the latter, who can smile sweetly even upon the Man he hates, when he is instructed or it is his Interest so to do, fawnd & flatterd one of the *Heads of the faction*, & at length approvd of him when he was elected a Councellor last May. To palliate this inconsistent Conduct it was previously given out that M^r H had deserted the faction, & became as they term each other, a Friend to Governm^t. But he had Spirit enough to refuse a Seat at the Board, & continue a Member of the House, where he has in every Instance joyned with the friends of the Constitution in Opposition to the Measures of a Corrupt Administration ; & in particular no one has discoverd more firmness against the Independency of the Govr & the Judges than he.

I have mentiond to Mr Cushing the Hint in your last concerning his not answering your Letter. I believe he will write you soon. The Gratitude of the friends to Liberty towards Mr Otis for his eminent Services in times past induces them to take all Occasions to show him Respect. I am much obligd to you for the friendship you have discoverd for him, in holding up to the View of the Publick his Generosity to Robinson.

Your Brother in Virginia has lately honord me with a Letter ; & I intend to Cultivate a Correspondence with him, which I am sure will be much to my Advantage.

As you have confided in me to recommend one or more Gentlemen of this place as Candidates for the Society of the Bill of Rights, I can with the greatest

Integrity nominate my two worthy & intimate Friends
J Adams & J Warren Esq^{rs} ; the one eminent in the
profession of the Law & the other equally so in that of
physick.   Both of them men of an unblemishd moral
Character & Zealous Advocates for the Common
Rights of Mankind.

TO RICHARD HENRY LEE.

[MS., American Philosophical Society; a text is in R. H. Lee, *Life of
Richard Henry Lee*, vol. i., pp. 88–90, and a draft is in the Samuel Adams
Papers, Lenox Library.]

BOSTON April 10 1773

SIR—·

Your Letter to me of the 4th Feb last, I receivd
with singular Pleasure ; not only because I had long
wishd for a Correspondence with some Gentleman in
Virginia, but more particularly because I had fre
quently heard of your Character and Merit, as a
warm Advocate for Virtue and Liberty.

I have often thought it a Misfortune, or rather
a Fault in the Friends of American Independence
and Freedom, their not taking Care to open every
Channel of Communication.   The Colonies are all
embarkd in the same bottom.   The Liberties of all
are alike invaded by the same haughty Power : The
Conspirators against their common Rights have in
deed exerted their brutal Force, or applied their insid
ious Arts, differently in the several Colonies, as they
thought would best serve their Purpose of Oppres
sion and Tyranny.   How necessary then is it ; that
All should be early acquainted with the particular

Circumstances of *Each*, in Order that the Wisdom &
Strength of the whole may be employd upon every
proper Occasion.   We have heard of Bloodshed &
even civil War in our Sister Colony North Carolina ;
And how strange is it, that the best Intelligence we
have had of that tragical Scene, has been brought to
us from England !

This Province, and this Town especially, have sufferd a great Share of Ministerial Wrath and Inso
lence : But God be thanked, there is, I trust, a Spirit
prevailing, which will never submit to Slavery: The
Compliance of New York in making annual Pro
vision for a military Force designed to carry Acts of
Tyranny into Execution :   The Timidity of some
Colonies and the Silence of others is discouraging :
But the active Vigilance, the manly Generosity and
the Steady Perseverance of Virginia and South Caro
lina, gives us Reason to hope, that the Fire of true
Patriotism will at length spread throughout the Con
tinent ; the Consequence of which must be the Acqui
sition of all we wish for.

The Friends of Liberty in this Town have lately
made a successful Attempt to obtain the explicit po
litical Sentiments of a great Number of the Towns in
this Province ; and the Number is daily increasing.
The very Attempt was alarming to the Adversaries ;
and the happy Effects of it are mortifying to them.
I would propose it for your Consideration, Whether
the Establishment of Committees of Correspondence
among the several Towns in every Colony, would
not tend to promote that General Union, upon which
the Security of the whole depends.

The Reception of the truly patriotick Resolves of the House of Burgesses of Virginia gladdens the Hearts of all who are Friends to Liberty. Our Committee of Correspondence had a special Meeting upon this Occasion, and determined immediately to circulate printed Copies in every Town in this Prov ince, in order to make them as extensively useful as possible. I am desired by them to assure you of their Veneration for your most ancient Colony, and their unfeigned Esteem for the Gentlemen of your Committee. This indeed is a small Return ; I hope you will have the hearty Concurence of every Assem bly on the Continent. It is a Measure that I think must be attended with great and good Consequences.

Our General Assembly is dissolved ; and Writs will soon be issued according to the Charter for a new Assembly to be held on the last Wednesday in May next. I think I may almost assure you that there will be a Return of such Members as will heart ily cooperate with you in your spirited Measures.

The most enormous Stride in erecting what may properly be called a Court of Inquisition in America, is sufficient to excite Indignation even in the Breast the least capable of feeling. I am expecting an au thentick Copy of that Commission, which I shall send to you by the first opportunity after I shall have re ceivd it. The Letter from the new Secretary of State to the Governor of Rhode Island, which possi bly you may have seen in the News papers, may be depended upon as genuine. I receivd it from a Gen- tleman of the Council in that Colony, who took it from the Original. I wish the Assembly of that little

Colony had acted with more firmness than they have done ; but as the Court of Enquiry is adjournd, they may possibly have another Tryal.

I have a thousand things to say to you, but am prevented by Want of Time ; having had but an hours Notice of this Vessels sailing. I cannot how ever conclude without assuring you, that a Letter from you as often as your Leisure will permit of it, will lay me under great Obligations.—

I am in strict Truth

Sir

Your most humble serv^t

ARTICLE SIGNED "CANDIDUS."

[*Boston Gazette*, April 12, 1773.]

Messieurs EDES & GILL,

PERHAPS no measure that has been taken by the Town of Boston during our present Struggles for Liberty, has thwarted the designs of our enemies more than their Votes and Proceedings on the 20th of November last.[1] If we take a Retrospect of two or three Years past, we shall find that what our "*pre tended* patriots*", as they were stiled in the Court Gazette, so zealously forewarn'd us of, has since turn'd out to be a Fact ; that every art would be made use of to lull the people of this Province and Continent into Security, in order that the Conspirators against our Rights and Liberties might carry on their Schemes and compleat their system of Tyranny with-

---

[1] Volume II., page 350.

out Opposition or Molestation.   The first part of
their plan, they imagin'd they had finish'd ; that is,
the Establishment of a Revenue : And though this
was far from being sufficient to answer their whole
purpose, they thought that if they could put the
people to sleep, they might the more easily add to
this revenue, at some future time, and plead the
present submission for a precedent.   They therefore
began upon the second and equally important part of
their plan, which was to appropriate the revenue they
had rais'd, to set up an Executive, absolutely inde
pendent of the legislative, which is to say the least,
the nearest approach to absolute Tyranny.

The Governor, who was the first American *Pen
sioner*, had now an exhorbitant Salary allowed him
out of the monies extorted from the people : And
although this was directly repugnant to the obvious
meaning, if not the very letter of the Charter, much
was said by *Chronus* and the Tribe of ministerial
Writers in Mr. *Draper's* paper, to reconcile it to the
people.   But the people, whom they generally in
their incubrations treated with an air of contempt, as
an unthinking herd, had a better understanding of
things than they imagined they had.   They were
almost universally disgusted with the Innovation,
while the advocates for it were yet endeavoring to
make the world believe, that the opposition to it arose
from a few men only, of "no property" and "desper
ate fortunes," who were "endeavouring to bring things
into confusion, that they might have the advantage
of bettering their fortunes by plunder."   Little did
they think that it was then known, as it now appears

in fact, that those who were assiduously watching for places, preferment and pensions, were in truth the very men of *no property*, and had no other way of mending their shattered fortunes, but by being the sharers in the spoils of their country.

Scarcely had the General Assembly the opportunity of expressing their full Sentiments of the mischievous tendency, of having a Governor absolutely depend ent on the Crown for his being and support, before the alarming News arriv'd of the Judges of the Superior Court being placed in the same Situation. This Insolence of Administration was so quickly re peated, no doubt from a full perswasion of the truth of the accounts received from their infatuated tools on this side of the atlantick, that the temper of the people would now admit of the experiment. But the News was like Thunder in the ears of all but a de testable and detested few : Even those who had been inclin'd to think favorably of the Governor and the Judges were alarm'd at it. And indeed what honest and sensible man or woman could contemplate it with out horror ! We all began to shudder at the Pros pect of the same tragical Scenes being acted in this Country, which are recorded in the English History as having been acted when their Judges were the meer Creatures, Dependents and tools of the Crown. Such an indignation was discover'd and express'd by almost every one, at so daring an Insult upon a free people, that it was difficult to keep our Resentment within its proper bounds. Many were ready to call for immediate Vengeance, perhaps with more zeal than discretion : How soon human Prudence and

Fortitude, directed by the wise and righteous Gover
nor of the world, may point out the time and the means
of successfully revenging the wrongs of America, I
leave to those who have been the Contrivers and
Abbettors of these destructive Measures, seriously
to consider.   I hope and believe that I live in a
Country, the People of which are too intelligent and
too brave to submit to Tyrants : And let me remind
the greatest of them all, "there is a degree of patience
beyond which human Nature will not bear"!

Amidst the general Anxiety the memorable Meet
ing was called, with Design that the Inhabitants
might have the Opportunity, of expressing their
Sense calmly and dispassionately ; for it is from such
a Temper of Mind, that we are to expect a rational,
manly and successful Opposition to the ruinous Plans
of an abandoned Administration :   And it is for this
Reason alone, that the petty Tyrants of this Country
have always dreaded and continue still to dread, a
regular Assembly of the People.

The desirable Effects of this Meeting, contemp
tible as it was at first represented to be, together with
the Prospect of what may be further expected from
it, may possibly be the subject of a future Paper.

Your s,

CANDIDUS.

April 10, 1773.

THE COMMITTEE OF CORRESPONDENCE OF BOSTON TO
JOHN WADSWORTH.[1]

[MS., Committee of Correspondence Papers, Lenox Library.]

BOSTON April 13 1773

SIR

The Committee of Correspondence of the Town of Boston have receivd a Letter from the respectable Inhabitants of the Town of Duxborough. Nothing can afford us greater pleasure than to find so noble a Spirit of Opposition to the Efforts of arbitrary power prevailing in so great a number of Towns in this province. And it gives us a particular Satisfaction that our worthy Brethren of Duxborough, who are settled upon the very spot which was first cultivated by our renowned Ancestors, inherit so great a Share of their heroick Virtues. It is as you justly observe an Affront to the Understanding of our Ancestors to suppose, that when they took possession of this Country, they consented, even tacitly, to be subject to the unlimited Controul of a Government without a Voice in it, the merciless Oppression of which was intollerable even when they had a Voice there. Your just Resentment of the Injuries done to us by the British parliament more especially in giving & grant ing our property & appropriating it to the most de structive purposes, without our Consent, and your resolution to oppose Tyranny in all its forms is worthy the Imitation of this Metropolis. We wish for & hope soon to see that Union of Sentiments in the several Towns throughout this province & in the American Colonies which shall strike a Terror in the

---

[1] Town Clerk of Duxbury.

hearts of those who would enslave us ; and together with a Spirit of union may God inspire us with that ardent Zeal for the support of religious & civil Lib erty which animated the Breasts of the first Settlers of the old Colony of Plymouth from whom the native Inhabitants of Duxborough have lineally descended. After the Example of those renowned Heroes, whose memory we revere, let us gloriously defend our Rights & Liberties, & resolve to transmit the fair Inherit ance they purchased for us with Treasure & Blood to their latest posterity.

THE COMMITTEE OF CORRESPONDENCE OF BOSTON TO
EZRA WHITMARSH.[1]

[MS., Committee of Correspondence Papers, Lenox Library.]

[April 13, 1773.]

SIR

The Selectmen of this Town have handed to us an attested Copy of a letter directed to them by order of the ancient Town of Weymouth. As it is the particular Department of the Committee of Corre spondence appointed by the Town, to return an Answer to this Letter we chearfully embrace the Opportunity ; and acknowledge the Candor of our Brethren of Weymouth in giving any Attention to the proceedings of this Town. The Town of Boston are deeply sensible that our publick Affairs as you justly observe are in a critical Scituation : yet our Intention was, not to obtrude *their* Opinions upon their Fellow-Countrymen, as has been injuriously

---

[1] Town Clerk of Weymouth.

said, but to be informd, if possible of their real Senti
ments, at a time when it was publickly & repeatedly
given out that this Country in general was perfectly
reconciled to the measures of the British Administra
tion.   It affords us pleasure to find it to be the Sense
of the Town of Weymouth that " Encroachments are
made upon our Rights & Liberties," & that they are
"disposed at all times to unite in every lawful &
proper measure for obtaining a redress of our Griev
ances."   Many of the Towns in this province have
expressd a just Abhorrence of the Attempts that
have been & still are made to deprive us of our in
estimable rights.   Their good Sense & generous
Zeal for the common Liberty is highly animating &
we would wish to emulate it.   We are sensible that
"much Wisdom is necessary to conduct us right,"
and we joyn in earnestly supplicating "that Wisdom
which is from above."   The Friendship to this Town
expressd in your Letter lays us under great Obligations.   No greater Blessing can be desired by this
Community than " Peace Prosperity & Happiness,"
and the Enjoyment of this Blessing depends upon
civil & religious Liberty.

THE COMMITTEE OF CORRESPONDENCE OF BOSTON TO
JOSEPH NORTH.[1]

[MS., Committee of Correspondence Papers, Lenox Library.]

BOSTON April 13 1773

SIR

The Votes of the plantation of Gardnerstown have
been laid before the Committee of Correspondence

---

[1] Clerk of the " plantation " of Gardnerstown.

of the Town of Boston by M[r] Samuel Adams to whom you were so kind as to transmit them. The notice which your plantation have taken of the State of the Rights & Grievances of this people publishd by this metropolis gives us great pleasure. So thorough a Sense of Liberty civil & religious so early discoverd in an Infant Body, affords an agreable prospect that the good Cause will be nobly defended & maintaind by it, when it shall arrive to a State of Maturity. We wish you the Blessings of Heaven in your Settlement; and we will exert our small Share of Influence in getting you protected from the savage hand of Tyranny, with which the whole British America has so long been contending. The resolves of the patriotick Assembly of Virginia accompany this Letter, & we doubt not you will par take of the general Joy they have given to all the friends of American Independence & freedom.

THE COMMITTEE OF CORRESPONDENCE OF BOSTON TO JOSIAH STONE.[1]

[MS., Committee of Correspondence Papers, Lenox Library.]

BOSTON April 13 1773

SIR

Your attested Copy of the proceedings of the Town of Framingham at a legal meeting on the 15th of March last has been receivd by the Committee of Correspondence of the Town of Boston.

The just resentment which your Town discovers at the power of Legislation for the Colonists assumed

---

[1] Town Clerk of Framingham.

by the British Parliament, and its exerting that power
in raising a revenue and applying it to purposes re
pugnant to the common Safety, and the resolution
of that town to defend our rights & Liberties purchasd with so much Blood & Treasure, must do them
honor in the Estimation of all who place a true Value
upon those inestimable Blessings.   May *He* who
gave this Land to our worthy forefathers, animate us
their posterity to defend it at all Hazards ; and while
we would not lose the Character of loyal Subjects to
a prince resolvd to protect us, we will yet never
forfeit that of Men determined to be free.

TO ARTHUR LEE

[R. H. Lee, *Life of Arthur Lee*, vol. ii., pp. 203, 204.]

BOSTON, April 22nd. 1773.

MY ESTEEMED FRIEND,—I have written you a long
epistle by this conveyance, and yet as the vessel is
detained by a contrary wind, I cannot help indulging
the mood I am in to chat a little more with you.
When I mentioned Mr. Hancock in my last, I forgot
to tell you that he is colonel of a company, called the
governor's company of cadets.   Perhaps in this view
only he was held up to Mr. Wilkes, when he was in
formed that he had deserted the cause.   But it should
be known it is not in the power of the governor to
give a commission for that company to whom he
pleases as their officers are chosen by themselves.
Mr. Hancock was elected by an unanimous vote ;
and a reluctance at the idea of giving offence to an

hundred gentlemen, might very well account for the governor giving the commission to Mr. H., without taking into consideration that most powerful of all other motives, *an instruction*, especially at a time when he vainly hoped he should gain him over. I have been the more particular, because I know our adversaries avail themselves much by propagating reports that persons who have signalized themselves as patriots have at length forsaken their country. Mr. Otis yesterday was engaged in a cause in the ad miralty on the side of Dawson, commander of one of the king's cutters. At this some of the minions of power triumph, and say they have got over to their side the greatest champion of our cause. I have not yet discovered in the faces of their masters, an air of exultation at this event; and indeed how can they boast of the acquisition of one, whom they themselves have been the most ready to expose as distracted.

I send you a complete printed copy of our contro versy with the governor, at the end of which you will observe some errors noted which escaped the press.

This letter goes under care of Mr. Cushing's to Dr. Franklin. The franks you favoured me with I shall make use of as necessity shall require.

I am yours affectionately,

TO ARTHUR LEE.

[R. H. Lee, *Life of Arthur Lee*, vol. ii., pp. 204, 205.]

BOSTON, May 6th, 1773.

MY DEAR SIR,—My last letter to you I sent by

Capt. Symmes, who sailed a few days ago. This town met yesterday, and made choice of their repre sentatives for the year ensuing. Enclosed is a copy of the town's instructions.[1] It is a very common practice for this town to instruct their representatives ; which among other good purposes serves to communicate their sentiments and spirit to the other towns, and may be looked upon as fresh appeals to the world. I perceive by the late London newspapers that the governor's first speech had arrived there, and had been very sensibly remarked upon by Junius Americanus. This warm and judicious advocate for the province I apprehend was mistaken in saying, that the supreme authority of the British parliament to legislate forces has been always acknowledged here ; when he reads the answer of the house to the speech, he will find the con trary clearly shown, even from Gov. Hutchinson's history. What will be the consequence of this con troversy, time must discover ; it must be placed to the credit of the governor, that he has quickened a spirit of enquiry into the nature and end of government, and the connexion of the colonies with Great Britain, which has for some time past been prevailing among the people. *Magna est veritas et prevalebit ;* I believe it will be hardly in the power even of that powerful nation to hold so inquisitive and increasing a people long in a state of slavery.

Pray write to me as often as you can find leisure, and be assured I am sincerely your friend and servant,

---

[1] The text is in *Boston Record Commissioners' Report*, vol. xviii., pp. 131-134.

TO THE SELECTMEN OF BOSTON.

[W. V. Wells, *Life of Samuel Adams*, vol. ii., p. 70 ; printed also in the *Historical Magazine*, vol. vii., p. January, 20, 1863.]

BOSTON, May 14, 1773.

GENTLEMEN,—-

I must beg the favor of you to present my un feigned regards to the town, and acquaint them that, by reason of bodily indisposition, I am unable to dis charge the duty they have been pleased to assign me as moderator of their meeting, which is to be held this day by adjournment. I am much obliged to the town for the honor done me, and esteem it a very great misfortune whenever it is not in my power to render them services proportionate to my own inclination.

With all due respect, I remain, gentlemen,

Your friend and fellow-citizen,

TO ARTHUR LEE.

[MS., Samuel Adams Papers, Lenox Library ; a text with modifications is in R. H. Lee, *Life of Arthur Lee*, vol. ii., pp. 205, 206.]

BOSTON May 17, 1773.

DEAR SIR/

My last went by Cap Calef, and inclosd a Copy of the Instructions of this Town to their representa tives. Our General Assembly will meet next Week, what kind of a Budget the Govr will then open is un certain ; It is whispered that he intends to bring about a Coalition of parties, but how he will attempt it I am at a loss to conceive. Surely he cannot think that the Body of this people will be quieted till there is an End put to the Oppressions they are under ; and he dares not to propose a Coalition on these Terms because it would disgust those who are the Instruments of & Sharers in the Oppression./ Besides I am inclind to think he never will be able to recover so much of the Confidence of the people as to make his Administration easy. A few of his Letters we have seen, but are restraind at present from publish ing them. Could they be made generally known, his Friends must desert him. It is a pity when the most important Intelligence is communicated with such Restrictions, as that it serves rather to gratify the Curiosity of a few than to promote the publick good. I wish we could see the Letters he has written since his Advancement to the Government. His friends give out that they are replete with tenderness to the province ; If so, *I speak with Assurance*, they are the reverse of those he wrote before.

I send you for your Amusement the Copy of a Vote passd by this Town at the Adjournment of their Meeting a few days ago and remain with Sincerity your friend.

You cannot write me too often.

TO ARTHUR LEE.

[R. H. Lee, *Life of Arthur Lee*, vol. ii., p. 192, under date of June 14, 1772.]

BOSTON, June 14th, [1773.]

DEAR SIR, —— I now enclose letters written by Thomas Hutchinson and Oliver —— and others of

less importance, the originals of which have been laid
before the house of representatives.[1] The house have
already resolved, by a majority of 101 out of 106
members, that the design and tendency of them is to
subvert the constitution and introduce arbitrary power
into the province.   They are now in the hands of a
committee to consider them farther, and report what
is still proper to be done.

I think there is now a full discovery of a combination of persons who have been the principal movers,
in all the disturbance, misery, and bloodshed, which
has befallen this unhappy country.   The friends of
our great men are much chagrined.

I am much engaged at present, and will write you
more fully by the next opportunity.   In the mean
time believe me to be with great esteem your un
feigned friend,

Wednesday, June 16th, 1773.—The enclosed resolves are to be considered by the house this afternoon.

THE COMMITTEE OF CORRESPONDENCE OF BOSTON TO
ELIJAH MORTON.[2]

[MS., Committee of Correspondence Papers, Lenox Library.]

BOSTON June 19 1773

SIR

The judicious and manly Resolves of the Town of
Hatfield, passd at the Adjournment of a legal meet-

---

[1] See *Journal of the House of Representatives, 1773-1774*, under dates of June
2, 3, 10, 16, 21, 22, 26, 28, 1773 ; cf. Bigelow, *Complete Works of Benjamin
Franklin*, vol. v., pp. 147–150, 152, 153, 205–207.

[2] Town clerk of Hatfield.

ing on the 31 of May last, have been laid before the Com^e of Correspondence for the Town of Boston. It affords us very great Satisfaction to find that the At tempts of this Town to state the common Rights of this Colony & the many grievances we labor under have been judgd by our Brethren of Hatfield to be an acceptable Service ; and the Thanks of that Town does great Honor to the metropolis. It has been the unremitted Endeavor of the Invaders of our Rights & the Tools they have employed, to prevail on the people to believe that there have been no Infringe ments made upon them ; and the artful Publications which have frequently issued from one of the presses in this Town in particular, had perhaps in some degree answerd their purpose. But we have the pleasure to assure you, that the Letters we have lately receivd from every part of the province, breath the true Sen timents & Spirit of Liberty. There seems to be in every town, an apprehension of fatal Consequences from "the illegal & unconstitutional measures which have been *adopted*, (as you justly express it) by the British ministry." Your Expression is indeed perti nent; for it has as we think abundantly appeard since you wrote, by some extraordinary Letters which have been publishd, that the plan of our Slavery was concerted here, & properly speaking "adopted by the British ministry." The plan indeed is concise ; first to take the people's money from them without their Consent & then to appropriate that money for the purpose of supporting an Executive independent of them and under the absolute Controul of the Crown or rather of the ministry. It was formerly the saying

of an English Tyrant " Let me have Judges at my
Command & make what Laws you please." And
herein he judgd wisely for his purpose, for what
Security can the people expect from the most salutary
Laws if they are to be executed by the absolute Dependents of a monarch.   The nation cannot then
wonder that not only the several Towns of this prov
ince in their more private Departments, but the
Representative body of the people in General Court
assembled, are so greatly alarmd at this finishing
Stroke of the System of Tyranny.   That Union of
Sentiments among the freemen of this Colony, that
firmness, and Resolution to make every constitutional
Stand against the Efforts of a corrupt administration
which appears in the proceedings of so many Towns
already publishd to the World, must afford full con
viction to the Earl of Dartmouth that the opposition
is not, as was represented to his predecessor in office,
an expiring Faction.   That the People of this province thus animated with a laudable Zeal, may be di
rected to the wisest measures for the Defence &
Support of their common Liberty is the ardent wish
of this Committee.

   We are with the warmest affection for our Country,
and a due regard to the Town of Hatfield

                    Sir

                         your assured friends
                         & humble Servants,

TO ARTHUR LEE.

[MS., Samuel Adams Papers, Lenox Library ; a text with modifications is in R. H. Lee, *Life of Arthur Lee*, vol. ii., pp. 206, 207.]

BOSTON June 21 1773

Sir

I wrote in very great Haste a few days ago, and then inclosd a printed Copy of Letters signd Tho Hutchinson, And^w Oliver & others, with a Copy of certain Resolutions formd by a Committee and brot into the House of Representatives. Those Resolutions have been since considerd by the House and with little Variation adopted as you^l see by the inclosd. Upon the last Resolve there was a Division 85 to 28 since which five of the minority alterd their minds, and two other members came into the House and desird to be counted so that finally there were 93 in favor & 22 against it. Many if not most of the latter voted for all the other resolves. A Petition & Remonstrance against Hutchinson & Oliver will be brot in I suppose this Week. I should think enough ap pears by these Letters to show that the plan for the ruin of American Liberty was laid by a few men born & educated amongst us, & governd by Avarice & a Lust of power.] Could they be removed from his Majestys Service and Confidence here, effectual Measures might then be taken to restore, " placidam sub Libertate Quietam." Perhaps however you may think it necessary that some on your side the Water should be impeachd & brot to condign punishment. In this I shall not differ with you.

I send you our last Election Sermon delivered by

Mr Turner. The Bishop of St Asaphs I have read with singular pleasure.

I remain sincerely your friend,

PETITION OF THE HOUSE OF REPRESENTATIVES OF MASSACHUSETTS TO THE KING. JUNE 23, 1773.

[MS., Samuel Adams Papers, Lenox Library.]

Province of Massachusetts Bay   June 23 1773[1]
To the Kings most Excellent Majesty
Most Gracious Sovereign
We your Majestys most loyal Subjects the Repre sentatives of your ancient Colony, in General Court legally assembled, by Virtue of your Majestys Writ under the Hand and Seal of the Governor beg leave to lay this our humble Petition before your Majesty ; earnestly beseeching that in your Royal Clemency, your Majesty would . . .

Nothing but a Sense of the Duty we owe to our Sovereign, and the Obligation we are under to con sult the Peace and Safety of the Province, could induce us to remonstrate to your Majesty, the Mal-Conduct of those, who, having been born & educated and constantly resident in the Province and who formerly have had ye Confidence & were loaded with ye honours of this People, your Majesty, we conceive, from the purest Motives of rendering the People most happy, was graciously pleasd to advance to the high est places of Trust and Authority in the province.

---

[1] Adopted by the House of Representatives by a vote of 80 to 11, after a motion to refer its consideration to the next session had been defeated by a vote of 73 to 13.

It has been with the greatest Concern and Anxiety, that your Majestys humble Petitioners have seen Discords & Animosities too long subsisting between your Subjects of the Parent State & those of the Colonies : And we have trembled with Apprehen sions that the Consequences naturally arising there from must at length prove fatal to both Countries.

Your Majesty will permit us humbly to suggest, that your Subjects here have been naturally inducd to believe, that the Grievances they have sufferd and still continue to suffer by the late measures of the British Administration, have been occasioned by your Majestys ministers & principal Servants being unfor tunately for us, either under strong prejudices against us, or misinformd in certain Facts of very interrest- ing Importance to us. It is for this Reason that former Houses of Representatives have from time to time prepared a true State of facts to be laid before your Majesty ; but their Petitions it is presumed, have by some means been prevented from reaching your Royal Hand.

/ Your Majestys Petitioners have at length had be fore them certain Papers, from which, they conceive it [1] may be made manifestly to appear that there has long been a Combination [2] of evil Men in this province, who have contemplated Measures and formd a Plan, to raise their own Fortunes and advance them selves to Posts of Power Honor & Profit, to the Destruction of the Character of the province, at

---

[1] As an alternative to the following six words, the draft has also, interlined, " is most reasonable to Suppose."

[2] The draft has also "Conspiracy," interlined.

the Expence of the Quiet of the Nation and to
the annihilating of the Rights & Liberties of the
American Colonies.

And we do with all due Submission to your Maj
esty, beg Leave particularly to complain of the Con
duct of his Excellency Thomas Hutchinson Esq[r]
Governor, and the Hon[be] Andrew Oliver Esq[r] Lieu
tenant Governor of this province, as having a natural
& efficacious Tendency to interrupt & alienate the
Affections of your Majesty our Rightful Sovereign
from this your loyal province; to destroy that Har
mony & Good Will between Great Britain and this
Colony which every honest Subject would wish to
establish; to excite the Resentment of the British
Administration against this Province; to defeat the
Endeavors of our Agents & Friends to serve us by a
fair Representation of our State of facts; and to
prevent our humble and repeated Petitions from
reaching the Ear of your Majesty & having their de
sired Effect. And finally that the said Tho[s] Hutch
inson & Andrew Oliver have been some of the chiefe
Instruments in the Introduction of a Fleet and Army
into this province to establish & perpetuate their
plans; whereby they have not only been greatly
instrumental of disturbing the peace & Harmony of
the Government and causing unnatural & hateful
Discords and Animosities between the several parts
of your Majestys Dominions, but are justly charge
able with all that Corruption of Morals in this Pro
vince, and all that Confusion Misery and Bloodshed
which have been the natural Effects of the posting of
Troops in a populous Town.

We do therefore most humbly beseech your Maj
esty, to give order that Time may be allowed to us to
support these our complaints by our Agents and
Council. And as the said Tho⁵ Hutchinson Esqʳ
and Andrew Oliver Esqʳ have by their above mentiond Conduct and otherwise rendered themselves
justly obnoxious to your Majestys loving Subjects,
we pray that your Majesty will be graciously pleasd
to remove them from their posts in this Government,
and place such good and faithful men in their Stead
as, your Majesty in your great Wisdom shall think
fit ————————

TO ARTHUR LEE.

[MS., Samuel Adams Papers, Lenox Library; a text with modifications is in
R. H. Lee, *Life of Arthur Lee*, vol. ii., pp. 207, 208.]

BOSTON June 28, 1773.

Dear Sir,

My last was by Cap. Collson by the way of
Bristol, inclosd in a frankd Cover. I then informd
you of the passing of a Number of Resolves in
the House of Representatives upon certain Letters
that had been under their Consideration. Since
which the House have by a Division of $\frac{82}{13}$, voted a
Petition & Remonstrance to the King praying that
Govʳ Hutchinson & Lᵗ Govʳ Oliver may be removd
from their Posts. A Copy of which is sent to Dʳ
Franklin by this Vessel, who is directed to apply to
Arthur Lee, Esqʳ and any other Gentleman as Coun
cil. Upon my motion the Dʳ was directed to make

application to you solely; but the next Day it was questiond in the House whether you were yet initiated into the Practice of Law, and the Addition was made upon a Doubt which I was sorry I had it not in my Power to remove.   However, you must be applyd to ; Every Friend of Liberty, or which is the same thing, nine-tenths of the House having the greatest Confidence in your Integrity and Abilities.

You have herewith inclosd a Copy of the proceedings of the Council upon the same Subject.

The People are highly incensd against the two impeachd Gentlemen.   They have entirely lost the Esteem of the publick.   Even some of their few friends are ashamd to countenance them.   The Govr, as he has been one of the most obligd, has provd himself to be a most ungrateful man.   He appears to me to be totally disconcerted.   I wish I could say humbled.

The House are now considering the Independency of the Judges; A Matter which every day grows still more serious, and employs much of the Attention of the People without Doors, as well as of the Members of the House.   I wish Lord Dartmouth & the rest of the Great officers of the Crown could be prevaild upon duly to consider that British Americans cannot long endure a State of Tyranny.

I expect the Genl Assembly will be up in a few Days.[1]   I will then write you more particularly.   In the mean time I remain

Your Friend,

---

[1] The General Court was prorogued June 29, to meet September 15; but the next session did not begin until January 26, 1774.

THE COMMITTEE OF CORRESPONDENCE OF BOSTON TO THE
COMMITTEE OF CORRESPONDENCE OF WORCESTER.

[MS., Committee of Correspondence Papers, Lenox Library.]

BOSTON, Septem[r] 11, 1773

GENTLEMEN

The happy fruit of the Appointment of Committees of Correspondence in almost every Town in this prov ince, is the Advantage that Each has of communicating any Matter of common Concern & Importance to a chosen Number of Men zealous for the publick Liberty, in any particular Town or County, where it may be specially requisite that such Intelligence sh[d] be given. In order to support our Cause, it is necessary that we attend to every part of the plan which our Enemies have concerted against it. In making Laws & raising revenues from us without our Consent, a Design is evidently apparent to render an American Legislative of little Weight ; and in appropriating such revenues to the support of Governor & Judges, it as evidently appears that there is a fixd Design to make our Ex ecutive dependent upon them & subservient to their own purposes. Every method is therefore to be usd that is practicable, in opposition to these two capital Grievances, which are the fountain from whence every other Grievance flows. All the Judges of the Superior Court, except the Chiefe Justice have receivd the Grants out of the province Treasury in full ; but this by no means makes it certain whether they intend for the future to depend upon the Crown for Support or upon the Grants of the Gen[l] Assembly. Indeed one of them viz M[r] Trowbridge has explicitly declared to the Speaker of the House of Representatives that he will receive his Salary from the province only, so long as he shall hold his Commission. The Chiefe Justice (Oliver) has been totally silent. So that neither of them except Mr Trowbridge has yet thought proper to comply with the just Expectation & Demand of the House of Representatives, upon which the Safety, & therefore we trust the Quiet of this people depends.

The Court is now sitting here ; and the Grand Jury have presented a Memorial to them, setting forth as we are informd, the Contempt with which the Grand Juries of the province have been treated in the Letters of Govr Hutchinson & others ; asserting the Inde pendence of Grand Juries as being accountable to none but God & their own Consciences for their Conduct ; claiming to themselves equal protection with the Court, & expecting that effectual measures will be taken to secure that most valueable Branch of our civil Constitution, from further Contempt. They have also represented to the Court, the great Uneasiness in the Minds of the people of this County & as they conceive of the whole province, by reason of the un certainty that yet remains, respecting the Dependence of the Judges on the Crown for Support, & their own Doubts & Difficulties on this Account ; & they pray that the Court w^d come to an explicit & publick Declaration thereupon.

This is the Substance of the Matter. We shall en- deavor to obtain a correct Copy, & in that Case you will see it publishd in the newspapers. In the mean time we would propose to you whether it would not be serving the Cause if every County would take

similar Measures.   And as the Court is to sit next in
your County,¹ & yours is the principal Town we have
written to your Committee only on this Subject, leav
ing it to your Discretion & good Judgment to take
such methods as shall be most proper.

TO JOSEPH HAWLEY.²

[MS., Samuel Adams Papers, Lenox Library.]

BOSTON Oct. 4ᵗʰ 1773

MY DEAR SIR/

I can not omit this Opportunity of submitting to
your Judgment, the Ideas I have of the present Dis
position of the British Administration towards this
Country; and I the rather do it at this time, because
as Matters seem to me to be drawing to a Crisis, it
is of the greatest Importance that we should have a
right Understanding of their Sentiments and Designs.
The "wild and extravagant Notions" (as they have
been lately called) of the supreme Authority of
Parliament " flowing from the Pen of an House of
Representatives " has greatly chagrind them ; as they
apprehend it has been the means of awakning that
Spirit of Opposition to their Measures, which from
the Information their Tools on this side of the Water
had given them, and the Confidence they had placed
in the Art and Address of Mʳ Hutchinson, they had

---

¹ Cf. Columbia University *Studies in History, Economics and Public Law*,
vol. vii., p. 58.

² The political leader of Northampton, Massachusetts.   His " Broken Hints "
is in Niles, *Principles and Acts*, p. 324.

flatterd themselves, had subsided, & would soon be extinguished. At the same time they are very sensible, that the impartial Part of the Nation, con sidering that the House were in a Manner forced to express their own Sentiments on the Subject, be they what they might, with Freedom are ready to excul pate them, and lay the whole Blame, if there be any, upon the Governor, for his Imprudent Zeal in bring ing a Matter into open Controversy which the Ministry had hoped to have settled in a silent Way. It is my Opinion that the present Administration even though the very good Lord Dartmouth is one of them, are as fixed in their Resolutions to carry this favorite point as any of their Predecessors have been; I mean to gain from us an implicit Acknowledgment of the Right of Parliament to make Laws binding upon us in all Cases whatever. The King who you know de termines by their Advice, has expressd his Dis pleasure at our late petitions because they held up Rights repugnant to this Right. Some of our Poli ticians would have the People believe that Adminis tration are disposd or determind to have all the Grievances which we complain of redressd, if we will only be quiet. But this I apprehend would be a fatal Delusion ; for I have the best Assurances, that if the King himself should make any Concessions or take any Steps contrary to the Right of Parliam' to tax us, he would be in Danger of embroiling himself with the Ministry ; and that under the present Prejudices of all about him, even the recalling an Instruction to the Governor is not yet likely to be advisd. Lord Dart mouth has indeed lately said in the House of Lords

as I have it from a Gentleman in London who receivd the Information from a peer who was present,
that " he had formd his plan of Redress, which he was
determind to carry *at the Hazard of his office.*" But
his Lordship might very safely make this Promise;
for from all that I have heard, his Plan of Redress is
built very much upon the Hopes that we may be prevaild upon, at least implicitly to yield up the Right,
of which his Lordship is as fixd in his Opinion, as
any other Minister. This I conceive they have had
in view from the year 1763; and we may well re
member, that when the Stamp Act was repeald, our
Friends in Parliam submitted as a Condition of the
Repeal, that the declaratory Act as it is called should
be passed, declaratory of the Right & Authority of
Parliament to make Laws binding upon us in all
Cases whatever. Till that time the Dispute had been
limitted to the Right of Taxation. By assuming the
Power of making Laws for America *in all Cases*, at
the time when the Stamp Act was repeald it was pro
bably their Design to secure, as far as they could do
it by an Act of their own, this particular Right of
Taxation thinking at the same time that if they could
once establish the Precedent in an Instance of so
much importance to us, as that of taking our Money
from us, they should thenceforward find it very easy
to exercise their pretended Right in every other Case.
For this Purpose in the very next Session if I mistake
not, they passed another revenue Act, for America;
which they have been endeavoring to support by
military parade, as well as by other Means, at an Expence to the Nation, as it is said of more than the

revenue yielded. And yet, in order to induce us to
acquiesce in or silently to submit to their Exercise of
this Right, they have even condescended to meet us
half way (as it was artfully given out) and lessened
this Revenue by taking off the Duty on Glass &
several other Articles. Mr George Grenville declared
that he would be satisfied with a *peper Corn*, but that
he must have *three;* which shows that he had a
stronger Sense of the Importance of establishing the
Power of Parliament, or as his own Words were, " of
securing the Obedience of the Colonies " than barely
of a Revenue. ⎰The Acknowledgment on our part of the
Right of Parliament has been their invariable Object:
And could they now gain this Acknowledgment from
us, tho it were but implicitly, they would willingly sacrifice the *present* revenue by a repeal of the Acts, and
for the present redress all our Grievances. I have
been assured that a Question has of late been pri
vately put by one in Administration upon whom much
Dependence is had by some persons, to a Gentleman
well acquainted with the Sentiments of the People of
this Province, Whether the present House of Repre
sentatives could not be prevaild on to rescind the
Answers of the last House to the Governors Speeches
relative to the supreme Authority of Parliament;
which Answers have been lookd upon as a Bar in the
Way of a Reconciliation and being informd that such
a measure on our part could by no means be expected,
I am apprehensive that Endeavors will be used to
draw us into an incautious mode of Conduct which
will be construed as in Effect receding from the Claim
of Rights of which we have hitherto been justly so

tenacious.   It has been given out, I suspect from the
Secrets of the Cabinet, that if we will now send home
decent temperate & dutiful petitions, even our im
aginary Grievances shall be redressd ; but let us con
sider what Ideas Administration have of Decency
Temperance & Dutifulness as applyd to this Case.
Our late petitions against the Independency of the
Governor & Judges were deemd indecent intemperate
& undutiful, not because they were expressd in ex
ceptionable Words, but because it was therein said
that by the Charter it plainly appeard to us to be
intended by the Royal Grantors that the General As
sembly should be the constituted Judge of the ade
quate Support of the Government of the province
and the Ways & Means of providing for the same ;
and further that this operation of an Act of parlia
ment, by which the People are taxed & the money is
appropriated & used for that purpose, derogates from
one of the most sacred Rights granted in the Charter,
& most essential to the Freedom of the Constitu
tion, & divests the Gen¹ Assembly of a most important
part of legislative Power and Authority expressly
granted therein, and necessary for the Good and Wel
fare of the province & the Support and Government
of the same.   The Subject Matter of our Complaint
was, not that a Burden greater than our proportion
was laid upon us by Parliament; such a Complaint
we might have made salva Authoritate parliamentaria:
But that the Parliament had assumed & exercisd the
power of taxing us & thus appropriating our money,
when by Charter it was the exclusive Right of the
General Assembly.   We could not otherwise have

explaind to his Majesty the Grievance which we meant
to complain of ; and yet he is pleasd in his answer to
declare that he has well weighd the *Subject Matter*
of the petitions—and is determined to support the
Constitution and to resist with firmness every At
tempt to derogate from the Authority of the *supreme
Legislature.*   Does not this imply that the parlia·
ment is the supreme Legislature & its Authority over
the Colonies the Constitution?   And that until we
frame our petitions so as that it may fairly be con
strued that we have at least tacitly conceded to it we
may expect they will be still disregarded or frownd
upon as being *not* decent temperate and dutifull?   We
may even be allowd to claim certain Rights and
exercise subordinate powers of Legislation like the
Corporations in England, subject to the universal
Controul of Parliam', and if we will implicitly acknow
ledge its Right to make Laws binding upon us in all
Cases whatever, that is, its absolute Sovereignty over
us the Acts we shall then complain of as *burdensome*
to us, shall be repeald, all Grievances redressd, and
Administration will flatter us that the right shall
never be exercisd but in a Case of absolute necessity
which shall be apparent to every judicious man in the
Empire.   To induce us to be thus submissive beyond
the bounds of reason & Safety their Lordships will
condescend to be familiar with us and treat us with
Cakes & Sugar plumbs.   But who is to determine
when the necessity shall be thus apparent?   Doubt
less the Parliam', which is supposd to be the supreme
Legislature will claim that prerogative; and then
they will for ever make Laws for us when they think

proper.   Or if the several Colony Assemblies are to signify that such necessity is apparent to every wise man within their respective Jurisdictions before the parliam⁺ shall exercise the Right, the point will be given up to us in Effect, that the Parliam⁺ shall not make a Law binding upon us in any Case until we shall consent to it, which their Lordships can in no wise be thought to intend.

But I must break off this abruptly.   I intend to write you further.   In the meantime I must beg to be indulgd with your Thots on these matters & remain with great regard,

Sir,

TO JOSEPH HAWLEY.

[MS., Samuel Adams Papers, Lenox Library.]

Boston Octob 13 1773

My dear Sir/

I lately wrote you a long Epistle upon our political Affairs; and although I fear I have put your patience to the Tryal, I can not withstand a strong Inclination to communicate more of my mind to you on the same Subject.   Perhaps it may be of Service to you, as it may afford you an opportunity of exercising that Charity or Candor which " beareth all things."

I have taken some pains to enquire into the true Character of the Minister in the American Depart ment.   And I find that all allow him to be a good man.   Goodness has rarely I fear been of late the Characteristick of his Majestys Ministers ; for which reason his Lordship is to be sure the more highly to be prizd. But it seems very necessary that Men in such elevated Stations should be great as well as good. The Promotion of a nobleman to this Department, who is famed in America for his Piety is easily ac counted for on the principles of modern Policy. How ever illy we may deserve it, the great men in England have an opinion of us as being a mightily religious People. Surely then it must be supposd that we shall place an entire Confidence in a Minister of the same Character. We find it is so in fact. How many were filled with the most sanguine Expectations, when they heard that the good Lord Dartmouth was en trusted with a Share in Administration? Little did they think that if his Lordship did not come in upon express terms, which however is doubted by some, yet without a Greatness of mind equal, perhaps superior to his Goodness, it will be impossible for him singly to stem the Torrent of Corruption. This requires much more Fortitude than I yet believe he is possessd of. Fain would I have him treated with great Decency & Respect, both for the Station he is in and the Char acter he sustains; but considering with whom he is connected, I confess that in regard to any power he will have substantially to serve us, I am an Infidel.

I do not agree with some of our Politicians who tell us that the Ministry are "sick of their Measures." I cannot but wonder that any prudent Man should be lieve this, while he sees not the least Relaxation of measures; but instead of it new Insult & Abuse. Is the Act of Parliament, made the last year, and the Appointment of Commissioners with Instructions to

put it in full Execution in the Rhode Island Affair, a
Ground of such a Beliefe? Can we think the East
India Company are so satisfied that Administration
are disposd to give up their Designs of establishing
Arbitrary Power, when no longer ago than the last
Session of Parliament they effected the Deprivation
of their Charter Rights, whereby they have acquired
so great an Addition of Power & Influence to the
Crown? Or are such Hopes to be gatherd from the
Treatment given to our own Petitions the last May,
when they were discountenancd for no other Reason
but because the Rights of our Charter were therein
pleaded as a Reason against a measure which if a little
while persisted in, will infallibly establish a Despotism
in the End? Surely this is not a time for us to tes
tify the least Confidence in the Spirit of the British
Government, or from flattering Hopes that their de
signs are to alter measures, to trust to their Discretion
or good Will.

I am apt to think that Ministry have two great
Events in Contemplation both which in all probability
will take place shortly. The one is a War & the other
a new Election of Parliament Men. In order to improve these Events to their own purpose, it will be
come necessary to sooth & flatter the Americans
with Hopes of Reliefe. In Case of a War, America
if in good Humour will be no contemptible Ally.
She will be able by her Exertions to annoy the Enemy
much. Her aid will therefore be courted. And to
bring her into this good Humour, the Ministry must
be lavish in promises of great things to be done for
her. Perhaps some Concessions will be made; but

these Concessions will flow from policy not from
Justice. Should they recall their Troops from the
Castle, or do twenty other seemingly kind things, we
ought never to think their Designs are benevolent to
ward us, while they continue to exercise the pretended
Right to tax us at their pleasure, and appropriate our
money to their own purposes. And this they have
certainly no Thought at present of yielding up. With
regard to the Election of another House of Commons,
that will not take place within these Eighteen months
unless a Dissolution of parliam' should happen before;
which has indeed been hinted, & may be the move
ment in order suddenly to bring on the Election
before the People are prepared for it. We are to sup
pose that an Attempt will be made to purchase the
Votes of the whole Kingdom. This will require much
Time and dexterous Management. The Ministry
have in a great Measure lost the Influence of London
and other great Corporations as well as that of the
East India Company by their late Treatment of that
powerful Body, whom Lord North now finds it neces
sary to coax and pascify. They will therefore be glad
to sooth America into a State of Quietness, if they
can do it without conceding to our Rights, that they
may have the Aid of the Friends of America when the
new Election comes on. And that America has many
Friends among the Merchants & Manufacturers the
Country Gentlemen & especially the Dissenters from
the establishd Church I am so well informd that I
cannot doubt. The last of these are so from generous
the others from private & selfish Principles. Such
Considerations as these will be strong Inducements

[to] them to make us fair & flattering Promises for the present; but Nothing I think will be so dangerous as for the Americans to withdraw their Dependence upon themselves & place it upon those whose constant En deavor for ten years past has been to enslave us, & who, if they can obtain a new Election of old Mem bers, it is to be feard, unless we keep up a perpetual Watchfulness, will, in another seven years, effect their Designs. The Safety of the Americans in my humble opinion depends upon their pursuing their wise Plan of Union in Principle & Conduct. If we persevere in asserting our Rights, the Time must come probably a Time of War, when our just Claims must be attended to & our Complaints regarded. But if we discoverd the least Disposition to submit our Claims to their Decision, it is my opinion that our Injuries will be in creasd ten fold. I conclude at present with assuring you that I am with sincere regard

Sir your Friend & hbl serv',

THE COMMITTEE OF CORRESPONDENCE OF MASSACHUSETTS TO OTHER COMMITTEES OF CORRESPONDENCE.[1]

[MS., Samuel Adams Papers, Lenox Library.]

PRO OF MASSACHUSETTS BAY
BOSTON Octob 21 1773

GENTLEMEN

The Committee of Correspondence appointed by the House of Representatives of this Province have

---

[1] The origin of this letter appears in the manuscript journal, preserved in the Boston Public Library, of the Committee of Correspondence, consisting of fifteen members, appointed by the House of Representatives of Massachusetts. At a meeting of the committee on June 28, 1773, a sub-committee, consisting of

been not altogether inattentive to the Design of their Institution. We have been waiting for Intelligence from Great Britain from whose injudicious Councils the common Grievances of the Colonies have sprang; in hopes that a Change in the American Department would have producd a happy Change in the meas ures of Administration; But we are sorry to say, that from the best Accounts that we have ob- taind the Ministry have been hitherto so far from radically redressing American Grievances that even the least Relaxation has not been advisd if thought of. On the Contrary, the British Parliament have been prorogud without taking the least Notice of the Affairs of America; while they have been curtailing the Charter of the East India Company in such a Manner & in such a Degree, as to indicate that they are much more intent upon increasing the power & Influence of the Crown than securing the Liberties of the Subject. At the same time, this Province has had a very recent Discovery of the unalterd Reso lution of the Ministry to pursue their plan of arbitrary

Adams, Hancock, Cushing, Phillips, and Heath, was appointed, to write to the Connecticut Committee of Correspondence and also to the committee of each assembly. The letter to Connecticut appears to have been approved at a meet ing of the sub-committee on July 4. At a meeting of the sub-committee on July 15 Adams was asked to draft a letter on general government to the com mittees of the neighboring governments. This letter was still unwritten on August 19, and on September 29 the sub-committee called a meeting of the full committee for October 20. On that date it was voted expedient to write a circular letter to the other committees, and in the afternoon of the same day Adams and Warren were appointed a sub-committee to draft such a letter. At the afternoon meeting on October 21 a draft was reported, read several times, and accepted; and it was voted that the chairman, with Adams and Heath, should sign the letters. The Journal is printed in *Proceedings* of Massachusetts Historical Society, 2d ser., vol. iv., pp. 85–90.

Power, in the Kings Answer to the Petitions of our
Assembly against the appropriation of the Revenue
raisd from the Colonies, for the purpose of rendering
our Governor & Judges dependent on the Crown.
In his Majestys Answer, we have nothing explicit,
but his Resolution to support the supreme Authority
of the British parliam^t to make Laws binding on the
Colonies (altho the petitions were supported by the
express Declarations of the Charter of the province)
and his great Displeasure, that principles repugnant
to that Right were therein held forth. Such an
Answer to such a petition affords the strongest
Grounds to conclude, that the Ministry are as firmly
resolvd as ever to continue the Revenue Acts &
apply the tribute extorted by Virtue of them from the
Colonies, to maintain the executive powers of the
several Governments of America absolutely in
dependent of their respective Legislatives; or
rather absolutely dependent on the Crown, which
will, if a little while persisted in, end in absolute
Despotism.

Such being still the temper of the British Ministry,
Such the Disposition of the parliament of Britain
under their Direction & Influence, to consider them
selves as *the Sovereign* of America, Is it not of the
utmost Importance that our Vigilance should increase,
that the Colonies should be united in their Sentiments
of the Measures of Opposition necessary to be taken
by them, and that in whichsoever of the Colonies any
Infringments are or shall be made on the common
Rights of all, that Colony should have the united
Efforts of all for its Support. This we take to be the

true Design of the Establishment of our Committees of Correspondence.

There is one thing which appears to us to be an Object worthy of the immediate Attention of the Colonies. Should a War take place, which is thought by many to be near at hand, America will then be viewd by Administration in a Light of Importance to Great Britain. Her Aids will be deemd necessary; her Friendship therefore will perhaps be even courted. Would it not then be the highest Wisdom in the sev eral American Assemblies, absolutely to withhold all kinds of Aid in a general War, untill the Rights & Liberties which *they ought to enjoy* are restored, & secured to them upon the most permanent founda tion? This has always been the Usage of a spirited House of Commons in Britain, and upon the best Grounds; for certainly protection & Security ought to be the unalterable Condition when Supplys are called for. With Regard to the Extent of Rights which the Colonies ought to insist upon, it is a Subject which requires the closest Attention & De liberation; and this is a strong Reason why it should claim the earliest Consideration of, at least, every Committee; in order that we may be prepared when time & Circumstances shall give to our Claim the surest prospect of Success. And when we consider how one great Event has hurried on, upon the back of another, such a time may come & such Circum stances take place sooner than we are now aware of. There are certain Rights which every Colony has explicitly asserted, & we trust they will never give up. *That* in particular, that they have the sole &

unalienable Right to give & grant their own money
& appropriate it to such purposes as they judge
proper, is justly deemd to be of the last Importance.
But whether even this Right, so essential to our Free
dom & Happiness, can remain . . . to us, while
a Right is claimed by the British parliament to make
Laws binding upon us in all Cases whatever, you will
certainly consider with Seriousness.   It would be de-
basing to us after so manly a Struggle for our Rights
to be contented with a mere *temporary* reliefe.   We
take the Liberty to present you with the State of
a Controversy upon that Subject, between the Gov
ernor of this province and the Assembly.   And as
the Assembly of this or some other Colony may pos
sibly be called into a further Consideration of it, we
should think our selves happy in a Communication of
such further Thoughts upon it, as we are perswaded
will upon a . . . occur to your Minds.   We are
far from desiring that the Connection between Britain
& America should be broken.   *Esto perpetua*, is our
ardent wish; but upon the Terms only of Equal Lib
erty.   If we cannot establish an Agreement upon
these terms, let us leave it to another & wiser Gen
eration.   But it may be worth Consideration that the
work is more likely to be well done, at a time when
the Ideas of Liberty & its Importance are strong in
Mens Minds.   There is Danger that these Ideas will
hereafter grow faint & languid.   Our Posterity may
be accustomd to bear the Yoke & being inured to
Servility they may even bow the Shoulder to the
Burden.   It can never be expected that a people, how
ever *numerous*, will form & execute a wise plan to

perpetuate their Liberty, when they have lost the Spirit & feeling of it.

We cannot close without mentioning a fresh In stance of the temper & Design of the British Minis try; and that is in allowing the East India Company, with a View of pacifying them, to ship their Teas to America. It is easy to see how aptly this Scheme will serve both to destroy the Trade of the Colonies & increase the revenue. How necessary then is it that Each Colony should take effectual methods to prevent this measure from having its designd Effects.[1]

GENTLEMEN

The foregoing Letter was unanimously agreed to by the Committee of Correspondence, and is in their name and by their order Transmitted to you by your most respectfull friends and humble Servants,

T: CUSHING   S: ADAMS   W: HEATH

P.S. It is the request of the Committee that the Con tents of this Letter be not made publick least our Com mon Enemies should counteract and prevent its design.

RESOLUTIONS OF THE TOWN OF BOSTON, NOVEMBER 5, 1773.

[*Boston Record Commissioners' Report*, vol. xviii., pp. 142, 143; a draft of the preamble, in the handwriting of Adams, is in the Mellen Chamberlain col lection, Boston Public Library.]

Whereas it appears by an Act of the British Parlia ment passed in the last Sessions, that the East India Company are by the said Act allowed to export their Teas into America, in such Quantities as the Lord of

---

[1] The remainder is not in the autograph of Adams.

the Treasury shall Judge proper[1] : And some People with an evil intent to amuse the People, and others thro' inattention to the true design of the Act, have so construed the same, as that the Tribute of three Pence on every Pound of Tea is not to be en acted by the detestable Task Masters there[2]—Upon the due consideration thereof, *Resolved*, That the Sense of the Town cannot be better expressed on this Occasion, than in the words of certain Judicious Re solves lately entered into by our worthy Brethren the Citizens of Philadelphia—wherefore

⁀*Resolved*, that the disposal of their own property is the Inherent Right of Freemen ; that there can be no property in that which another can of right take from us without our consent ; that the Claim of Parliament to tax America, is in other words a claim of Right to buy[3] Contributions on us at pleasure -——

2ᵈ· That the Duty imposed by Parliament upon Tea landed in America, is a tax on the Americans, or levying Contributions on them without their consent -——

3ᵈ· That the express purpose for which the Tax is levied on the Americans, namely for the support of Government, the Administration of Justice, and the defence of His Majestys Dominions in America, has a direct tendency to render Assemblies useless, and to introduce Arbitrary Government and Slavery -——

4ᵗʰ· That a virtuous and steady opposition to the Ministerial Plan of governing America, is absolutely necessary to preserve even the shadow of Liberty, and

---

[1] At this point the draft includes the words, "without the same having been exposed to sale in the Kingdom of Great Britain."

[2] The draft reads "here."

[3] The town record should apparently read "lay."

is a duty which every Freeman in America owes to his Country to himself and to his Posterity -——

5th That the Resolutions lately come by the East India Company, to send out their Teas to America Subject to the payment of Duties on its being landed here, is an open attempt to enforce the Ministerial Plan, and a violent attack upon the Liberties of America ——

6$^{th.}$ That it is the Duty of every American to oppose this attempt --——

7$^{th.}$ That whoever shall directly or indirectly coun tenance this attempt, or in any wise aid or abet in unloading receiving or vending the Tea sent or to be sent out by the East India Company while it remains subject to the payment of a duty here is an Enemy to America ——

8$^{th.}$ That a Committee be immediately chosen to wait on those Gentlemen, who it is reported are ap pointed by the East India Company to receive and sell said Tea, and to request them from a regard to their own characters and the peace and good order of this Town and Province immediately to resign their appointment.

THE COMMITTEE OF CORRESPONDENCE OF BOSTON
TO THE COMMITTEE OF CORRESPONDENCE
OF ROXBURY.

[MS., Committee of Correspondence Papers, Lenox Library.]

BOSTON Novr 9, 1773.

GENTLEMEN

The Town of Boston has for a few days past been greatly alarmd with hearing of the marching of the Soldiers posted at Castle Island from day to day in

Companies through the neighboring Towns armd. The pretence is that they are sickly & require such Exercise ; But why then should they be thus armd ? It is justly to be apprehended there are other Designs, which may be dangerous to our common Liberty. It is therefore the Request of the Committee of Corre spondence for this Town, that you would give us your Company at Faneuil Hall on Thursday next at three o'Clock, joyntly to consult with them on this alarm ing occasion ——

We are Gentⁿ

your Fellow Countrymen,

TO ARTHUR LEE.

[R. H. Lee, *Life of Arthur Lee*, vol. ii., pp. 208, 209.]

BOSTON, Nov. 9th, 1773.

MY DEAR SIR,—I have but just time to enclose you a newspaper, by which you will see that Lord Sh— —ne was not mistaken when he said that "things began to wear a very serious aspect in this part of the world." I wish that Lord Dartmouth would believe, that the people here begin to think that they have borne op pression long enough, and that if he has a plan of reconciliation he would produce it without delay ; but his lordship must know, that it must be such as will satisfy Americans. One cannot foresee events ; but from all the observation I am able to make, my next letter will not be upon a trifling subject.

I am with great respect, your friend,

TO THE SELECTMEN OF BOSTON.

[MS., Mellen Chamberlain Collection, Boston Public Library.[1]]

BOSTON Nov[r] 17, 1773

GENTLEMEN

Whereas the Freeholders & other Inhabitants of this Town did at their last Meeting make application to Richard Clarke Esq[r] & Sons who are supposd to be the persons to whom the East India Companys Tea is to come consignd; And request them to resign their Appointment to which they returnd for Answer that they were uncertain upon what Terms the said Tea would be sent to them, and what Obligations they should be laid under.   And Whereas by a Vessell now arrived from London (in which is come a Passenger a Son of the said M[r] Clarke) there is Advice that said Tea is very soon expected.

It is therefore the Desire of us the Subscribers that a Meeting of the Town may be called, that an other Application may be made to the same persons requesting as before; it being probable that they can now return a definite Answer.

We are Gentlemen

Your humble serv[ts]

THE COMMITTEE OF CORRESPONDENCE OF BOSTON TO THE COMMITTEE OF PLYMOUTH.

[MS., Committee of Correspondence Papers, Lenox Library.]

BOSTON Dec[r] 17, 1773

GENTLEMEN

The Com[e] of Correspondence for this Town duly rec[d] your Letter of the 14th & note the important Con-

[1] All in the autograph of Adams, and signed by Adams and twenty-four others. Cf., *Boston Record Commissioners' Report*, vol. xviii., p. 147.

tents. We inform you in great Haste that every
Chest of Tea on board the three Ships in this Town
was destroyed the last Evening without the least In
jury to the Vessels or any other property. Our Enemies must acknowledge that these people have acted
upon pure & upright Principle. The people at the
Cape will we hope behave with propriety and as be
comes Men resolved to save their Country.[1]

THE COMMITTEE OF CORRESPONDENCE OF BOSTON TO
OTHER COMMITTEES OF CORRESPONDENCE.

[MS., Committee of Correspondence Papers, Lenox Library.[2]]

BOSTON 17th Decer 1773.

GENTLEMEN,

Yesterday we had a greater meeting of the Body
than ever, the Country coming in from twenty miles
round, & every step was taken, that was practicable
for returning the Teas. The moment it was known
out of doors that Mr Rotch could not obtain a pass
for his Ship by the Castle, a number of people huz-
za'd in the Street, and in a very little time every
ounce of the Teas on board of the Capts Hall, Bruce
& Coffin, was immersed in the Bay, without the least
injury to private property. The Spirit of the People
on this occasion surprisd all parties who view'd the
Scene.

We conceived it our duty to afford you the most

---

[1] At the foot of the draft is written the following. also in the handwriting of
Adams: & to Sandwich with this Addition— " We trust you will afford them
your immediate Assistance & Advice."

[2] Merely the subscription and addresses are in the autograph of Adams.
Noted as sent " by Mr Revere " to " Mr Mifflin & Geo Clymer " at Philadel
phia and " Phillip Livingston & Sam Broom " at New York.

early advice of this interesting event by express which
departing immediately obliges us to conclude.

In the Name of the Com^e,

TO ARTHUR LEE.

[R. H. Lee, *Life of Arthur Lee*, vol. ii., pp. 212, 213.]

BOSTON, Dec. 25th, 1773.

MY DEAR SIR,—I wrote you a few days past by
Capt. Scott, and then promised to write farther by
the next opportunity; but not having heard of the
sailing of this vessel till this moment, I have only
time to recommend a letter written and directed to
you by John Scollay, Esq. a worthy gentleman and
one of the selectmen of this town. He desires me to
apologise for his addressing a letter to one who is a
perfect stranger to him, and to assure you that he is
persuaded there is no gentleman in London who has
the liberties of America more warmly at heart, or is
more able to vindicate them than yourself. You see
the dependence we have upon you.

Excuse this *short epistle*, and be assured that as I
am a friend to every one possessed of public virtue,
with affection I must be constantly yours,

TO ARTHUR LEE.

[R. H. Lee, *Life of Arthur Lee*, vol. ii., pp. 209-212.]

BOSTON, Dec. 31, 1773.

MY DEAR SIR,—I am now to inform you of as
remarkable an event as has yet happened since the

commencement of our struggle for American liberty. The meeting of the town of Boston, an account of which I enclosed in my last, was succeeded by the arrival of the ship Falmouth, Captain Hall, with 114 chests of the East India Company's tea, on the 28th of November last. The next day the people met in Faneuil hall, without observing the rules prescribed by law for calling them together ; and although that hall is capable of holding 1200 or 1300 men, they were soon obliged for the want of room to adjourn to the Old South meeting-house ; where were assembled upon this important occasion 5000, some say 6000 men, con sisting of the respectable inhabitants of this and the adjacent towns. The business of the meeting was conducted with decency, unanimity, and spirit. Their resolutions you will observe in an enclosed printed paper. It naturally fell upon the correspondence for the town of Boston to see that these resolutions were carried into effect. This committee, finding that the owner of the ship after she was unloaded of all her cargo except the tea, was by no means disposed to take the necessary steps for her sailing back to London, thought it best to call in the committees of Charlestown, Cambridge, Brookline, Roxbury, and Dorchester, all of which towns are in the neighbour hood of this, for their advice and assistance. After a free conference and due consideration, they dispersed. The next day, being the 14th, inst. the people met again at the Old South church, and having ascertained the owner, they *compelled* him to apply at the custom house for a clearance for his ship to London with the tea on board, and appointed ten gentlemen to see it performed ; after which they adjourned till Thursday the 16th. The people then met, and Mr. Rotch in formed them that he had according to their injunction applied to the collector of the customs for a clearance, and received in answer from the collector that he could not consistently with his duty grant him a clearance, until the ship should be discharged of the dutiable article on board. It must be here observed that Mr. Rotch had before made a tender of the tea to the consignees, being told by them that it was not practicable for them at that time to receive the tea, by reason of a constant guard kept upon it by armed men ; but that when it might be practicable, they would receive it. He demanded the captain's bill of lading and the freight, both which they refused him, against which he entered a regular protest. The people then required Mr. Rotch to protest the refusal of the collector to grant him a clearance under these circumstances, and thereupon to wait upon the governor for a permit to pass the castle in her voyage to London, and then adjourned till the afternoon. They then met, and after waiting till sun-setting, Mr. Rotch returned, and acquainted them that the governor had refused to grant him a passport, thinking it inconsistent with the laws and his duty to the king, to do it until the ship should be qualified, notwithstanding Mr. Rotch had acquainted him with the circumstances above mentioned. You will observe by the printed proceedings, that the people were resolved that the tea should not be landed, but sent back to London in the same bottom ; and the property should be safe guarded while in port, which they punctually performed. It cannot therefore be fairly said that the destruction of the property was in their contemplation. It is proved that the consignees, together with the collector of the customs, and the governor of the province, prevented the safe return of the East India Company's property (the danger of the sea only excepted) to London. The people finding all their endeavours for this purpose thus totally frustrated, dissolved the meeting, which had consisted by common estimation of at least seven thousand men, many of whom had come from towns at the distance of twenty miles. In less than four hours every chest of tea on board three ships which had by this time arrived, *three hundred and forty-two* chests, or rather the contents of them, was thrown into the sea, without the least injury to the vessels or any other property. The only remaining vessel which was expected with this detested article, is by the act of righteous heaven cast on shore on the back of Cape Cod, which has often been the sad fate of many a more valuable cargo. For a more particular detail of facts, I refer you to our worthy friend, Dr. Hugh Williamson, who kindly takes the charge of this letter. We have had great pleasure in his company for a few weeks past; and he favoured the meeting with his presence.

You cannot imagine the height of joy that sparkles in the eyes and animates the countenances as well as the hearts of all we meet on this occasion; excepting the disappointed, disconcerted Hutchinson and his tools. I repeat what I wrote you in my last; if lord Dartmouth has prepared his plan let him produce it speedily; but his lordship must know that it must

be such a plan as will not barely amuse, much less
farther irritate but conciliate the affection of the
inhabitants.

I had forgot to tell you that before the arrival of
either of these ships, the tea commissioners had
preferred a petition to the governor and council,
praying "to resign themselves and the property in
their care, to his excellency and the board as guard
ians and protectors of the people, and that measures
may be directed for the landing and securing the
tea," &c. I have enclosed you the result of the
council on that petition. He (the governor) is now,
I am told, consulting *his* lawyers and books to make
out that the resolves of the meeting are treasonable.
I duly received your favours of the 23d June, of the
21st July and 13th October,[1] and shall make the best
use I can of the important contents.

Believe me to be affectionately your friend,

P.S.—Your letter of the 28th August is but this
moment come to hand. I hope to have leisure to
write you by the next vessel. Our friend Dr. Warren
has written to you by this[2]; you will find him an
agreeable and useful correspondent.

---

[1] Under date of October 13, 1773, Lee had written to Adams: "Every day
gives us new light and new strength. At first it was a tender point to question
the authority of parliament over us *in any case* whatsoever; time and you have
proved that their right is equally questionable *in all cases* whatsoever. It was
certainly a great stroke, and has succeeded most happily." R. H. Lee, *Life
of Arthur Lee*, vol i., pp. 236, 237.

[2] Under date of December 21, 1773. The text is in *Ibid.*, vol. ii., pp.
262, 263.

TO JOHN PICKERING, JUNIOR.[1]

[MS., Samuel Adams Papers, Lenox Library.]

BOSTON Jany 8 1774

SIR/

As the General Assembly will undoubtedly meet on the 26th of this Month, the Negroes whose Petition lies on file and is referrd for Consideration, are very sollicitous for the Event of it. And having been informd that you intended to consider it at your Leisure Hours in the Recess of the Court, they earnestly wish you would compleat a Plan for their Reliefe. And in the mean time, if it be not too much Trouble, they ask it as a favor that you would by a Letter enable me to communicate to them the general outlines of your Design.

> I am with sincere Regard,
> Sir, your humble Servt

TO ARTHUR LEE.

[MS., Samuel Adams Papers, Lenox Library.]

Jan 25 1774

The sending the East India Companies Tea into America appears evidently to have been with Design of the British Administration, and to complete the favorite plan of establishing a Revenue in America. The People of Boston and the other adjacent Towns endeavored to have the Tea sent back to the place from whence it came & then to

---

[1] Of Salem, Mass. Upon a later letter from Pickering to Adams is endorsed in the autograph of Adams : " Letter from M^r J Pickerin an honest & sensible Friend of ye Liberty of his Country."

prevent the Design from taking Effect. Had this been done in Boston, as it was done in New York & Philadelphia, the Design of the Ministry would have been as effectually prevented here as in those Colonies and the property would have been saved. Governor Hutchinson & the other Crown officers having the Command of the Castle by which the Ships must have passed, & other powers in their Hands, made use of these Powers to defeat the Intentions of the people & succeeded ; in short the Governor who for Art & Cunning as well as an inveterate hatred of the people was inferior to no one of the Cabal ; both encouragd & provoked the people to destroy the Tea. By refusing to grant a Passport he held up to them the alternative of destroying the property of the East India Com pany or suffering that to be the sure means of unhinging the Security of property in general in America, and by delaying to call on the naval power to protect the Tea, he led them to determine their Choice of Difficulties. In this View of the Matter the Question is easily decided who ought in Justice to pay for the Tea if it ought to be paid for at all.

The Destruction of the Tea is the pretence for the unprecedented Severity shown to the Town of Boston, but the real Cause is the opposition to Tyranny for which the people of that Town have always made themselves remarkeable & for which I think this Country is much obligd to them. They are suffering the Vengeance of Administration in the Common Cause of America.

RESOLUTION OF THE HOUSE OF REPRESENTATIVES OF
MASSACHUSETTS.   MARCH 1, 1774.[1]

[*Journal of the House of Representatives, 1773, 1774*, p. 219.]

Whereas Peter Oliver,[2] Esq ; Chief Justice of the
Superior Court of Judicature, &c. hath declined any
more to receive the Grants of this House for his
Services, and hath informed this House by a Writing
under his Hand, that he hath taken and received
a Grant from his Majesty for his Services, from the
fifth Day of July 1772, to the fifth day of January
1774 ; and that he is resolved for the future to re
ceive the Grants from his Majesty that are or shall
be made for his said Services, while he shall continue
in this Province as Chief Justice :

Therefore, *Resolved*, That this House will not
proceed to make a Grant to the said Peter Oliver,
Esq ; for his Services for the Year past.

THE COMMITTEE OF CORRESPONDENCE OF BOSTON TO THE
COMMITTEE OF CORRESPONDENCE OF MARBLEHEAD. [3]

[MS., Committee of Correspondence Papers, Lenox Library.]

BOSTON March 24 1774

GENTLEMEN

The Bearer of this Mr Wm Goddard has brot us
Letters from our worthy Brethren the Committees of
Correspondence of New York Newport and Provi
dence, recommending to our Consideration the Expe-

---

[1] On March 1, 1774, the House of Representatives voted that Adams should
prepare a resolution stating the reason for omitting the usual grant to Peter
Oliver.   He reported the same day, and his report was accepted.

[2] For the articles of impeachment against Peter Oliver, see *Massachusetts
Gazette*, March 3, 1774, and *Annual Register*, 1774, pp. 224–227.

[3] Intended also for the Committees of Correspondence at Salem, Portsmouth
and Newbury Port.

diency of making an Effort to constitute & support
a Post throughout America in the room of that which
is now establishd by an Act of the British Parliament.
When we consider the Importance of a Post, by which
not only private Letters of Friendship and Commerce
but *publick Intelligence* is conveyd from Colony to
Colony, it seems at once proper & necessary that
such an one should be establishd as shall be under the
Direction of the Colonies ; more especially when we
further consider that the British Administration &
their Agents have taken every Step in their Power
to prevent an Union of the Colonies which is so
necessary for our making a successful opposition to
their arbitrary Designs, and which depends upon a
free Communication of the Circumstances and Senti
ments of each to the others, and their mutual Councils
Besides, the present Post Office is founded on an Act
of the British Parliament and raises a revenue from
us without our Consent, in which View it is equally
as obnoxious as any other revenue Act, and in the
time of the Stamp Act as well as since it has been
pleaded as a Precedent against us. And though we
have appeard to acquiesce in it, because the office was
thought to be of publick Utility, yet, if it is now made
use of for the purpose of stopping the Channels of
publick Intelligence and so in Effect of aiding the
measures of Tyranny, as Mr Goddard informs us it
is, the necessity of substituting another office in its
Stead must be obvious. The Practicability of doing
this throughout the Continent is to be considerd.
We by no means despair of it. But as it depends
upon joynt Wisdom & Firmness our Brethren of

New York are sollicitous to know the Sentiments of the New England Colonies. It is therefore our earnest Request that you would take this matter so interresting to America into your consideration, & favor us by the return of Mr Goddard with your own Sentiments, and as far as you shall be able to collect them, the Sentiments of the Gentlemen of your Town & more particularly the Merchants and Traders. And we further request that you would, if you shall judge it proper, communicate your Sentiments in a Letter by Mr Goddard to the Committees of Correspondence of New York & Philadelphia &c. It is our present opinion that when a plan is laid for the effectual Establishment and Regulation of a Post throughout the Colonies upon a constitutional Footing, the Inhab itants of this Town will heartily joyn in carrying it into Execution. We refer you for further particulars to Mr Goddard, who seems to be deeply engagd in this attempt, not only with a View of serving himself as a Printer, but equally from the more generous motive of serving the Common Cause of America. We wish Success to the Design and are with cordial Esteem,

                    Gentlemen,
                         Your Friends & fellow Countrymen,

TO ELBRIDGE GERRY.

[J. T. Austin, *Life of Elbridge Gerry*, vol. i., pp. 36-39.]

                                   BOSTON, March 25, 1774.

My Dear Sir,

While the general court was sitting I received a letter from you relating to the unhappy circumstances

the town of Marblehead was then in ; but a great
variety of business, some of which was very import
ant, prevented my giving you a convincing proof at
that time, of the regard with which I am ever disposed
to treat your favours. Besides, if it had been in my
power to have aided you with advice, I flattered my
self, from the information I afterwards had, that the
storm, though it raged with so much violence, would
soon spend itself, and a calm would ensue. The
tumult of the people is very properly compared to the
raging of the sea. When the passions of a multitude
become headstrong, they generally will have their
course : a direct opposition only tends to increase
them ; and as to reasoning, one may as well expect
that the foaming billows will hearken to a lecture of
morality and be quiet. The skilful pilot will care
fully keep the helm, and so steer the ship while the
storm continues, as to prevent, if possible, her receiv
ing injury.

When your petition was read in the house, I was
fearful that our enemies would make an ill improve
ment of it. I thought I could discover in the counte
nances of some a kind of triumph in finding that the
friends of liberty themselves, were obliged to have re
course even to military aid, to protect them from the
fury of an ungoverned mob. They seemed to me to
be disposed to confound the distinction, between a
lawless attack upon property in a case where if there
had been right there was remedy, and the people's
rising in the necessary defence of their liberties, and
deliberately, and I may add rationally destroying
property, after trying every method to preserve it, and

when the men in power had rendered the destruction of that property the only means of securing the prop erty of *all*.

It is probable that such improvement may have been made of the disorders in Marblehead, to preju dice or discredit our manly opposition to the efforts of tyranny ; but I hope the friends of liberty will pre vent any injury thereby to the common cause : and yet, I cannot but express some fears, that parties and animosities have arisen among the brethren ; because I have just now heard from a gentleman of your town, that your committee of correspondence have resolved no more to act ! I am loath to believe, nay, I cannot yet believe, that the gentlemen of Marble- head, who have borne so early and so noble a testi mony to the cause of American freedom, will desert that cause, only from a difference of sentiments among themselves concerning a matter which has no relation to it. If my fears are groundless, pray be so kind as to relieve them, by writing to me as soon as you have an opportunity. I shall take it as the greatest act of friendship you can do me. Indeed the matter will soon be put to the trial ; for our committee, without the least jealousy, have written a letter to your's, by Mr. God- dard, who is the bearer of this. The contents we think of great importance, and therefore I hope they will have the serious consideration of the gentlemen of your committee.

I am, with strict truth,

Your's affectionately,

THE COMMITTEE OF CORRESPONDENCE OF MASSACHUSETTS
TO BENJAMIN FRANKLIN.[1]

[*Seventy-Six Society Publications. Papers Relating to Massachusetts*, pp.
186-192. A draft is in the Committee of Correspondence Papers, Lenox
Library. A manuscript text, with autograph signatures, is in the library of the
Massachusetts Historical Society.]

BOSTON, March 31st, 1774.

SIR :

By the inclosed Papers you will observe the pro
ceedings of the two Houses of Assembly in the late
session with regard to the Justices of the Superior
Court. The conduct of Administration in advising
an annual Grant of the Crown to the Governor and
the Judges whereby they are rendered absolutely de
pendent on the Crown for their being and support,
had justly and very thoroughly alarmed the appre
hensions of the people. They clearly saw that this
measure would complete the Tragedy of American
Freedom, for they could conceive of no state of sla
very more perfect, than for a Parliament in which they
could have no voice to claim a power of making Laws
to bind them in all cases whatever, and to exercise
that assumed Power in taking their money from them
and appropriating it for the support of Judges who
are to execute such laws as that parliament should
see fit to make binding upon them, and a Fleet and
Army to enforce their subjection to them. No dis
cerning Minister could expect that a people who had
not entirely lost the Spirit and Feeling of that Lib
erty wherewith they had before been made free, would
tamely and without a struggle submit to be thus dis
graced and enslaved by the most powerful and haughty

---

[1] Signed by Samuel Adams, John Hancock, William Phillips and William
Heath.

Nation on Earth. They heard with astonishment that his Majesty, *their own sovereign* as well as the sovereign of Britain, had been advised by his servants to signify his displeasure at the decent temperate and humble Petitions of their Representatives, for the re dress of this intolerable Grievance merely because they held up principles founded in nature, and con firmed to British Subjects by the British Constitution, and to the subjects in this Province by a sacred char ter granted to the inhabitants by his illustrious pre decessors for themselves their Heirs and successors forever. They regretted that the Influence of the good Lord Dartmouth upon whose exertions they had placed a confidence could not prevail to gain the Royal attention to their just Complaints being as sured that could his Majesty be truly informed, that the express intention of the Royal Charter was to establish and confirm to his subjects in this Province all the liberties of his natural born subjects within the Realm, to all Intents, Purposes and Constructions whatsoever, they should soon rejoice in the full re dress of their Grievances and that he would revoke his Grants to his Governor and Judges and leave the Assembly to support his Governor in the Province in the way and manner prescribed in the Charter accord ing to ancient and uninterrupted usage and conform able to the true spirit of the British Constitution.

The People however forbore to take any extraor dinary Measures for the Removal of this dangerous innovation, and trusted to the Prudence and forti tude of their Representatives by whose Influence four of the Judges have been prevailed upon to renounce

the Grants of the Crown and to declare their Resolu
tion to depend upon the Grants of the Assembly for
their future services. The Chief Justice has acted a dif
ferent part. The House of Representatives have
addressed the Governor and Council to remove him
from his Office ; they have impeached him of High
Crimes and misdemeanors, the Governor has refused,
even though requested by the Council, to appoint a
time to determine on the matter, and finally the House
have Resolved that they have done all in their Power
in their capacity to effect his removal and that the
Governor's refusal was presumed to be because he
received *his* support from the Crown.

As the Papers inclosed contain so fully the Senti
ments of the two Houses concerning this important
matter, it is needless to make any observations
thereon. The Assembly is prorogued and it is
expected will soon be Dissolved. Doubtless the
People who in general are greatly agitated with the
conduct of the Governor, will *at least* speculate very
freely upon a subject so interesting to them. They
see with resentment the effect of the Governor's in
dependency, That he is resolved to save a favorite
(with whom he has a connection by the intermarriage
of their children) and therein to set a precedent for
future Independent Governors to establish any cor
rupt officers against the remonstrances of the Repre
sentative Body. They despair of any Constitutional
remedy, while the Governor of the Province is thus
dependant upon Ministers of State against the
most flagrant oppressions of a corrupt Officer. They
take it for certain that *such* a Governor will forever

screen the conduct of *such* an officer from examination
and prevent his removal, if he has reason to think it
is expected he should so do by those upon whose
favor he depends.   On the other hand his Majesty's
Ministers, unless they are blinded by the plausible
Colourings of designing men may see, that by the
present measures the People are provoked and irri
tated to such a degree, that it is not in the Power of
a Governor (whom they look upon as a mere Instru
ment of Power) though born and educated in the
Country, and for a long time possessed of a great
share of the confidence and affections of the People
now to carry a single point which they the ministers
can recommend to him.   And this will always be the
case let who will be Governor while by being made
totally dependent on the Crown or perhaps more
strictly speaking upon the Ministry, he is thus aliened
from the People for whose good he is and ought to
be appointed.   In such a state what is to be expected
but warm and angry Debates between the Governor
and the two Houses (while the Assembly is sitting
instead of the joint consultation for the public Wel
fare) and violent commotions among the People?   It
will be in vain for any to expect that the people of
this Country will now be contented with a partial and
temporary relief, or that they will be amused by
Court promises while they see not the least relaxation
of Grievances.   By the vigilance and activity of
Committees of Correspondence among the several
towns in the Province they have been wonderfully
enlightened and animated.   They are united in sen
timent and their opposition to unconstitutional Meas-

ures of Government is become systematical, Colony communicates freely with Colony. There is a com mon Affection   *   *   *   *   *   *   *   *   *   *   *   *   *   whole continent is now become united in sentiment and opposition to tyranny. Their old good will and affection for the Parent Country is not however lost, if she returns to her former moderation and good humor their affection) will revive. They wish for nothing more than per-, manent union with her upon the condition of equal'. liberty. This is all they have been contending for / and nothing short of this will or ought to satisfy them. When formerly the Kings of England have encroached upon the Liberties of their Subjects, the subjects have thought it their Duty to themselves and their Posterity to contend with them until they were restored to the footing of the Constitution. The events of such struggles have sometimes proved fatal to Crowned Heads—perhaps they have never issued but Establishments of the People's Liberties. In those times it was not thought reasonable to say, that since the King had claimed such or such a Power the People *must* yield it to him because it would not be for the Honor of his Majesty to recede from his Claim. If the People of Britain must needs flatter themselves that they collectively are the Sovereign of America, America will never consent that they should govern them arbitrarily, or without known and stipulated Rules. But the matter is not so considered here : Britain and the Colonies are con sidered as distinct Governments under the King. Britain has a Constitution the envy of all Foreigners,

to which it has ever been the safety as well of Kings
as of subjects steadfastly to adhere. Each Colony
has also a Constitution in its Charter or other Insti
tution of Government; all of which agree in this that
the fundamental Laws of the British Constitution
shall be the Basis. That Constitution by no means
admits of Legislation without representation. Why
then should the Parliament of Britain which not
withstanding all its Ideas of transcendant Power
must forever be circumscribed within the limits of that
Constitution, insist upon the right of legislation for
the people of America without their having Representation there? It cannot be justified by their
own Constitution. The Laws of Nature and Reason
abhor it; yet because she has claimed such a Power,
her Honor truly is concerned still to assert and ex
cise it, and she may not recede. Will such kind of
reasoning bear the test of Examination! Or rather
will it not be an eternal disgrace to any nation which
considers her Honor concerned to employ Fleets and
Armies for the Support of a claim which she cannot
in Reason defend, merely because she has once in
anger made such a Claim? It is the misfortune of
Britain and the Colonies that flagitious Men on both
sides the Water have made it their Interest to foment
divisions, Jealousies, and animosities between them,
which perhaps will never subside until the Extent of
Power and Right on each part is more explicitly
stipulated than has ever yet been thought necessary,
and although such a stipulation should prove a
lasting advantage on each side, yet considering that
the views and designs of those men were to do infinite

mischief and to establish a Tyranny upon the Ruins of a free constitution they deserve the vengeance of the public, and till the memory of them shall be erased by time, they will most assuredly meet with the exe crations of Posterity.

Our Lieutenant Governor Oliver is now dead.[1] This event affords the Governor a Plea for postponing his voyage to England till further orders. Had the Government by the absence of *both* devolved on the Council, his Majesty's service (which has been fre quently pleaded to give a Colouring to measures de structive of the true Interests of his Subjects) would we are persuaded, have been really promoted. Among other things the Grants of the House which in the late session were repeated for the services of our Agents would have been passed. There is a degree of Insult in the Governor's refusal of his consent to those Grants, for as his refusal is grounded upon the Hopes that our Friends will thereby be discouraged from further serving us, it is as much as to say that there will be no Agents unless the Assembly will be content with such as he shall prescribe for their choice. The House by a Message urged the Gover- nor to enable them to do their Agents Justice but in vain. This and other instances serve to show that the Powers vested in the Governor are exercised to injure and Provoke the People.

We judge it to be the expectation of the House of Representatives that you should warmly solicit the Earl of Dartmouth for his Interest that as well as other instructions which are grievous to us, more

---

[1] Cf. *Literary Diary of Ezra Stiles*, vol. i., pp. 436, 437.

particularly those which relate to the disposition of
our public   *   *   *   *   *   that which
restrains the Governor from consenting   *   *
     *   *   *   to the Agents may be recalled.
And his Lordship ought to consider his Interest in
this particular not as a *personal* favor done to you
but as a piece of Justice done to the Province ; and
in the same light we strongly recommend it to your
own Consideration especially as we hope for a change
in the Government.

We now write to you by the direction of the
House of Representatives to the Committee of
Correspondence, and are with very great Regard,
　　In the name of the Committee
　　　　　　Sir,
　　　　Your most humble servants,

TO JAMES WARREN.

[MS., Samuel Adams Papers, Lenox Library.]

BOSTON March 31 1774

My Dear Sir

I have been for some time past waiting for the
Arrival of a ship from London, that I might have
something of Importance to communicate to you.
No ship has yet arrived. I cannot however omit
writing to you by our worthy Friend Mr Watson, by
whom I rec^d your obliging Letter of the 27 Instant.

Altho we have had no Arrival from Lond^n directly
to this place, we have heard from thence by the way of
Philadelphia as you have observd in the News papers.
The Account they first receivd of our opposition to

the East India Act, as it is called, particularly the transactions at Liberty Tree, they treated with Scorn & Ridicule; but when they heard of the Resolves of the Body of the people at the old South Meeting house, the place from whence the orders issued for the removal of the Troops in 1770, they put on grave Countenances. No Notice is taken of America in the Kings Speech. Our Tories tell us to expect Regiments [to be] quarterd among us. What Measures an injudicious Ministry, (to say the least of them) will take, cannot easily at present be foreseen; it will be wise for us to be ready *for all Events*, that *we may make the best Improvement of them*. It is probable that Mr Hutchinson will make the Death of his Brother Oliver a plea for postponing a Voyage to London, and if Troops should arrive *it may be best that he should be here.*—I never suffer my Mind to be ever much disturbd with Prospects. Sufficient for the Day is the Evil thereof. It is our Duty at all Hazards to preserve the publick Liberty. Righteous Heaven will graciously smile on every manly and rational Attempt to secure that best of all his Gifts to Man, from the ravishing Hand of lawless & brutal Power.

Mr Watson will inform you, what Steps [the] Com^e of Correspondence have taken with regard to the Establishment of a Post Office upon constitutional Principles. Mr Goddard, who brot us Letters from New York, Newport & Providence relating to that Subject, is gone with Letters from us to the principal trading Towns as far as Portsmouth. I will acquaint you with the State of the Affair when he returns, and

our Com^e will I doubt not, then write to yours. The
Colonies must unite to carry thro such [a] Project, and
when the End is effected it will be a pretty grand
Acquisition.

I refer you also to Mr Watson, who can inform you
respecting one of your Protecters who has been in
Town. The Tryumph of your Tories as well as ours
will I hope be short. We must not however boast as
he that putteth off the Harness. H—n is politically
sick and [I] fancy despairs of returning Health. The
"law learning" Judge I am told is in the Horrors and
the late Lieutenant (joynt Author of a late Pamphlet
intitled *Letters* &c.) a few Weeks ago "died & was
buried". —Excuse me from enlarging at present. I
intend to convince you that I am "certainly a Man
of my Word"—In the mean time with Assurance of
unfeigned Friendship for Mrs Warren and your agreable Family, in which Mrs Adams joyns, I remain

Yours Affectionately,

THE COMMITTEE OF CORRESPONDENCE OF BOSTON TO THE
COMMITTEE OF CORRESPONDENCE OF MARBLEHEAD.[1]

[MS., Committee of Correspondence Papers, Lenox Library; a text, with
slight modifications, is in J. T. Austin, *Life of Elbridge Gerry*, vol. i., pp.
39-42.]

BOSTON April 2^d 1774

GENTLEMEN

Yesterday we receivd your Letter dated the 22^d of
March, wherein we have the disagreeable Intelligence
of your "having resignd the several offices in which
you have acted for the Town" of Marblehead, and

[1] Addressed to "Azor Orne Esqr & other Gentlemen of the Committee of
Correspondence for Marblehead."

that you shall "accept them no more—without material Alteration in the Conduct of the Inhabitants."

When we heard of the unhappy Circumstances of
that Town—The Contest that had arisen to so great
a Degree of Violence on Account of the Hospital
lately erected there, it gave us great Concern and
Anxiety, lest it might issue to the Prejudice of the
Common Cause of American Freedom. We were
apprehensive that the Minds of the Zealous Friends
of that good Cause, being warmly agitated in such a
Controversy, would become thereby disaffected to
each other, and that the Advantage which we have
hitherto experienced from their united Efforts would
cease. We are confirmd that our Fears were not ill
grounded, by your relinquishing a Post, which, in our
Opinion, and we dare say in the Opinion of your
Fellow Townsmen you sustaind with Honor to your
selves and Advantage to your Country. But Gentle
men, Suffer us to ask, Whether you well considerd,
that although you derivd your Being as a Committee
of Correspondence from that particular Town which
appointed you, yet in the Nature of your office, while
they continued you in it you stood connected in a pe
culiar Relation with your Country. If this be a just
View of it, Should the ill Conduct of the Inhabitants
of Marblehead towards you, influence you to decline
serving the publick in this office, any more than that
of the Inhabitants of this or any other Town ? And
would you not therefore have continued in that office,
though you had been obligd to resign every other
office you held under the Town, without Injury to
your own Reputation ? Besides will the Misfortune

end in this Resignation? Does not the Step natur
ally lead you to withdraw your selves totally from the
publick Meetings of the Town, however important to
the Common Cause, by which the other firm Friends
to that honorable Cause may feel the Want of your
Influence and Aid, at a time when, as you well ex
press it "a *fatal* Thrust may be aimed at our Rights
and Liberties," and it may be necessary that all should
appear, & "as one Body" oppose the Design & de
feat the Rebel Intent? Should not the Disorders
that have prevaild and still prevail in the Town of
Marblehead, have been a weighty Motive rather for
your taking Measures to strengthen your Connections
with the People than otherwise; that you might in
Conjunction with other prudent Men, have employed
your Influence & Abilities in reducing to the Exer
cise of Reason those who had been governd by Pre
judice and Passion, & they have brought the Contest
to an equitable & amicable Issue, which would cer
tainly have been to your own Satisfaction. If Difficulties stared you in the Face, it is a good Maxim
Nil desperandum; and are you sure that it was im
practicable for you, by Patience and Assiduity, to
have restored "Order & Distinction" and renderd
the publick offices of the Town again respectable?

It is difficult to enumerate all the Instances in
which our Enemies, as watchful as they are inveter
ate, will make an ill Improvement of your Letter of
resignation. And therefore we earnestly wish that a
Method may yet be contrived for the Recalling of it
consistent with your own Sentiments. We assure
our Selves that personal Considerations will not be

sufferd to have an undue Weight in your Minds, when the publick Liberty in which is involvd the Happiness of your own as well as the Children of those who have ill treated you, & whom to rescue from Bondage will afford you the most exalted Pleasure, is in Danger of suffering Injury.

We wish most ardently that by the Exercise of Moderation & Prudence the Differences subsisting among the good People of Marblehead may be settled upon righteous Terms. And as we are informd that the Town at their late Meeting did not see Cause to make Choice of other Gentlemen in your Room in Consequence of your declining to serve any longer as a Committee of Correspondence, we beg Leave still to consider & address you in that Character.

We are with unfeigned Respect,

TO ARTHUR LEE.

[R. H. Lee, *Life of Arthur Lee*, vol. ii., pp. 215-220.]

BOSTON, April 4th, 1774.

MY DEAR SIR,—My last letter to you I delivered to the care of Dr. Williamson, who sailed with Capt. —————in December last. The general assembly has since been sitting, and the important subject of the judges of the superior court being made dependent on the crown for their salaries, was again taken up by the house of representatives with spirit and firmness. The house had in a former session passed divers resolutions expressing their sense of the dangerous tendency of this innovation, and declaring that unless the justices should renounce the sal-

aries from the crown, and submit to a constitutional
dependence upon the assembly for their support,
they would proceed to impeach them before the gov
ernor and council.   One of them, Mr. Trowbridge,
very early in the session, in a letter to the speaker,
expressed his former compliance with that resolve,
which letter was communicated to the house and voted
satisfactory.   The other four had taken no notice of
the resolve.   The house therefore having waited from
the 26th of January, which was the first day of the
session, till the 1st of February, then came to a
resolution, that unless they should conform to their
order on or before the fourth of the same month,
farther proceedings would be had on such neglect.
The effect of this resolve was, that three of them,
viz:—Hutchinson, (a brother to him who is called
governor),——, —————, made similar declarations to that of Trowbridge, which were also
voted satisfactory.   Mr. Justice Oliver, who is a
brother of the lieutenant-governor, and is connected
with the governor by the marriage of their children,
came to a different determination; which occasioned
a controversy between the governor and the two
houses, inserted at large in the enclosed papers.
Therein you will see that the governor has treated
the petitions, complaints, and remonstrances of the re
presentative body, with haughty contempt.   The
people view it with deep resentment as an effect of
his independency; whereby he is aliened from them,
and become a fitter instrument in the hands of the
ministry to carry into effect their destructive plans.
They are irritated to the highest degree, and despair

of any constitutional remedy against the oppressions of a corrupt officer, while the governor, *be he who he may*, is thus dependent on ministers of state.   They have ever since the trial of Preston and his soldiers been murmuring at the conduct of the superior court, and the partiality which many say is so clearly dis covered in causes between revenue officers and the government, abettors, and other subjects.   Indeed, the house of representatives two or three years ago passed a resolution that such conduct in several in stances had been observed, as appears in their printed journals.   To give you some idea of what the temper of that court has been, a lawyer [1] of great eminence in the province, and a member of the house of repre sentatives, was thrown over the bar a few days ago, because he explained in a public newspaper the sentiments he had advanced in the house when he had been misrepresented ; and a young lawyer of great genius in this town, who had passed the regular course of study, (which is more than can be said of the chief-justice) has been and is still refused by the governor, only because he mentioned the name of Hutchinson with freedom, and that not in court, but in a Boston town-meeting some years before.   And to show you from whence this influence springs, I must inform you that not long ago the governor, the lieutenant-governor, and three of the judges, which make a majority of the bench, were nearly related ; and even now the governor has a brother there, and is brother-in-law to the chief-justice.   Such combi nations are justly formidable, and the people view

---

[1] Joseph Hawley, Esq., of North Hampton.

them with a jealous eye. They clearly see through a system formed for their destruction. That the parliament of Britain is to make laws, binding them in all cases whatsoever; that the colonies are to be taxed by that parliament without their own consent; and the crown enabled to appropriate money for the support of the executive and arbitrary powers; that this leaves their own assembly a body of very little significance; while the officers of government and judges, are to be totally independent of the legislature, and altogether under the control of the king's ministers and counsel lors; and there an union will be effected, as dangerous as it will be powerful; the whole power of government will be lifted from the hands into which the consti tution has placed it, into the hands of the king's min isters and their dependents here. This is in a great measure the case already ; and the consequences will be, angry debates in our senate, and perpetual tumults and confusions abroad ; until these maxims are en tirely altered, or else, which God forbid, the spirits of the people are depressed, and they become inured to disgrace and servitude. This has long been the prospect in the minds of speculative men. The body of the people are now in council. Their opposition grows into a system. They are united and resolute. And if the British administration and government do not return to the principles of moderation and equity, the evil which they profess to aim at preventing by their rigorous measures, will the sooner be brought to pass, viz:—*the entire separation and independence of the colonies.*

Mr. Cushing obliged me with a sight of your letter

to him of the 22d Dec. last. I think I am not so
clearly of opinion as you seem to be, that "the decla
ratory act is a mere nullity," and that therefore "if
we can obtain a repeal of the revenue acts from
1764, without their pernicious appendages, it will be
enough." Should they retract the exercise of their
assumed power, you ask when will they be able to
renew it? I know not when, but I fear they will soon
do it, unless, as your worthy brother in Virginia in a
letter I yesterday received from him expresses him
self, "we make one uniform, steady effort to secure
an explicit bill of rights for British America." Let
the executive power and right on each side be therein
stipulated, that Britain may no longer have a power
or right to make laws to bind us, in all cases whatso
ever. While the claim is kept up, she may exercise
the power as often as she pleases; and the colonies
have experienced her disposition to do it too plainly
since she in anger made the claim. Even imaginary
power beyond right begets insolence. The people
here I am apt to think will be satisfied on no other
terms but those of redress; and they will hardly think
they are upon equitable terms with the mother
country, while by a solemn act she continues to claim
a right to enslave them, whenever she shall think fit
to exercise it. I wish for a permanent union with
the mother country, but only on the principles of
liberty and truth. No advantage that can accrue to
America from such an union can compensate for the
loss of liberty. The time may come sooner than they
are aware of it, when the being of the British nation,
I mean the being of its importance, however strange

it may now appear to some, will depend on her union with America. It requires but a small portion of the gift of discernment for any one to foresee, that provi dence will erect a mighty empire in America; and our posterity will have it recorded in history, that their fathers migrated from an *island* in a distant part of the world, the inhabitants of which had long been revered for wisdom and valour. They grew rich and powerful; these emigrants increased in numbers and strength. But they were at last absorbed in luxury and dissipation; and to support themselves in their vanity and extravagance they coveted and seized the honest earnings of those industrious emigrants. This laid a foundation of distrust, animosity and hatred, till the emigrants, feeling their own vigour and independence, dissolved every former band of con nexion between them, and the *islanders* sunk into obscurity and contempt.

May I whisper in your ear that you paid a compli ment to the speaker when you told him you "always spoke under the correction of his better judgment." I admire what you say to him, and I hope it will have a good impression on his mind; *that we shall be re spected in England exactly in proportion to the firmness and strength of our opposition.*

I am sincerely your friend,

As Capt. Wood is now about to sail, there is not time to have copies of the papers; I will send them by the next opportunity. In the mean time I refer you to Dr. Franklin, to whom they are sent by this vessel.

TO ARTHUR LEE.

[R. H. Lee, *Life of Arthur Lee*, vol. ii., pp. 220, 221.]

BOSTON, April , 1774.

MY DEAR SIR,—Capt. Wood being still detained, I have the opportunity of acknowledging your favour of the 22d Dec. last,[1] which is just now come to my hand. As Mr. Cushing received your letter of the same date near three weeks ago, I am at a loss to conjecture the reason of my not receiving it at the same time.

I do not depend much upon Lord Dartmouth's inclination to relieve America, upon terms which we shall think honourable; upon his ability to do it, I have no dependence at all. He might have said with safety, when called upon by Lord Shelburne, that he had prepared a plan to pursue at the hazard of his office; for I have reason to believe it was grounded upon the hopes that we could be prevailed upon, at least impliedly, to renounce our claims. This would have been an acceptable service to the ministry, and would have secured to him his office. No great advantage can be made against us from the letter which you mention to Lord Dartmouth from the two houses of our assembly; for upon a review of it I think the most that is said in it is, that if we are brought back to the state we were in at the close of the last war, we shall be as easy as we then were. I do not like any thing that looks like accommodating our language to the humour of a minister; and am fully of your opinion that "the harmony and concurrence of the colonies, is of a thousand times more importance in our dispute,

---

[1] R. H. Lee, *Life of Arthur Lee*, vol. i., pp. 238-240.

than the friendship or patronage of any great man in England."

At the request of our friend, Mr. Hancock, I beg your acceptance of an oration delivered by him on the fifth of March last. I intend to write to you again very soon; in the mean time I remain your assured friend,

TO JOHN DICKINSON.

[MS., Samuel Adams Papers, Lenox Library.]

BOSTON April 21 1774

SIR /

I take the Liberty to inclose an Oration deliverd on the last Anniversary of the 5th of March 1770, by Mr Hancock; which I beg you to accept as a Token of my great Regard for you. This Institution in a great Measure answers the Design of it, which is, to preserve in the Minds of the People a lively Sense of the Danger of standing Armies. We are again threatned with that great Evil; the British Ministry being highly provoked at the Conduct of the People here in destroying the East India Companys Tea. They shut their Eyes to what might appear obvious to them, that the Governors Refusal to suffer it to repass our Castle, compelled to that Extremity. The Disappointment of the Ministry, and, no doubt, the Govrs aggravated Representations, have inflamed them to the highest Degree. May God prepare this People for the Event, by inspiring them with Wisdom and Fortitude! At the same time they stand in Need of all the Countenance that their Sister Colonies can afford them; with whom to cultivate and strengthen an Union, was a great object in View. *We* have borne a double Share of ministerial Resentment, in every Period of the Strug gle for American Freedom. I hope this is not to be attributed to our having, in general, imprudently acted our Part. Is it not rather owing to our having had constantly, Governors and other Crown officers resid ing among us, whose Importance depended solely upon their blowing up the flame of Contention? We are willing to submit our Conduct to the Judgment of our Friends, & would gladly receive their Advice.

Coll Lee the Bearer of this Letter and Mr Dalton his Companion, are travelling as far as Maryland. They are Gentlemen of Fortune and Merit; and will be greatly disappointed if they should miss the Pleas ure of seeing the common Friend of America, The Pennsylvania Farmer. Allow me, Sir, to recommend them to you, and to assure you that I am with great Sincerity,

Your affectionate Friend and humble serv^t,

TO ELBRIDGE GERRY.

[J.T. Austin, *Life of Elbridge Gerry*, vol. i., pp. 45, 46.]

BOSTON, May 12, 1774.

MY DEAR SIR,

I duly received your excellent letter of this day, while I was in town-meeting. I read it there, to the great satisfaction of my fellow townsmen, in as full a town-meeting as we have ever had. I think you and the worthy colonel Orne must by no means refuse to come to the general assembly. Every consideration is to give way to the public. I cannot see how you can reconcile a refusal to your own principles. Excuse my honest freedom. I can write no more at present, being now in committee of correspondence upon matters of great importance. This waits on you by Mr. Oliver Wendel, who is one of a committee of this town to communicate with the gentlemen of Salem and Marblehead, upon the present exigency.

I am, in haste, your friend,

————————

TO THE COMMITTEE OF CORRESPONDENCE OF PORTSMOUTH, NEW HAMPSHIRE.

[MS., Public Record Office, London. [1]]

BOSTON 12th May 1774.

GENTLEMEN

I am Desired by the freeholders and other Inhab itants of this Town to enclose you an attested copy of their Vote passed in Town meeting Legally Assembled this day—The Occasion of this meeting is most Alarming: we have receiv'd a Copy of an Act of the British Parliament—which is inclosed, wherein it appears that the Inhabitants of this Town have been Tryed condemn'd and are to be punished by shutting up the Harbour and otherways, without their having been called to Answer for, nay, for ought that appears without their having been accused of any crime committed by them, for no such crime is alleged in the Act—the town of Boston is now Suffering the stroke of Vengeance in the Common cause of America, I hope they will sustain the Blow with

---

[1] The copy from which the text is printed was an enclosure in a letter of Governor Wentworth, dated June 8, 1774.

Becoming Fortitude, and that the Effect of this cruel act Intended to intimidate and subdue the Spirits of all America will by the joint efforts of all be frustrated.

The people receive this Edict with indignation ; it is expected by their Enemies, and fear'd by some of their Friends, that this town singly will not be able to support the cause under so severe a Tryal—as the very Being of every Colony considered as a free people depends upon the event a thought so Dishonor able to our Brethren cannot be entertain'd as that this town will be left to struggle alone.

Your Hum^e S^t

THE TOWN OF BOSTON TO THE COLONIES.[1]

[MS., Committee of Correspondence Papers, Lenox Library.]

Boston May 13th : 1774

I am desired by the Freeholders and other Inhab itants of this Town to inclose you an Attested Copy of their Vote passed in Town Meeting legally assem bled this day.[2] The Occasion of this Meeting is most alarming : We have receivd the Copy of an Act of the British Parliament (which is also inclos'd) wherein it appears that the Inhabitants of this Town have been tryed and condemned and are to be punished by the shutting up of the Harbour, and other Ways, without their having been called to answer for, nay,

---

[1] The letter was signed by Adams, but only the annotations at the end are in his autograph. Another draft is also in the Committee of Correspondence Papers. The final text of the letter as sent to the Committee of Correspond ence of Connecticut, with the subscription and signature in the autograph of Adams and the body of the letter in the autograph of Thomas Cushing, is in Emmet MS., No. 344, Lenox Library, and is printed in *Bulletin* of New York Public Library, vol. ii., p. 201.

[2] *Boston Record Commissioners' Report*, vol. xviii., pp. 173, 174.

for aught that appears without their having been even accused of any crime committed by them ; for no such Crime is alledgd in the Act.

The Town of Boston is now Suffering the Stroke of Vengeance in the Common Cause of America. I hope they will sustain the Blow with a becoming for titude ; and that the Effects of this cruel Act, in tended to intimidate and subdue the Spirits of all America will by the joynt Efforts of all be frustrated.

The People receive this Edict with Indignation. It is expected by their Enemies and feard by some of their Friends, that this Town singly will not be able to support the Cause under so severe a Tryal. As the very being of every Colony, considerd as a free People depends upon the Event, a Thought so dis honorable to our Brethren cannot be entertaind, as that this Town will now be left to struggle alone.

General Gage is just arrivd here, with a Commis· sion to supercede Govr Hutchinson. It is said that the Town of Salem about twenty Miles East of this Metropolis is to be the Seat of Government—that the Commissioners of the Customs and their numerous Retinue are to remove to the Town of Marblehead a Town contiguous to Salem and that this if the Gen eral shall think proper is to be a Garrisond Town. Reports are various and contradictory.

I am &c.

Sent to the Com^e of Correspondence for

Connecticutt	⎫	by Mr Revere—and in that sent
New York	⎪	to Philadelphia there were Cop-
New Jersey	⎰	ies of the Vote of the Town
& Philadelphia	⎭	inclosd for the Colonies to the

Southward of them which they were desired to forward with all possible Dispatch with their own Sentiments.

to

Rhode Island ⎱ Post
Providence ⎰

Portsmouth　　p Ditto

to Peyton Randolph Esqʳ to be communicated by him to the Gentlemen in Virginia which was sent by Mʳ Perez Moulton as far as Philadelphia to be thence forwarded by the Post.

THE COMMITTEE OF CORRESPONDENCE OF BOSTON TO THE COMMITTEE OF CORRESPONDENCE OF PHILADELPHIA.[1]

[MS., Committee of Correspondence Papers, Lenox Library.]

BOSTON May 13 1774

GENTLEMEN

We have just receivd the Copy of an Act of the British Parliament passd in the present Session whereby the Town of Boston is treated in a Manner the most ignominious cruel and unjust. The Parliaament have taken upon them, from the Represen tations of our Governor & other Persons inimical to and deeply prejudiced against the Inhabitants, to try, condemn and by an Act to punish them, *unheard;* which would have been in Violation of *natural Justice*

---

[1] Intended also for the Committees of Correspondence of New York, New Jersey, Rhode Island, Connecticut, and Portsmouth. An endorsement upon the draft also states that it was written with the concurrence of the Committees of Correspondence of Charlestown, Cambridge, Brookline, Newton, Roxbury, Dorchester, Lexington, and Lynn. *Cf. Proceedings,* Bostonian Society, 1891, pp. 39, 40.

even if they had an acknowledgd Jurisdiction. They
have orderd our port to be entirely shut up, leaving
us barely so much of the Means of Subsistence as to
keep us from perishing with Cold and Hunger; and
it is said, that [a] Fleet of British Ships of War is to
block up our Harbour, until we shall make Restitu
tion to the East India Company, for the Loss of their
Tea, which was destroyed therein the Winter past,
Obedience is paid to the Laws and Authority of
Great Britain, and the Revenue is duly collected.
This Act fills the Inhabitants with Indignation. The
more thinking part of those who have hitherto been
in favor of the Measures of the British Government,
look upon it as not to have been expected even from
a barbarous State. This Attack, though made immedi
ately upon us, is doubtless designd for every other
Colony, who will not surrender their sacred Rights &
Liberties into the Hands of an infamous Ministry.
Now therefore is the Time, when *all* should be united
in opposition to this Violation of the Liberties of *all*.
Their grand object is to divide the Colonies. We
are well informd, that another Bill is to be brought
into Parliament, to distinguish this from the other
Colonies, by repealing some of the Acts which have
been complaind of and ease the American Trade;
but be assured, *you* will be called upon to surrender
your Rights, if ever they should succeed in their At
tempts to suppress the Spirit of Liberty *here*. The
single Question then is, Whether *you* consider Boston
as now suffering in the Common Cause, & sensibly
feel and resent the Injury and Affront offerd to her?
If you do, (and we cannot believe otherwise) May

we not from your Approbation of our former Con duct, in Defence of American Liberty, rely on your suspending your Trade with Great Britain at least, which, it is acknowledgd, will be a great, but necessary Sacrifice, to the Cause of Liberty, and will effectually defeat the Design of this Act of Revenge. If this should be done, you will please to consider it will be, though a voluntary Suffering, greatly short of what we are called to endure under the immediate hand of Tyranny.

We desire your Answer by the Bearer; and after assuring you, that, not in the least intimidated by this inhumane Treatment we are still determind to maintain to the utmost of our Abilities the Rights of America we are,

Gentlemen,

your Friends & Fellow Countrymen,

TO JAMES WARREN.

[*Collections* of Massachusetts Historical Society, 4th ser., vol. iv., pp. 390–392 ; a draft, with several variances, is in the Samuel Adams Papers, Lenox Library.]

BOSTON, May 14, 1774.

My Dear Sir,

This Town has received the Copy of an Act of the British Parliament, wherein it appears that we have been tried and condemned, and are to be punished, by the shutting up of the harbor and other marks of revenge, until we shall disgrace ourselves by servilely yielding up, in effect, the just and righteous claims of America. If the Parliament had a Right to pass such an *edict*, does it not discover the want of every moral

principle to proceed to the destruction of a commu
nity, without even the accusation of any crime com
mitted by such community? And for any thing that
appears, this is in fact the case. There is no crime
alleged in the Act, as committed by the Town of
Boston. Outrages have been committed within the
Town, and therefore the community, as such, are to
be destroyed, without duly inquiring whether it de
served any punishment at all. Has there not often
been the same kind of reason why the Port of London
should be shut up, to the starving of hundreds of
thousands, when their own mobs have surrounded
the Kings Palace? But such are the councils of a
nation, once famed and revered for the character of
humane just and brave.

The people receive this cruel edict with abhorrence
and indignation. They consider themselves as suffering the stroke ministerial—I may more precisely
say, Hutchinsonian vengeance, in the common cause
of America. I hope they will sustain the blow
with a becoming fortitude, and that the cursed de
sign of intimidating and subduing the spirits of all
America, will, by the joint efforts of *all*, be frustrated.
It is the expectation of our enemies, and some of our
friends are afraid, that this Town, *singly*, will not be
able to support the cause under so severe a trial.
Did not the very being of every sea-port town, and
indeed of every Colony, considered as a free people,
depend upon it, I would not even then entertain a
thought so dishonorable of them as that they would
leave us now to struggle alone.

I enclose you a copy of a vote, passed by this Town

at a very full meeting yesterday, which stands ad
journed till Wednesday next, to receive the report of
a committee appointed to consider what is proper
further to be done.   The inhabitants in general abhor
the thought of paying for the tea, which is one condi
tion upon which we are to be restored to the grace
and favor of Great Britain.   Our Committee of Cor
respondence have written letters to our friends in the
Southern Colonies, and they are about writing to the
several towns in this Province.   The merchants of
Newburyport have exhibited a noble example of public
spirit, in resolving that, if the other sea-port Towns
in this Province alone, will come into the measure,
they will not trade to the southward of South Caro
lina, nor to any part of Great Britain and Ireland, till
the harbor of Boston is again open and free ; or till
the disputes between Britain and the Colonies are
settled, upon such terms as all rational men ought to
contend for.   This is a manly and generous resolu
tion.   I wish Plymouth, which has hitherto stood
foremost, would condescend to second Newburyport.
Such a determination put into practice would alter the
views of a nation, who are in full expectation that
Boston will be unthought of by the rest of the conti
nent, and even of this Province, and left, as they are
devoted, to ruin.   The heroes who first trod on your
shore, fed on clams and muscles, and were contented.
The country which they explored, and defended with
their richest blood, and which they transmitted as an
inheritance to their posterity, affords us a super
abundance of provision.   Will it not be an eternal
disgrace to this generation, if it should now be sur-

rendered to that people who, if we might judge of them by one of their laws, are barbarians. *Impius haec tam culta novalia miles habebit? Barbarus has segetes?* If our brethren feel and resent the affront and injury now offered to this town ; if they realize of how great importance it is to the liberties of all America that Boston should sustain this shock with dignity ; if they recollect their own resolutions, to defend the public liberty *at the expense of their fortunes and lives*, they cannot fail to contribute their aid by a temporary suspension of their trade.

I am your friend,

TO SILAS DEANE.[1]

[MS., Samuel Adams Papers, Lenox Library; a text, with variations, is in *Correspondence of Samuel B. Webb*, W. C. Ford, vol. i., pp. 23, 24.]

BOSTON May 18 1774

SIR

The Committee of Correspondence for the Town of Boston have had before them a Letter signd by yourself in behalf of the Committee of the Hon[bl] House of Deputies of the Colony of Connecticutt, and I am desired by our Committee to return them their hearty Thanks, for the readiness they discover to support this Town, now called to stand in the Gap and suffer the vengeful Stroke of the hand of Tyranny, or, which God forbid, succumb under it. I trust in God, we shall never be so servile as to submit to the ignominious Terms of the cruel Edict ; aided by our Sister Colonies, we shall be able to acquit ourselves, under this severe Tryal, with Dignity. But that Aid must

---

[1] Addressed to Deane at Hartford, Connecticut.

be speedy, otherwise we shall not be able to keep up
the Spirits of the more irresolute amongst us, before
whom the crafty Adversaries are already holding up
the grim Picture of Want and Misery. It is feard
by the Committee that a Conferrence of Committees
of Correspondence from all the Colonies, cannot be
had speedily enough to answer for the present Emer
gency. If your hon[bl] Committee shall think it proper
to use their Influence with the Merchants in the Sea
port Towns in Connecticutt to withhold—& prevail
with those of each town for themselves—their Trade
with Great Britain and Ireland and every Part of the
West Indies, to commence at a certain time (say on the
14th June next) it will be a great Sacrifice indeed, but
not greater than Americans have given the World
Reason to expect from them when called to offer it
for the preservation of the publick Liberty. One
years virtuous forbearance w[d] succeed to our wishes.
[1] What would this be in Comparison with the Sacrifice
our renowned Ancestors made that they might quietly
enjoy their Liberties civil & religious? They left,
many of them, affluence in their Native Country,
crossd an untryed Ocean, encounterd the Diffi
culties of cultivating a howling wilderness, defended
their Infant Settlements against a most barbarous
Enemy with their richest Blood.

Your Sentiment that Boston is "suffering in the
common Cause" is just and humane. Your obliging
Letter has precluded any Necessity of urging your
utmost Exertions, that Connecticut may at this
Juncture act her part in the Support of that common

---

[1] The following two sentences are stricken out in the draft.

Cause, though the Attack is made more immediately on the Town of Boston.   Being at present pressd for time I cannot write so largely as I feel disposd to do. I must therefore conclude with assuring you that I am with very great Regard for your Com^e

    Sir

        your sincere Friend and Fellow Countryman,

TO STEPHEN HOPKINS.[1]

[MS., Samuel Adams Papers, Lenox Library.]

BOSTON May 18 1774

SIR

You have without Doubt heard of the Edict of the British Parliament to shut up the Harbour of Boston, the Injustice & Cruelty of which cannot be parralled[sic] in the English History.   Injustice, in trying condemn ing and punishing upon the mere Representations of interrested Men, without calling the Party to answer ; and Cruelty in the Destruction of a whole Commu nity only because it is alledgd that Outrage has been committed in it, without the least Enquiry whether the Community have been to blame.   The Town of Boston now suffer the Stroke of ministerial Ven geance in the Common Cause of America ; and I hope in God they will sustain the Shock with Dig nity.   They do not conceive that their Safety con sists in their Servile Compliance with the ignominious Terms of this barbarous Act.   Supported by their Brethren of the Sister Colonies I am perswaded they will nobly defeat the diabolical Designs of the com-

---

[1] See vol. ii., page 389. *Cf.* Frothingham, *Life of Joseph Warren*, pp. 312, 313.

mon Enemies. ' If the Spirit of American Liberty is suppressd in this Colony, which is undoubtedly the Plan, where will the Victory lead to and end ? I need not urge upon *you* the Necessity of the joynt Efforts of all in the Defence of this single Post. I know your great Weight and Influence in the Colony of Rhode Island, and intreat that you would now employ it for the common Safety of America. I write in great Haste and am with sincere affection,

Your friend,

I shall esteem a Letter from you a very great favor.

TO ARTHUR LEE.

[R. H. Lee, *Life of Arthur Lee*, vol. ii., pp. 221-223 ; a draft is in the Samuel Adams Papers, Lenox Library; a text is in Force, *American Archives*, 4th ser., vol. i., p. 332.]

BOSTON, May 18th, 1774.

My Dear Sir,—The edict of the British parlia ment, commonly called the Boston Port Act, came safely to my hand. For flagrant injustice and bar barity, one might search in vain among the archives of Constantinople to find a match for it. But what else could have been expected from a parliament, too long under the dictates and control of an administra tion, which seems to be totally lost to all sense and feeling of morality, and governed by passion, cruelty, and revenge. For us to reason against *such* an act, would be idleness. Our business is to find means to evade its malignant design. The inhabitants view it, not with astonishment, but indignation. They dis· cover the utmost contempt of the framers of it ; while they are yet disposed to consider the body of the nation (though represented by such a parliament) in the character they have sustained heretofore, humane and generous. They resent the behaviour of the merchants in London, those I mean who receive their bread from them, in infamously deserting their cause at the time of extremity. They can easily believe that the industrious manufacturers, whose time is wholly spent in their various employments, are misled and imposed upon by such miscreants as have un gratefully devoted themselves to an abandoned min istry, not regarding the ruin of those who have been their best benefactors. But the inhabitants of this town must and will look to their own safety, which they see does not consist in a servile compliance with the ignominious terms of this barbarous edict. Though the means of preserving their liberties should distress and even ruin the British manufacturers, they are resolved (but with reluctance) to try the experi ment. To this they are impelled by motives of self-preservation. They feel humanely to those who must suffer, but being innocent are not the objects of their revenge. They have already called upon their sister colonies, (as you will see by the enclosed note) who not only feel for them as fellow-citizens, but look upon them as suffering the stroke of ministerial ven geance in the common cause of America ; that cause which the colonies have pledged themselves to each other not to give up. In the mean time I trust in God this devoted town will sustain the shock with dignity ; and supported by their brethren, will glori ously defeat the designs of their common enemies. Calmness, courage, and unanimity prevail. While they are resolved not tamely to submit, they will by refraining from any acts of violence, avoid the snare that they discover to be laid for them, by posting regiments so near them. I heartily thank you for your spirited exertions. Use means for the preservation of your health. Our warmest gratitude is due to lords Camden and Shelburne. Our dependence is upon the wisdom of the few of the British nobility. We suspect studied insult, in the appointment of the person who is commander-in-chief of the troops in America to be our governor; and I think there appears to be in it more than a design to insult upon any specious pretence. We will endeavour by circumspection and sound prudence, to frustrate the diabolical designs of our enemies.

I have written in haste, and am affectionately your friend,

TO ELBRIDGE GERRY.

[J.T. Austin, *Life of Elbridge Gerry*, vol. i., pp. 46, 47.]

BOSTON, May 20, 1774.

DEAR SIR,

I have just time to acquaint you that yesterday our committee of correspondence received an express from New York, with a letter from thence, dated the 15th instant, informing that a ship arrived there after a passage of twenty-seven days from London, with the detested act for shutting up this port; that the citizens of New York resented the treatment of Boston, as a most violent and barbarous attack on the rights of all America; that the general cry was, let the port of New York voluntarily share the fate of Boston;

that the merchants were to meet on Tuesday last, and it was the general opinion that they would entirely suspend all commercial connexion with Great Britain, and not supply the West Indies with hoops, staves, lumber, &c. ; that they hoped the merchants in this and every colony would come into the measure, as it was of the last importance.

Excuse me, I am in great haste,

Your friend,

THE COMMITTEE OF CORRESPONDENCE OF BOSTON TO THE COMMITTEE OF CORRESPONDENCE OF MARBLEHEAD.

[MS., Committee of Correspondence Papers, Lenox Library.]

BOSTON May 22 1774

DEAR SIR

We have just receivd your favor of this Date by the Hands of Mr Foster. We cannot too highly applaud your Sollicitude & Zeal in the Common Cause. The News you mention as having been receivd here from New York by the Post is without Foundation. We have receivd a Letter from New York dated the Day before the Post came out from that City, advising us that there was to be a meeting of the merchants there on the Tuesday following (last Tuesday)--that by a Vessel which had arrivd there from London the Citizens had receivd the barbarous Act with Indignation—that no Language could express their Abhorrence of this additional Act of Tyranny to all America—that they were fully perswaded that America was attackd & intended to be enslavd by their distressing & subduing Boston—that a Compliance with the provision of the Act will only be a temporary Reliefe from a particular Evil, which must end in a general Calamity—that many timid People in that City who have interrested themselves but very little in the Controversy with Great Britain express the greatest resentment at the Conduct of the Ministry to this Town and consider the Treatment as if done to them—and that this is the general Sense of the Inhabitants—that it was the general Talk that at the Meeting of the Merchants it would be agreed to suspend commercial Connection with Great Britain— also to stop the Exportation of Hoops Staves Heading & Lumber to the English Islands, & export no more of those Articles to foreign Islands than will be sufficient to bring home the Sugar Rum & Mo lasses for the Return of American Cargoes, and we are to be advisd of the Result of the meeting, which we expect very soon. The Express which we sent to New York had not arrivd when this left the City.

We have receivd Letters by the post from Portsm[t] in New Hampshire, from Hartford Newport Provi dence Westerly &c. all expressing the same Indig nation and a Determination to joyn in like measures— restrictions on their Trade.

Hutchinsons minions are endeavoring to promote an address to him. The *professd* design is to desire his Friendship ; but we take it rather to be a Design of his own, that when he arrives in England he may have *the Shaddow* of Importance. It is carried on in a private Way—and is said to be signd by not fifty— Names of little Significance here may serve to make a Sound abroad.

We are sorry to hear that Mr Hooper is throwing his Weight & Influence into the Scale against us. We can scarcely believe it. If it be true we would desire to know of him whether he would advise the Town of Boston to give up the rights of America. We conclude in haste,

We are credibly informd that in the address to Hutchinson are these remarkeable Words " We see no harm in your Letters and approve of them." The most intelligent & respectable merchants among those who have been reputed Tories have refused to sign it.

TO CHARLES THOMSON.[1]

[MS., Samuel Adams Papers, Lenox Library.]

BOSTON May 30 1774

MY DEAR SIR,

I receivd your very obliging Letter by the hands of Mr Revere. I thank you for the warm Affection you therein express for this Town, your Zeal for the Common Cause of America, and your prudent and salutary Advice. I hope in God that this People will sustain themselves under their pressing Difficulties with Firmness. It is hard to restrain the Resentment of some within the proper Bounds, and to keep others who are more irresolute from sinking. While we are resolved not tamely to comply with the humiliating terms of the barbarous Edict, I hope, by refraining from every Act of Violence we shall avoid the Snare that is laid for us by the posting of Regiments so

---

[1] Later secretary of the Continental Congress.

near us. We shall endeavor by Circumspection to frustrate the diabolical Designs of our Enemies.

Our Committee of Correspondence will write an Answer to the Letter they receivd from yours by this opportunity. In order that you may have an Under standing of our Appointment I think it necessary to inform you, that we are a Committee, not of the Trade, but of the whole Town ; chosen to be as it were out-guards to watch the Designs of our Enemies. We were appointed near two years ago, and have a Cor respondence with almost every Town in the Colony. By this Means we have been able to circulate the most early Intelligence of Importance to our Friends in the Country, & to establish an Union which is formidable to our Adversaries.

But it is the Trade that we must at present depend upon for that *speedy* Reliefe which the Necessity of this Town requires. The Trade will forever be divided when a Sacrifice of their Interest is called for. By far the greater part of the Merchants of this place are & ever have been steadfast in the Cause of their Country ; but a small Number may defeat the good Intentions of the rest, and there are some Men among them, perhaps more weak than wicked, who think it a kind of Reputation to them to appear zealous in Vindication of the Measures of Tyranny, and these it is said are tempted by the Commissioners of the Cus toms, with Indulgencies in their Trade. Nevertheless it is of the greatest Importance that some thing should be done for the immediate Support of this Town. A Congress is of absolute Necessity in my Opinion, but from the length of time it will take to bring it to pass,

I fear it cannot answer for the present Emergency. The Act of Parliament shuts up our Port. Is it not necessary to push for a Suspension of Trade with Great Britain as far as it will go, and let the yeomanry (whose Virtue must finally save this Country) resolve to desert those altogether who will not come into the Measure. This will certainly alarm the Manufacturers in Britain, who felt more than our Enemies would allow, the last Nonimportation Agreement. The virtuous forbearance of the Friends of Liberty may be powerful enough to command Success. Our Enemies are already holding up to the Tradesmen the grim Picture of Misery and Want, to induce them to yield to Tyranny. I hope they will not prevail upon them but this is to be feard, unless their Brethren in the other Colonies will agree upon Measures of *speedy* Support and Reliefe.

It gives me the greatest pleasure to find our worthy Friend the Farmer[1] at the head of a respectable Committee. Pray let him know that I am fully of his Sentiments. Violence & Submission would at this time be equally fatal.

I write in the utmost haste.

Your affectionate Friend,

You will see in some of our Papers of this day an infamous Address to Hutchinson signd by a Number who call themselves Merchants Traders & others. In this List of Subscribers are containd the Names of his party taken after abundance of Pains from every Class of Men down to the lowest. I verily

---

[1] John Dickinson. *Cf.*, page 104.

believe I could point out half a Score Gentlemen in Town able to purchase the whole of them. For their understanding I refer you to the Address itself. There is also another Paper of this Kind subscribed by those who call themselves Lawyers. It was re· fused with Indignation by some who for Learning & Virtue are acknowledgd to be the greatest Orna ments of that Profession. The Subscribers are taken from all parts of the Province. A few of them are allowed to be of Ability—others of none—others have lately purchasd their Books and are now about to read. This List you will observe is headed by one of our Judges of the Admiraltry, & seconded by another—there is also the Solicitor General (a Wed- derburne in Principle but not equal to him in Ability) the Advocate General &ᶜ &ᶜ. The whole Design of these Addresses is to prop a sinking Character in England.

TO SILAS DEANE.

[MS., Samuel Adams Papers, Lenox Library.]

BOSTON May 31 1774

SIR/

I receivd your favor of the 26 Instant by the hands of Mʳ Revere. I am glad to find that it is fully the Opinion of your Committee, that some immediate and effectual Measures are necessary to be taken for the Support of this Town. I have just now received Intelligence (and I am apt to believe it) that several Regiments are to be posted in the Town. What can this mean but to pick a Quarrel with the Inhabit-

ants, and to provoke them to take some violent Steps
from whence they may have a specious Pretence to
carry Matters to the greatest Extremity. We shall
be hard pressd ; and it will be difficult for us to pre
serve among the people that Œquanimity which is
necessary in such arduous Times. The only Way
that I can at present think of to bring the Ministry
to their Senses, is to make the people of Great Brit
ain share in the Misfortunes which they bring upon
us ; and this cannot be done so speedily as the Emer
gency calls for, but by a Suspension of Trade with
them. I think that should be pushd as far as it will go
& as speedily as possible. Although the interrested
& disaffected Merchants should not come into it,
great Success may attend it. Let the yeomanry of
the Continent, who only, under God, must finally
save this Country, break off all commercial Connec
tion whatever with those who will not come into it.
A Congress appears to me to be of absolute Neces
sity, to settle the Dispute with Great Britain if she
by her violent and barbarous Treatment of us, should
not totally quench our Affection for her, and render
it impracticable. I hope no Hardships will ever in
duce America to submit to voluntary Slavery. I
wish for Harmony between Britain & the Colonies ;
but only upon the Principles of Equal Liberty.

Our Assembly was unexpectedly adjournd on Sat
urday last till the seventh of June, then to meet at
Salem. By this Means I am prevented mentioning
a Congress to the Members. I wish your Assembly
could find it convenient to sit a fortnight longer, that
we might if possible act in Concert. This however

is a sudden Thought. I have written in the utmost haste, and conclude, with great Regard to the Gentle men of the Committee.

Sir,

Your Friend & fellow Countryman,

TO WILLIAM CHECKLEY.

[MS., Samuel Adams Papers, Lenox Library.]

BOSTON June 1 1774

My dear Sir

It was with singular pleasure that I rec^d a Letter from you by Mr Howe, and another since by your worthy Townsman. I began to think you had at last entirely forgot me. I sincerely congratulate you on the birth of a Daughter. May God preserve her life & make her a Blessing in the World. Assure Mrs Checkley of our kind Regards for her. I hope she will enjoy a better State of Health than she has had in time past. You have now devolvd upon you the weighty Cares of a Parent; you will perhaps find it difficult "to train up the Child in the way it should go" in an Age of Levity Folly and Vice. Doubtless you will consider your self more interrested than ever in the Struggles of your Country for Liberty, as you hope your Infant will outlive you, and share in the Event. Your native Town which I am perswaded is dear to you, is now suffering the Vengeance of a cruel and tyrannical Administration; and I can assure you she suffers with Dignity. She scorns to own herself the Slave of the haughtiest nation on earth; and rather than submit to the humiliating Terms of an

Edict, barbarous beyond Precedent under the most absolute monarchy, I trust she will put the Malice of Tyranny to the severest Tryal. It is a consolatory thought, that an Empire is rising in America, and will not *this* first of June be rememberd at a time, how soon God knows! when it will be in the power of this Country amply to revenge its Wrongs. If Britain by her multiplied oppressions is now accelerating that Independency of the Colonies which she so much dreads, and which in process of time must take place, who will she have to blame but herself? We live in an important Period, & have a post to maintain, to desert which would be an unpardonable Crime, and would entail upon us the Curses of posterity. The infamous Tools of Power are holding up the picture of Want and Misery; but in vain do they think to intimidate us; the Virtue of our Ancestors inspires us—they were contented with Clams & Muscles. For my own part, I have been wont to converse with poverty; and however disagreable a Companion she may be thought to be by the affluent & luxurious who never were acquainted with her, I can live happily with her the remainder of my days, if I can thereby contribute to the Redemption of my Country.

The naval Power of Britain has blocked up this Harbour; but the Laws of Nature must be alterd, before the port of Salem can become an equivalent. The most remote inland Towns in the province feel the want of a mart, & resent the Injury done to themselves in the Destruction of Boston. The British Minister appears to me to be infatuated. Every step he takes seems designd by him to divide us, while the necessary Tendency is to unite. Our Business is to make Britain share in the miseries which she has unrighteously brought upon us. She will then see the Necessity of returning to moderation & Justice.

Adieu,

RESOLUTIONS OF THE HOUSE OF REPRESENTATIVES OF MASSACHUSETTS.

[MS., Committee of Correspondence Papers, Lenox Library.]

IN THE HOUSE OF REPRESENTATIVES June 17 1774

Whereas the Towns of Boston and Charlestown are at this time suffering under the Hand of Power, by the shutting up the Harbour by an armed Force, which in the opinion of this House is an Invasion of the said Towns evidently designd to compel the In habitants thereof to a Submission to Taxes imposed upon them without their Consent : And Whereas it appears to this House that this Attack upon the said Towns for the Purpose aforesaid is an Attack made upon this whole Province & Continent which threat ens the total Destruction of the Liberties of all British America : It is therefore Resolvd as the clear opinion of this House, that the Inhabitants of the said Towns ought to be relievd ; and this House do recommend to all, and more especially to [the] In habitants of this Province to afford them speedy and constant Reliefe in such Way and Manner as shall be most suitable to their Circumstances till the sense &

advice of our Sister Colonies shall be known : In full
Confidence that they will exhibit Examples of Pa
tience Fortitude and Perseverance, while they are
thus called to endure this oppression, for the Preser
vation of the Liberties of their Country.

After Debate accepted

THE COMMITTEE OF CORRESPONDENCE OF BOSTON TO ELBRIDGE GERRY.

[J. T. Austin, *Life of Elbridge Gerry*, vol. i., pp. 48, 49.]

BOSTON, June 22, 1774.

SIR,

The committee of correspondence take this first
opportunity to make their most grateful aknowledg-
ments of the generous and patriotic sympathy of our
brethren, the worthy merchants and traders of the
town of Marblehead, as well those who have already
subscribed for our relief, as those who express their
readiness to serve the trade of Boston.   Our sense
of their favour, as it respects individuals, is strong
and lively ; but the honour and advantage thereby
derived to the common cause of our country, are so
great and conspicuous, that private considerations
of every kind recede before them.

ARTICLE SIGNED "CANDIDUS."

[*Boston Gazette*, June 27, 1774.]

Messieurs EDES & GILL,

FROM an Extract of a Letter from a Southern

Colony, and the Publications in last Thursday's Gaz
ette, it is very evident a Scheme has been concerted
by some Persons to frustrate any Attempts that might
be made to suspend our Trade with Great-Britain,
till our most intolerable Grievances are redressed.
The Scheme appears to be, to *seem* to agree to the
Suspension in Case all agreed, and then by construing
some Passage in a Letter from the Committee of
another Province, that they had *not agreed*, to declare
that the conditional Signers were *not holden*. A
GAME or two of such Mercantile Policy would soon
have convinced the World that Lord North had a
just Idea of the Colonies ; and that notwithstanding
their real Power to prove a Rope of Hemp to him,
they were a Rope of Sand in Reality, among them
selves. I would beg Leave to ask the voluminous
Querists referr'd to. whether they conceive a Non-
consumption Agreement would ever have been tho't
of in the Country, could our Brethren there have
persuaded themselves that the Merchants were in
earnest to suspend Trade the little Time there was
between our receiving the Port Bill, and the Appoint
ment of a Congress, or any other general Measure
come into, from which a radical Relief might be
expected? 2. Whether the Trade in their last Meet
ing declaring, That their *conditional* Agreement was
dissolved, on Pretence that Advices from New York
and Philadelphia were totally discouraging, was not
highly unbecoming a People whose peculiar Circum
stances rendered it their duty to stop their Trade to
Great Britain the Moment the Port-Bill reached the
Shore of America? 3. Whether they conceive the

Committee of Boston planned the Non-consumption Agreement, and sent it first into the Country for their Adoption? or rather, whether the Country, enraged at their preposterous Management, did not originate the Plan and press the Committee to have it digested, printed and recommended throughout the Colony? 4. I would enquire whether a Backwardness in the Province, actually suffering, to come into the only peaceful Measure that remains for our Extrication from Slavery, would not naturally excuse every other Province from taking one Step for the common Salvation? 5. Whether in that Case all the Trade of the Province, whether consisting of Spring, Summer or Fall Importations, would in the End be worth an Oyster-Shell? 6. Whether all the Bugbears started against the Worcester Covenant, as holding up the taking a solemn Oath to "withdraw all Commercial Connexions," which our honest Commentators tell the People means even to deny buying or selling Greens or Potatoes to them, does not betray a great want of that Candor and manly Generosity, which is expected from well-bred and reasonable Citizens? 7. Whether the suggestion that the Boston Merchants ceasing to Import, will throw the Trade into the Hands of Importers in other Provinces, is not utterly unbecoming an Inhabitant of that Town, into which the Beneficence of the whole Continent is ready to flow in the most exemplary Manner? For Shame! Self Interested Mortals, cease to draw upon your worthy Fellow Citizens the just Resentment of Millions. If there may be Some Punctilios wrong in the Non-consumption Agreement, the united Wisdom of the Continent

will surely be capable of setting Matters right at the
general Congress; and no Gentleman Trader, be his
Haste ever so great to get Rich, need distress himself
so mightily about the Profits of one Fall-Importation,
if the constant Clamour of the Trade for two Years
past, that they did Business for nothing, had any
Foundation.

CANDIDUS.

TO CHARLES THOMSON.

[MS., Samuel Adams Papers, Lenox Library.]

BOSTON JUNE 30 1774

SIR

Your Letter by order of your Committee directed
to Mr Cooper with the inclosed Resolves came to my
hand this day.   I shall as soon as possible call a Com
mittee of the Town who are appointed to consider of
Ways and Means for the Employment of the poor,
and to appropriate and distribute such Donations as
our generous friends shall make for the Reliefe of
those Inhabitants who may be deprivd of the Means
of Subsistence by the Operation of the Port Bill.
This Committee consists of the standing Overseers of
the poor who are to act in Concert with others who
had been before appointed for the purposes above
mentiond, as you will observe by the inclosed Votes
of the Town. The principal Reason assignd in the
Vote for joyning the Overseers is because by an Act
of this province they are a corporate body empowerd
to receive Monies &c for the Use of the poor, but
those Gentlemen have since informd the others of

the joynt Committee that they cannot consistently with the Act of their Incorporation admit of any but their own Body in the Distribution of the Monies that may at any time come into their hands for the Use of the poor. They are heartily desirous of acting in Concert agreable to the Vote of the Town but consider themselves as under Restraint by the Law. The Donors may if they please consign their Dona tions to any one Gentleman (William Phillips Esqr) to be appropriated for the *Employment* or *Reliefe* of such Inhabitants of the Town of Boston as may be deprived of the Means of Subsistence by the Oper ation of the Act of Parliament commonly stiled the Boston Port Bill, at the best Discretion of the Over seers of the poor of Boston joynd by a Committee appointed by said Town to consider of Ways and Means for the Employment of the poor.

I have given my private Sentiment, and am with great Respect & Gratitude to the Gent^l of the City & County of Philadelphia,

Your friend & fellow Countryman,[1]

TO THE COMMITTEE, OF CORRESPONDENCE OF NORWICH.[2]

[MS., Committee of Correspondence Papers, Lenox Library.]

BOSTON July 11 1774.

GENTLEMEN

Your obliging Letter directed to the Committee of Correspondence for the Town of Boston came just

---

[1] In the interval before the date of the next letter an article signed "Candidus" was published in the *Massachusetts Spy*, July 7, 1774. This is attrib uted to Adams by W. V. Wells, and portions are printed in his *Life of Samuel Adams*, vol. ii., pp. 187, 197.

[2] Addressed to "Jed Huntington, Chris Leffingwell, Theoph Rogers Esq^{rs}."

now to my hand ; and as the Gentleman who brought
it is in haste to return, I take the Liberty of writing
you my own Sentiments in Answer, not doubting but
they are concurrent with those of my Brethren.   I
can venture to assure you that the valueable Donation
of the worthy Town of Norwich will be receivd by
this Community with the warmest Gratitude and disposd of according to the true Intent of the generous
Donors.   The Liberality of the Sister Colonies will
I trust support & comfort the Inhabitants under the
pressure of enormous Power, & enable them to en
dure affliction with that Dignity which becomes those
who are called to suffer in the Cause of Liberty &
Truth.   The Manner of transmitting the Donation
will be left to your Discretion ; and that it may be con
ducted according to the Inclination of the Town, I
beg Leave to propose, that it be directed to some one
Gentleman (say William Phillips Esqʳ) *to be disposd
of for the* Employment *or* Reliefe *of such Inhabitants
of the Town of Boston as may become Sufferers by
means of an Act of the British Parliament called the
Boston Port bill, at the Discretion of the Overseers of
the Poor of said Town joynd with a Committee ap
pointed to consider of Ways & Means for the Em-
ploymᵗ of such Poor.*   The Part which the Town of
Norwich takes in this Struggle for American Liberty
is truly noble ; and this Town rejoyces with you in
the Harmony Moderation & Vigor which prevails
throughout the united Colonies.

    You may rely upon it that there is no Foundation
for the Report that the Opposition gains Ground upon
us.   The Emissaries of a Party which is now reduced

to a very small Number of Men, a great Part of
whom are in Reality Expectants from & in Connec
tion with the Revenue, are daily going out with such
idle Stories; but whoever reads the Accounts of the
Proceedings of our Town Meetings, which I can
assure you have been truly stated in the News papers
under the hand of the Town Clerk, will see that no
Credit is due to such Reports.

I shall lay your Letter before the Committee of
Correspondence who will write to you by the first
opportunity.   In the mean time I am in Sincerity
            Your obliged Friend &
                Fellow Countryman,

TO RICHARD HENRY LEE.

[MS., American Philosophical Society[1]; a draft is in the Samuel Adams Paper,
    Lenox Library; an undated text is in R. H. Lee, *Life of R. H. Lee*, vol.
    i., pp. 99–101.]

BOSTON July 15th 1774

I have lately been favour'd with three Letters from
you, and must beg you to attribute my omitting to
make a due Acknowledgment till this Time, to a Mul
tiplicity of Affairs to which I have been oblig'd to
give my constant Attention.

The unrighteous and oppressive Act of the British
Parliament for shutting up this Harbour, although
executed with a Rigour beyond the Intent even of
the Framers of it, has hitherto faild, and I believe
will continue to fail of the Effect which the Enemies

---

[1] In this instance the body of the letter actually sent, from which this text is
taken, is not in the autograph of Adams, only the subscription, signature, and
address being in his hand.   The draft is wholly in his autograph.

of America flatter'd themselves it would have. The Inhabitants still wear chearful countenances. Far from being in the least Degree intimidated they are resolved to undergo the greatest Hardships, rather than Submit in any Instance to the Tyrannical Act. They are daily encouraged to persevere, by the Intelligence which they receive from their Brethren not of this Province only, but of every other Colony, that they are consider'd as suffering in the common Cause; and the Resolution of *all*, to support them in the Conflict. Lord North had no Expectation that we should be thus Sustained; on the Contrary he trusted that Boston would be left by all her Friends to Struggle and fall alone.—He has therefore made no Preparation for the Effects of an Union. From the Information I have had from Intelligent Persons in England, I verily believe the Design was to seize some Persons here, and send them Home; but the Steadiness and Prudence of the People, and the unexpected Union of the Colonies, evidenc'd by liberal Contributions for our Support, have disconcerted them; and they are at a loss how to proceed further. Four Regiments are now encamp'd on our Common, and more are expected; but I trust the People will, by a circumspect Behavior, prevent their taking occasion to Act. The Port Bill, is follow'd by two other Acts of the British Parliament; ,the one for regulating the Government of this Province, or rather totally to destroy our free Constitution and substitute an absolute Government in its Stead; the other for the more *impartial* Administration of Justice or as some term it for the screening from Punishment any Soldier who

shall Murder an American for asserting his Right. A
Submission to these Acts will doubtless be requir'd
and expected ; but whether General Gage will find it
an easy thing to *force* the People to submit to so
great and fundamental a Change of Government, is a
Question I think, worthy his Consideration—Will
the People of America consider these measures, as
Attacks on the Constitution of an Individual Province
in which the rest are not interested ; or will they view
the model of Government prepar'd for us as a Sistem
for the whole Continent. Will they, as unconcern'd
Spectators, look upon it to be design'd only to top off
the exuberant Branches of Democracy in the Consti
tution of this Province? Or, as part of a plan to
reduce them all to Slavery? These are Questions, in
my Opinion of Importance, which I trust will be
thoroughly weighed in a general Congress.—May
God inspire that intended Body with Wisdom and
Fortitude, and unite and Prosper their Councils !

The People of this Province are thoroughly Sensi
ble of the Necessity of breaking off all Commercial
Connection with the Country, whose political Coun
cils direct to Measures to enslave them. They how
ever *the Body* of the Nation, are being kept in
profound Ignorance of the Nature of the Dispute be
tween Britain and the Colonies ; and taught to believe
that we are a perfidious & rebellious People.

It is with Reluctance that they come into any
Resolutions, which must distress those who are not
the objects of their Resentment but they are urg'd
to it from Motives of Self-preservation, and therefore
are signing an agreement in the several Towns, not

to consume any British Goods which shall be imported after the last of August next ; and that they may not be impos'd upon, they are to require an Oath of those from whom they shall hereafter purchase such Goods. It is the Virtue of the Yeomanry that we are chiefly to depend upon. Our Friends in Maryland talk of withholding the Exportation of Tobacco ; this was first hinted to us by the Gentlemen of the late House of Burgesses of Virginia who had been called together after the Dissolution of your Assembly—This would be a Measure greatly interesting to the Mother Country.

Should America hold up her own Importance to the Body of the Nation and at the same Time agree in one general Bill of Rights, the Dispute might be settled on the Principles of Equity and Harmony restored between Britain and the Colonies.

I am with great Regard
Your Friend & Fellow Countryman

TO NOBLE WYMBERLEY JONES.[1]

[MS., Samuel Adams Papers, Lenox Library.]

BOSTON July 16 1774

GENTLEMEN

Having receivd Information that the respectable Inhabitants of the Town of Savannah have expressd a Degree of Uneasiness, as considering themselves neglected in the general Application which the distressd Town of Boston have made to the Colonies in

---

[1] Of Savannah, Georgia. *Cf.*, C. C. Jones, *Biographical Sketches*, pp. 124–136; and C. C. Jones, *History of Georgia*, vol. ii., p. 166 and *passim*.

America for Advice and Assistance in their present painful Struggle with the hand of Tyranny, I beg Leave to assure you that by express Direction of the Town of Boston a Letter was addressd to the Gen tlemen of Savannah upon the first Intelligence of the detestable Port Bill. Permit me to add Gentlemen that the Committee of Correspondence for the Town of Boston at whose Request I now write, set too high a Value upon your Advice and esteem a general Union of too great Importance, to neglect any Steps at this alarming Crisis, which may have a Tendency to effect so desirable a Purpose.

They have this additional Motive to invite all the Colonies into one firm Band of Opposition to the oppressive Measures of the British Administration, that they look upon this Town as conflicting for all. The Danger is general; and should we succumb under the heavy Rod now hanging over us, we might be esteemd the base Betrayers of the Common Interest.

We are informd that the Infant Colony of West Florida has contended for the Right of an annual Choice of Representatives. A noble Exertion cer tainly if it has taken place. Being your Neighbors, be pleasd to convey to them our warmest Regards, and encourage them in the Pursuit of so important an Object.

Your Correspondence with the Committee of this Town will always be esteemd a singular Gratification.

I am in their Behalf

Gentlemen

Your Friend and

Fellow Countryman

Sir

Having had your Name and Character mentiond to me as a warm and able Friend to the Liberties of America, I have taken the Liberty to address the foregoing Letter to your Patronage & beg the favor of you to communicate the same to the other Friends of Liberty in Georgia and to assure you that I am with very great Regard,

Your very humble Servt,

TO CHRISTOPHER GADSDEN.[1]

[MS., Samuel Adams Papers, Lenox Library.]

BOSTON July 18 1774

My dear Sir

I have lately receivd several Letters from you for which I am much obliged. It cannot but afford Pleasure to an observing American to find, that the British Administration, by every Measure they take for the Suppression of the Spirit of Liberty in the Colonies, have promoted, till they have at length established a perfect Union ; which, if it continues, must effect the Destruction of their cursed Plans of arbitrary Power.—The Boston Port bill is a parliamentary Punishment of this People, designd, as Lord North expressd himself, to convince America that they are in earnest.—What will his Lordship think, when he finds, that his "spirited Measures" have not the designd Effect, wch was to intimidate us—that America is also *in Earnest* and the whole Continent united in an effectual Measure, which they have always

---

[1] *Cf.*, Vol. i., page 108.

in their Power to adopt, to distress the Trade of
Britain, & thereby bring her to her Senses. The
Premier little thought of this united Resentment, and
therefore has made no Preparation against the Effects
of it.   He promisd himself that the Colonies would
view the fate of Boston as unconcernd Spectators,
and leave her to fall under the Scourge of ministerial
Vengeance.   The noble and generous Part which all
are taking & particularly South Carolina on this
Occasion must convince him that the British Colo
nists in North America are an inseperable Band
of Brothers, each of whom resents an Attack upon
the Rights of one as an Attack upon the Rights of
all.   The Port bill is followed by two others; One
for cutting the Charter of this Province into Shivers,
and the other to encourage Murderers by skreening
them from Punishment.   What short Work these
modern Politicians make with solemn Compacts
founded on the Faith of Kings!   The Minds of this
People can never be reconciled to so fundamental a
Change of their civil Constitution; and I should think
that General Gage, allowing that he has but a small
Share of Prudence, will hardly think of risqueing
the horrible Effects of civil War, by suddenly attempt
ing to force the Establishm^t of a Plan of civil Gov
ernment which must be shocking to all the other
Colonies even in the Contemplation of it; but the
more so, as they must consider themselves to be
deeply interrested in the Attempt.—I pray God
that he may not wantonly exercise the exorbitant
Power intended to be, if not already, put into his
Hands.—If the Wrath of Man is a little while

restraind, it is possible that the united Wisdom of
the Colonists, may devise Means in a peaceable Way,
not only for the Restoration of their own Rights and
Liberties, but the Establishment of Harmony with
Great Britain, which certainly must be the earnest
Desire of Wise and good Men.   I am

Yours affectionately,

TO CHRISTOPHER GADSDEN AND L. CLARKSON.

[MS., Samuel Adams Papers, Lenox Library.]

BOSTON July 18 1774

GENTLEMEN

We have received your polite and obliging Letter
of the 28 June inclosing Bill of lading for 194 whole
& 21 half barrills Rice on board the sloop Mary John
Dove Master which is safely arrived at Salem.   So
very generous a Donation of twenty Gentlemen only
of the Town of Charlestown, towards the Reliefe of
the Sufferers by the cruel & oppressive Port bill,
demands our most grateful Acknowledgments ; and
the Assurances you give us of the kind Disposition
of our worthy Friends in South Carolina towards the
Inhabitants of this Town will, we are perswaded,
greatly encourage them to bear up under that oppres
sive Ministerial Vengeance which they are now called
to endure for the common Cause of America.   Sup
ported as we are by our Brethren in all the Colonies,
we must be ungrateful to them as well as lost to the
feelings of publick Virtue should we comply with the
Demands to surrender the Liberty of America.   We
think you may rely upon it that the People of [this]

Province in general will joyn in any proper M[easures] that may be proposed for the restoration & Establish ment of the Rights of America, and of that Harmony with the Mother Country upon the principles of equal Liberty so much desired by all wise & good Men. . A Non Importation of British Goods is (with a few Ex ceptions) universally thought a salutary and an effica- tious Measure; and in order to effectuate such a Meas. ure the yeomanry in the Country (upon whom under God we are to depend) are signing agreements to re strict themselves from purchasing & consuming them. We applaud and at the same time [are] animated by the patriotick Spirit of our Sister Colonies. Such an union we believe was little expected by Lord North and we have Reason to hope therefore that he has not thought of making any Preparation against the Effects of it. The Resolution & Magnanimity of the Colonists and the Firmness Perseverance & Prudence of the People of this insulted Town astonishes our Adversaries, & we trust will put them to a Loss how to proceed further.

We shall dispose of the valueable Donation as you direct, in such Manner as we shall judge most con- ducible to the Intention of the generous Donors, to whom be pleasd to present our kind Regards and be assured we are Gentlemen their and your sincere & obliged Friends and

Fellow Countrymen

THE COMMITTEE OF CORRESPONDENCE OF BOSTON TO THE
COMMITTEE OF CORRESPONDENCE OF COLRAIN.

[MS., Committee of Correspondence Papers, Lenox Library.]

BOSTON July 18 1774

GENTLEMEN/

We receivd your favor by the hand of Mr Wood,
and observe the Art of the Tories in your part of the
Province to make the People believe the Non Con
sumption Agreement is a Trick of the Merchants of
this Town, that they may have the Advantage of
selling off the Goods they have on hand at an exorbi
tant Rate. So far is this from the Truth, that the
Merchants importing Goods from England, a few
excepted, were totally against the Covenant. They
complaind of it in our Town Meeting as a Measure
destructive to their Interest. Some of them have
protested against it as such ; and they are now using
their utmost Endeavors to prevent it. Can it then
be rationally said by the Advocates for Tyranny
that it is a Plan laid by the Merchants? The Enemies
of our Constitution know full well that if there are
no Purchasers of British Goods there will be no
Importers. On the Contrary if the People in the
Country will purchase there are People in the City
avaricious enough to import. Hence it is that they
are so agitated with the Non Consumption Agree
ment that they will not hesitate at any rate to
discredit it.

We highly applaud your Zeal for the Liberties of
your Country and are with great Regard
Your friends & fellow Countrymen,

TO ANDREW ELTON WELLS.[1]

[MS., Samuel Adams Papers, Lenox Library.]

BOSTON July 25 1774

MY DEAR BROTHER · ̀ᴌ   , ᛁ

I beg you to believe me when I tell you that inces
sant publick Business has prevented my writing to
you as often as my own Inclination would lead me
to do it.   I assure you I feel an exquisite Pleasure in
an epistolary Chat with a private Friend, and I never
contemplate a little Circle but I place you and your
Spouse as two, or I had rather say, *one.*—But con
sider my Brother, or to use a dearer Apellation my
Friend, consider our Native Town is in Disgrace.
She is suffering the Insolence of Power.   But she
prides herself in being calld to suffer for the Cause
of American Freedom and rises superior to her proud
oppressors, she suffers with Dignity ; and while we
are enduring the hard Conflict, it is a Consolation to
us that thousands of little Americans who cannot at
present distinguish between the Right hand & the
left, will reap the happy Fruits of it ; and among
these I bear particularly in my mind my young
Cousins of your Family.

Four Regiments are encampd upon our Common,
while the Harbour is blockd up by Ships of War.
Nothing is sufferd to be waterborn in the Harbour
excepting the Wood and Provisions brot in to keep
us from actually perishing.   By such Oppressions the
British Administration hope to suppress the Spirit of
Liberty in this place ; but being encouragd by the

----

[1] *Cf.*, Vol. II., page 337.

generous Supplys that are daily Sent to us the Inhabi
tants are determind to hold out and appeal to the
Justice of the Colonies & of the World—trusting in
God that these things shall be overruled for the
Establishment of Liberty Virtue & Happiness in
America—Your Sister is in tollerable Health and
together with my Son & Daughter send their affection
ate respects to your self Mrs Wells & your family—
I am sincerely

Yours,

TO PETER TIMOTHY.[1]

[MS., Samuel Adams Papers, Lenox Library.]

BOSTON July 27 1774

SIR/

I wrote to you by this Conveyance ; since which
nothing new has occurred here, saving that this Town
a ta legal Meeting yesterday [2] orderd a circular Letter
to be sent to all the Towns and Districts in the
province a Copy of which is inclosed. If the two
Acts therein referrd to take place, there will not be
even the Shadow of Liberty left in this Province ; and
our Brethren of the Sister Colonies will seriously con
sider whether it be not the Intention of a perverse
Administration to establish the same System of
Tyranny throughout the Colonies. There will shortly
be forty or fifty dozen of Hoes and Axes shipd to
your address by a worthy citizen & Merchant of this
Town Mr Charles Miller—The Makers are Men of
approvd Skill and fidelity in their Business and will

---

[1] *Cf.* Vol. II., page 64.
[2] *Boston Record Commissioners' Report*, vol. xviii., pp. 186, 187.

warrant their Work by affixing their names thereon–
The original Cost of the Axes will be 40/ & the Hoes
36/ sterling p^r Dozen, and I dare say they will be in
every respect better than any imported from abroad.

I am with due Regard

Y^r friend & Countryman

TO FISHER GAY.[1]

[*Collections* of Massachusetts Historical Society, 4th ser., vol. iv., pp. 14, 15.]

BOSTON, July 29th, 1774.

SIR,

I am desired by the Committee of the Town of
Boston, appointed to receive the Donations made by
our sympathizing brethren, for the employment or
relief of such inhabitants of this Town as are more
immediate sufferers by the cruel act of Parliament
for shutting up this harbor, to acquaint you that our
friend, Mr. Barrett, has communicated to them your
letter of the 25th instant, advising that you have
shipped, per Captain Israel Williams, between three
and four hundred bushels of rye and Indian corn for
the above mentioned purpose, and that you have the
subscriptions still open, and expect after harvest to
ship a much larger quantity. Mr. Barrett tells us,
that upon the arrival of Captain Williams, he will
endorse his bill of lading or receipt to us.

The Committee have a very grateful sense of the
generosity of their friends in Farmington, who may
depend upon their donations being applied agreeable
to their benevolent intention, as it is a great satisfac-

---

[1] A member of the committee of Farmington, Connecticut.

tion to the Committee to find the Continent so united in opinion. The Town of Boston is now suffering for the common liberties of America, and while they are aided and supported by their friends, I am per suaded they will struggle through the conflict, firm and steady.

I am, with very great regard, Gentlemen,

Your friend and countryman,

TO EZEKIEL WILLIAMS.[1]

[*Collections* of Massachusetts Historical Society, 4th ser., vol. iv., pp. 19, 20.]

BOSTON, July 29th, 1774.

SIR,

Your very obliging letter of the 25th instant, directed to the Selectmen or Overseers of the Poor of the Town of Boston, has been by them communi cated to a Committee of this Town appointed to receive the donation made for the employment or relief of such inhabitants as are or may be more im mediate sufferers by the cruel Act of Parliament for shutting up our harbor. This, at the desire and in the name of this Committee, I am very gratefully to acknowledge the generosity of the Town of Wethers- field, in the donation made by them, for the purpose above mentioned, consisting of 34¾ bushels of wheat, 248½ of rye, and 390 of Indian corn, which your letter informs is forwarded by Capt. Israel Williams, and for their kind intentions still further. They may be assured that their beneficence will be applied to the

---

[1] Of Wethersfield, Connecticut.

purpose for which they have designed it.   This Town is suffering the stroke of ministerial vengeance, as they apprehend, for the liberties of America, and it affords them abundant satisfaction to find that they have the concurrent sentiments of their brethren in the sister Colonies in their favor, evidenced by the most liberal acts of munificence for their support. While they are thus encouraged and supported, I trust they will never be so ungrateful to their friends, as well [as] so lost to a sense of virtue, as to "give up the glorious cause."   They have need of wisdom and fortitude to confound the devices of their enemies, and to endure the hard conflict with dignity.   They rejoice in the approaching general American Con gress, and trust that, by the divine direction and bless ing, such measures will be taken as will " bring about a happy issue of the present glorious struggle," and secure the rights of America upon the permanent principles of equal liberty and truth.

I am, with very great regard to the Gentlemen of your Committee, Sir, your friend and fellow-country man,

TO THE COMMITTEE OF CORRESPONDENCE OF MARBLE-
HEAD.

[*Collections* of Massachusetts Historical Society, 4th ser., vol. iv., pp. 30–32.]

BOSTON, August 2d, 1774.

GENTLEMEN,
The Commitee for Donations yesterday received your kind letter, by the hands of Mr. Gatchel, ac-

quainting them of the very generous present made to
the sufferers in this Town by the unrighteous and
cruel Act of the British Parliament, commonly called
the Port Bill. They had before received one barrel of
olive oil. Mr. Gatchel delivered them £39 1s. 3d. in
cash, and this day the fish in eleven carts, and the
remainder of the oil came to hand. I am desired by
that Committee to express their warmest gratitude to
the Gentlemen of Marblehead, who have so liberally
contributed on this occasion, and to assure them that
it will be applied in a manner agreeable to the inten
tion of the charitable donors.

It was in all probability the expectation of Lord
North, the sister Colonies would totally disregard the
fate of Boston, and that she would be left to suffer
and fall alone. Their united resolution, therefore, to
support her in the conflict, will, it is hoped, greatly
perplex him in the further prosecution of his oppres
sive measures, and finally reduce him to the necessity
of receding from them. While we are thus aided by
our brethren, you may depend upon it that we shall
not disgrace the common cause of America, by any
submissions to the barbarous edict. Our inhabitants
still wear cheerful countenances, and they *will* be
supported by the beneficence of our friends, notwith
standing one of your addressers meanly insinuated to
a gentleman of South Carolina, at Salem, yesterday,
that they would receive no benefit from the large dona
tion of rice received from that place. Such an intima·
tion discovers a degree of depravity of heart which can
not easily be expressed. I have received a letter from
your [Committee] to our Committee of Correspond-

ence, which I shall lay before them at their meeting this evening.

I am, in behalf of the Committee of Donations, Gentlemen, your friend and fellow-countryman,

P. S. Mr. Phillips, a carter, with about fifteen quintals of fish and the remainder of the oil, is not yet come in, but is expected every hour.

TO JOSEPH GILBERT.[1]

[*Collections* of Massachusetts Historical Society, 4th ser., vol. iv., p. 37.]

BOSTON, August 3d, 1774.

SIR,

The Committee appointed by this Town to receive donations for the relief of our poor, suffering by the shutting up this port, have this day received by the hands of Mr. Roger Wellington, 8½ bushels of rye and 10 bushels Indian corn, as a donation from sev eral gentlemen of Brookfield ; but as we received no letter advising us who we are particularly obliged to for this kind present, we take this opportunity to request you will please to return the sincere thanks of this Town to all those Gentlemen that contributed towards this donation. We esteem it a confirmation of that union and friendship which subsists at this time, and is of the utmost importance to secure the rights and liberties of this Province and indeed of all Amer ica. We shall endeavor to distribute the donations of our friends to the best advantage to promote indus try and harmony in this Town. Wishing you the rewards that attend the generous,

We are, with great respect and gratitude, Sir, your friends and servants,

---

[1] Of Brookfield, Massachusetts.

TO FISHER GAY.

[*Collections* of Massachusetts Historical Society, 4th ser., vol. iv., pp. 15, 16.]

BOSTON, August 4th, 1774.

SIR,

Your favor of 25th July, directed to John Barrett, Esq., has been laid before the Committee to receive and distribute Donations, and has been answered, July 29th,[1] which [we] trust you will duly receive. Since which Capt. Williams has arrived and delivered to the Committee's Treasurer, one hundred and sixteen and half bushels of rye, and one hundred and ninety bushels of Indian corn, as a donation from our generous, patriotic friends in Farmington. This Committee, in the name of the Town, return you and our other friends their most grateful acknowledgments, and assure [you we] shall do our utmost to distribute it, agreeable to the benevolent intentions of the contributors. As Capt. Williams brought us no letter, nor had any particular directions about the freight of the grain, the Committee immediately agreed to pay the same, and offered it to Capt. Williams, but he chose rather to suspend the receiving of it until further day. You may be assured that the friends of Liberty and a righteous government are firm and steady to the common cause of American rights. We are in hopes to keep our poor from murmuring, and that, by the blessing of Heaven, we shall shortly be confirmed in that freedom for which our ancestors entered the wilds of America.

With the greatest respect we are, Sir, your friends and fellow-countrymen. By order of the Committee

---

[1] *Cf.* page 148.

appointed to receive Donations for the employment or relief of the sufferers by the Boston Port Bill.

TO THE COMMITTEE OF CORRESPONDENCE OF BOSTON.

[MS., Samuel Adams Papers, Lenox Library.]

PHILAD^E Sept. 14 1774.

GENTLEMEN

I have been waiting with great Impatience for a Letter from the Committee of Correspondence for the Town of Boston upon whose Wisdom and Judgment I very much rely. The Congress is resolved into Committees and Sub-Committees and all seem fully sensible of the intollerable Grievances which the Col onies are struggling under, and determined to procure effectual redress. The Subject Matter of their De bates I am restraind upon Honor from disclosing at present; but I may assure you that the Sentiments of the Congress hitherto discoverd and the Business assignd to the several Committees are such as per fectly coincide with your Expectations.

The Spirit of our Countrymen does them great Honor—Our Brethren of the County of Middlesex have resolvd nobly, and their resolutions[1] are read by the several Members of this Body with high Applause.

It is generally agreed that an opposition to the new Mode of Government ought to be maintaind. A warm Advocate for the Cause of Liberty to whom America is much obligd for his former Labors told me that he was fully of Opinion that no officer under the new Establishment ought to be acknowledgd; on

---

[1] The proceedings are in *Journals of each Provincial Congress of Massachu-setts*, pp. 609-614.

the other hand that each of them should be warned against exercising any Authority upon pain of *the utmost* Resentment of the people. It is therefore greatly to his Satisfaction to observe the Measures that have been taken. I am pleasd to hear that a provincial Congress is proposd, and cannot but prom ise my self that the firm manly and persevering Opposition of that single province will operate to the total frustration of the villainous Designs of our Tyrants and their Destruction.

I hope the Committee will continue to act up to their Dignity and Importance.—I am yet of Opinion that Heaven will honor them with a great Share of the Merit of saving the Rights of all America. May God inspire them with Wisdom & Fortitude. I must beg them to excuse this hasty Effusion of an honest heart, having been just now (while in a Committee) informd that a Vessell is immediately about to sail to Marblehead. Pray let me hear from the Committee— being as you all know *a Man of Fortune*, you need not fear puting me to the Expence of postage— direct to Mr Saml Smith and Sons Merch^ts in this City. I conclude with my warmest Prayers to the Supreme Being for the Salvation of our Country, your Friend Fellow Countryman & Fellow Labourer,

TO CHARLES CHAUNCY.

[Force, *American Archives*, 4th ser., vol. i., p. 793.]

PHILADELPHIA, September 19,[1] 1774.

REVEREND SIR :

_ I have had the pleasure of receiving a letter from

---

[1] The date is given as September 18 in Frothingham, *Life and Times of Jo seph Warren*, p. 367.

you since my arrival in this city. Our friend, Mr. Quincy, informed me before I left Boston, of his in tention to take passage for England. I am persuaded he may do great service to our country there. Agree ably to his and your requests, I have desired gentle men here to make him known to their friends and correspondents.

Last Friday Mr. Revere brought us the spirited and patriotick Resolves of your County of Suffolk.[1] We laid them before the Congress. They were read with great applause, and the Enclosed Resolutions were unanimously passed, which give you a faint idea of the spirit of the Congress. I think I may assure you that America will make a point of supporting Boston to the utmost. I have not time to enlarge, and must therefore conclude with assuring you that I am, with great regard, your affectionate and humble servant,

TO JOSEPH WARREN.

[R. Frothingham, *Life and Times of Joseph Warren*, p. 377; a draft is in the Lenox Library.]

PHILADELPHIA, September, 1774.

My Dear Sir

Your letter of the 12th instant, directed to Mr. Cushing and others, came duly to hand. The subject of it is of the greatest importance. It is difficult, at this distance, to form a judgment, with any degree of accuracy, of what is best to be done. The eastern and western counties appear to differ in sentiment with regard to the two measures mentioned in your letter. This difference of sentiment might produce

---

[1] *Journals of each Provincial Congress of Massachusetts*, pp. 601-609.

opposition, in case either part should be taken. You know the vast importance of union. That union is most likely to be obtained by a consultation of depu ties from the several towns, either in a House of Representatives or a Provincial Congress. But the question still remains, which measure to adopt. It is probable that the people would be most united, as they would think it safest, to abide by the present form of government,—I mean according to the char ter. The governor has been appointed by the Crown, according to the charter ; but he has placed himself at the head of a different constitution. If the only constitutional council, chosen last May, have honesty and courage enough to meet with the representatives chosen by the people by virtue of the last writ, and jointly proceed to the public business, would it not bring the governor to such an explicit conduct as either to restore the general assembly, or give the two Houses a fair occasion to declare the chair vacant? In which case the council would hold it till another governor should be appointed. This would immedi ately reduce the government prescribed in the charter; and the people would be united in what they would easily see to be a constitutional opposition to tyranny. You know there is a charm in the word "consti tutional."

TO JOSEPH WARREN.

[R. Frothingham, *Life and Times of Joseph Warren*, pp. 377, 378 ; a draft is in the Lenox Library.]

PHILADELPHIA, September 25, 1774.

MY DEAR SIR,—I wrote you yesterday by the post.

A frequent communication at this critical conjuncture is necessary. As the all-important American cause so much depends upon each colony's acting agreeably to the sentiments of the whole, it must be useful to you to know the sentiments which are entertained here of the temper and conduct of our province. Heretofore we have been accounted by many, intemperate and rash ; but now we are universally applauded as cool and judicious, as well as spirited and brave. This is the character we sustain in congress. There is, however, a certain degree of jealousy in the minds of some, that we aim at a total independency, not only of the mother-country, but of the colonies too ; and that, as we are a hardy and brave people, we shall in time overrun them all. However groundless this jealousy may be, it ought to be attended to, and is of weight in your deliberations on the subject of your last letter. I spent yesterday afternoon and evening with Mr. Dickinson. He is a true Bostonian. It is his opinion, that, if Boston can safely remain on the defensive, the liberties of America, which that town has so nobly contended for, will be secured. The congress have, in their resolve of the 17th instant, given their sanction to the resolutions of the county of Suffolk, one of which is to act merely on the defensive, so long as such conduct may be justified by reason and the principles of self-preservation, but *no longer.* They have great dependence upon your tried patience and fortitude. They suppose you mean to defend your civil consti tution. They strongly recommend perseverance in a firm and temperate conduct, and give you a full pledge of their united efforts in your behalf. They have not yet come to final resolutions. It becomes them to be deliberate. I have been assured, in private conversation with individuals, that, if you should be driven to the necessity of acting in the defence of your lives or liberty, you would be justified by their constituents, and openly supported by all the means in their power; but whether they will ever be pre vailed upon to think it necessary for you to set up another form of government, I very much question, for the reason I have before suggested. It is of the greatest importance, that the American opposition should be united, and that it should be conducted so as to concur with the opposition of our friends in England. Adieu,

THE CONTINENTAL CONGRESS TO GENERAL GAGE.[1] [OCTO-BER, 1774.]

[MS., Samuel Adams Papers, Lenox Library.]

TO GENERAL GAGE.

Sir

The Delegates from his Majestys several Colonies of New Hampshire   *   *   *   *
*   *   *   *   *   *   *

assembled in general Congress in the City of Phila delphia take the Liberty of addressing you upon Sub jects of the last Importance, to your own Character, Happiness and Peace of Mind, to his Majestys Ser-

---

[1] Endorsed : " This was offered to the Co ᵐittee of Congress to be reported as a Remonstrance to Genˡ Gage." On October 6, 1774, Adams, Lynch and Pendleton were appointed a committee to draft a letter to General Gage. The committee reported October 10 ; the letter was amended and ordered to be signed. The text, dated October 10, 1774, and finally approved October 11, is in *Journals* of Continental Congress (Edit. of 1904), vol. i., pp. 60, 61. The reply of Gage is in *ibid.*, pp. 114, 115.

vice, to the Wellfare of that Province over which you preside and of all North America, and, perhaps, of the whole British Empire.

The Act of the British Parliament for shutting up the Harbour of Boston is universally deemd to be ,unjust and cruel ; and the World now sees with As tonishment & Indignation the Distress which the Inhabitants of that loyal though devoted Town are suffering under the most rigid Execution of it.

There are two other Acts passed in the present Session of Parliament, the one for regulating the Government of the Province of Massachusetts Bay and the other entitled an Act for the more impartial Administration of Justice in the same Province ; the former of these Acts was made with the professed Purpose of materially altering the Charter of that Province granted by his Majesties Royal Predecessors King William & Queen Mary for themselves their Heirs &c forever ; and both or either of them if put into Execution will shake the Foundations of that free & happy Constitution which is the Birthright of English Subjects, and totally destroy the inestimable Blessing of Security in Life Liberty and Property.

By your own Acknowledgment, the refusal of the People to yield obedience to these Acts is far from being confind to a Faction in the Town of Boston.   It is general through the province.   And we do now assure your Excellency, that this Refusal is vindicable, in the opinion of this Congress, by the Laws of Reason and Self preservation ; and the People ought to be and will be supported in it by the united Voice and Efforts of all America.

We are fully convinced that the Town of Boston and Province of the Massachusetts Bay are suffering in the righteous Cause of America, while they are nobly exerting themselves in the most spirited opposition to those oppressive Acts of Parliament and Measures of Administration which are calculated to annihilate our most sacred & invalueable Rights.

It is with the deepest Concern that we observe, that while this Congress are deliberating on the most effectual Measures for the restoration of American Liberty and a happy Harmony between the Colonies and the parent State, so essentially necessary to both, your Excellency is erecting Fortifications round the Town of Boston, whereby well grounded Jealousies are excited in the Minds of his Majesties faithful Subjects and apprehensions that all Communication between that Town & the Country will be cut off, or that this Freedom will be enjoyed at the Will of an Army.

Moreover we would express to your Excellency the just Resentment which we feel at the Indignities offerd to our worthy fellow Citizens in Boston and the frequent Violations of private property by the Soldiers under your Command. These Enormities committed by a standing Army, in our opinion, unlawfully posted there in a time of Peace, are irritating in the greatest Degree, and if not remedied, will endanger the involving all America in the Horrors of a civil War! Your Situation Sir is extremely critical. A rupture between the Inhabitants of the Province over which you preside and the Troops under your Command would produce Consequences of the most serious Nature: A Wound which would never be heald!⁄ It would probably establish Animosities between Great Britain & the Colonies which time would never eradicate! In order therefore to quiet the Minds & remove the Jealousies of the people, that they may not be driven to such a State of Desperation as to quit the Town & fly for Shelter to their Friends and Countrymen, we intreat you from the Assurance we have of the peaceable Disposition of the Inhabitants to desist from further fortifications of the Town, and to give orders that a free & safe Communication between them & the country may be restored & continued.

TO THOMAS YOUNG.

[MS., Samuel Adams Papers, Lenox Library.]

PHILADELPHIA Octob [17] 1774

MY DEAR SIR—

I have receivd your favors of 29th Sept and 11th Instant, the latter of which is just come to hand. The Affidavit inclosd confirms the report in Boston about the beginning of July, of a Mans being seizd by the Soldiery, put under Guard & finally sent to England. But what Remedy can the poor injurd Fellow obtain in his own Country where *inter Arma silent Leges!* I have written to our Friends to provide themselves without Delay with Arms & Ammunition, get well instructed in the mili tary Art, embody themselves & prepare a complete Set of Rules that they may be ready in Case they are called to defend themselves against the violent At-

tacks of Despotism. Surely the Laws of Self Preser
vation will warrant it in this Time of Danger &
doubtful Expectation. One cannot be certain that a
distracted Minister will yield to the Measures taken
by the Congress, though they should operate the
Ruin of the National Trade, until he shall have made
further Efforts to lay America, as he impiously
expressd it "prostrate at his Feet."

I believe you will have seen before this reaches
you, some further Resolves of the Congress relative
to my native Town & Province together with a Letter
to Gage. They were sent to the Com^e of Corre
spondence in Boston by Mr Revere who left us a
Week ago, and I suppose are or will be publishd in
the papers—you will therein see the sense of the
Gentlemen here of the Conduct of the General and the
"dignified Scoundrels," and of the opposition made
to the tyrannical Acts. I think our Countrymen discover the Spirit of Rome or Sparta. I admire in
them that Patience which you have often heard one
say is characteristick of the Patriot. I regretted your
Removal from Boston when you first informd me of
it, but I trust it will be for the publick Advantage.
Wherever you may be I am very sure you will im
prove your ten Talents for the publick Good. I pray
God to direct and reward you.

I am with due regard to Mrs Young,
                    affectionately yours,

TO PETER V. LIVINGSTON.[1]

[MS., Samuel Adams Papers, Lenox Library.]

BOSTON 21 Nov' 1774

SIR

When I was at New York in August Last I was informd by a Gentleman of that City (I think it was yourself but am not certain of it) that a Quantity of Rice had arrivd from South Carolina consignd to his Care for the Benefit of the Sufferers in this Town by Means of the Port Bill.—If it is under your Direction, I am very sure it will be disposd of in the best Man ner for the benevolent Use for which it was intended. My only Design in troubling you with this Letter is to be ascertaind of the Matter, and of the Situation the Rice is in, having been also informd, if I mistake not, that some of it had been dammaged.—A Line from you by the Post will much oblige me.

I am with great Respect
Sir your most humble Servant,

TO THE UNION CLUB.[2]

[*Collections* of Massachusetts Historical Society, 4th ser., vol. iv., pp. 168, 169.]

BOSTON, 16th December, 1774.

GENTLEMEN,

I am directed by the Committee of the Town of Boston, appointed to receive and distribute the dona tions that are made for the relief and employment of such as are, or may become sufferers by means of the Boston Port Bill, to return their sincere thanks to the members of the Union Club, in the Town of Salem, for

---

[1] Of New York.
[2] Of Salem, Massachusetts.

the generous contribution they made, and transmitted by their worthy brother, Mr. Samuel King. It is an unspeakable consolation to the inhabitants of this de voted Town, that amidst the distress designed to have been brought upon them by an inhuman, as well as arbitrary Ministers, there are many whose hearts and hands are open for their relief. You, gentlemen, are among the happy number of those, of whom it is said, the blessing of him that is ready to perish hath come upon us, and through your liberality the widow's heart to sing for joy.

Our friends have enabled us to bear up under oppression, to the astonishment of our enemies. May Heaven reward our kind benefactors ten-fold; and grant to us wisdom and fortitude, that during this hard conflict we may behave as becomes those who are called to struggle in so glorious a cause; and, by our patience and perseverance, at length frustrate the de signs of our country's inveterate foes. You may rely upon it that your donation will be applied by the Committee to the benevolent purpose for which you intended it.

Be assured that I am, in truth and sincerity, your friend and humble servant,

TO PETER T. CURTENIUS.[1]

[*Collections* of Massachusetts Historical Society, 4th ser., vol. iv., p. 165; a text, with slight changes, is in Force, *American Archives*, 4th ser., vol. i., pp. 1106, 1107.]

BOSTON, Jan. 9th, 1775.

GENTLEMEN,

The Committee appointed by the inhabitants of

[1] Of New York.

this Town, to receive and distribute the donations of our friends for the benefit of the sufferers by the Boston Port Bill, acknowledge your several favors of 7th and 17th of December last, enclosing invoices of flour, &c., amounting, with charges, to one thousand and sixty-two pounds, 9/6, which, agreeable to your kind wishes, are come safe to hand. I am directed by the Committee to request that you would assure our benefactors, the citizens of New York, of their warmest gratitude for the very seasonable relief they have afforded to their afflicted brethren in this place, by such generous donations, in this most difficult time of the year. While we acknowledge the superintendency of divine Providence, we feel our obligations to the sister Colonies. By their liberality, they have greatly chagrined the common enemies of America, who flattered themselves with hopes that before this day they should starve us into a compliance with the insolent demands of despotic power. But the people, relieved by your charitable contributions, bear the indignity with becoming patience and fortitude. They are not insensible of the injuries done them as men, as well as free Americans; but they restrain their just resentment from a due regard to the common cause.

The Committee beg the favor of you, gentlemen, to return their thanks to our worthy brethren of Marble Town, for the valuable donation received from them.

I am, with due acknowledgments for the care you have taken, in the name of the Committee, Gentle men, your obliged friend and servant,

DONATIONS COMMITTEE OF BOSTON TO THE PUBLIC.[1]

[*Collections* of Massachusetts Historical Society, 4th ser., vol. iv., pp. 277, 278 ; a text, dated January 20, is in Boston *Gazette*, January 23, 1775, and in Force, *American Archives*, 4th ser., vol. i., p. 1172.]

BOSTON, January 13.

The printers in this and the other American Col onies are requested to insert the following in their several News Papers.

TO THE PUBLIC.

The Committee appointed by the Town of Boston, to receive and distribute donations for the charitable purpose of relieving and employing the sufferers by means of the Act of Parliament commonly called the Boston Port-Bill, from a due regard to their own characters and that of the Town under whose appoint ment they act, as well as for the sake of the said sufferers, who depend upon the continual beneficence of their friends for necessary relief ; think themselves obliged, in this public manner, to contradict a slan derous report raised by evil minded persons, spread in divers parts of this Province, and perhaps more extensively through the continent. The report is, that "each Member of the Committee is allowed six shillings, and, as some say, half a guinea, for every day's attendance ; besides a commission upon all the donations received, and other emoluments for their trouble." The Committee, therefore, thus openly declare, that the above mentioned report is in every part of it groundless and false ; and that they have

[1] Signed by Samuel Adams as chairman. The authorship is not determined.

hitherto attended and acted in their office, and still continue so to do, without any intention, hope, or desire, of receiving any other reward in this life, but the pleasure which results from a consciousness of having done good.—So satisfied are they of their own *disinterested* motives and conduct in this regard, that they can safely appeal to the Omniscient Being for their sincerity in this declaration.

And whereas the committee have this evening been informed, by a letter from the country, of another report equally injurious, viz. that "the Committee have employed poor persons in working for themselves, and gentlemen of fortune with whom they are particularly connected in their private concerns, and paid them out of the donations received"; the Committee do, with the same solemnity, declare the said report to be as false as it is scandalous.

They were early apprehensive that the enemies of *Truth* and *Liberty*, would spare no pains to misrepresent their conduct and asperse their characters ; and therefore, that they might always have it in their power to vindicate themselves, they have constantly kept regular books, containing records of the whole of their proceedings ; which books, as the Committee advertised the public some months ago, are open for the inspection of such as are inclined to look into and examine them.

The Committee now challenge any person whatever, to make it appear, that there is a just foundation for such reports. Until this reasonable demand is complied with, they confide in the justice of the public, that no credit will be given to reports, so injurious to the Committee, and to this oppressed and insulted people.

If the friends of truth will inform the Committee of any reports they may hear, tending to defame the Committee, and by that means to discourage further donations for the benevolent purpose of relieving the sufferers above-mentioned, it will be acknowledged as a particular favor.

Sign'd by Order of the Committee,

TO ARTHUR LEE.

[MS., Samuel Adams Papers, Lenox Library.]

BOSTON Jan 29 1775

My dear Sir/

Upon my Return from the Continental Congress at Philadelphia I had the Pleasure of receiving your Letter of the . . . I beg you would attribute my not having acknowledgd the favor before this time, to continual Avocations which the Necessity of the Times have required.

When the cruel Edict for shutting up this Harbour took place, which was in a very short time after we had any notice that such a Measure was intended, the Inhabitants of the Town met in Faneuil Hall and, as you have long ago heard, resolvd to suffer all the hardships intended by it, rather than submit to its unrighteous as well as ignominious Terms. Supported by the most liberal Donations from their Brethren in all the Colonies, they suffer the Suspension of their Trade & Business with Patience and even laugh at this feeble Effort of their Enemies to force them to

The Act for regulating the Government of this
Province and the Murder Act as it is commonly
called soon followd the Port Act; and General Gage,
whether from his own Motives or the Instructions of
the Minister, thought proper to assemble all the
Kings Troops then on the Continent, in this Town
and has declared to the Selectmen & others his Reso
lution to put the Acts in Execution. The People on
the other hand resolve that they will not submit to
them and the Continent applauds them herein. The
new appointed Councellors and others who have
· openly avowd the Measures of Administration being
conscious that Mr Gage was not mistaken when he
publickly declared under his Hand, that the Oppo
sition to these Acts was general through the Province,
have fled to this Town for Protection. Thus we
appear to be in a state of Hostility. The General
with . . . Regiments with a very few Adherents on
one side & all the rest of the Inhabitants of the Province backd by all the Colonies on the other! The
People are universally disposd to wait till they can
hear what Effect the Applications of the Continental
Congress will have, in hopes that the new Parliament
will reverse the Laws & measures of the old, abolish
that System of Tyranny which was pland in 1763
(perhaps before), confirm the just Rights of the
Colonies and restore Harmony to the British Empire.
God grant they may not be disappointed! Lest they
should be, they have been, & are still exercising
themselves in military Discipline and providing the
necessary Means of Defence. I am well informd that
in every Part of the Province there are selected

Numbers of Men, called Minute Men—-that they are well disciplind & well provided—and that upon a very short Notice they will be able to assemble a formidable Army. They are resolvd however not to be the Aggressors in an open Quarrel with the Troops; but animated with an unquenchable Love of Liberty they will support their righteous Claim to it, to the utmost Extremity. They are filled with Indignation to hear that Hutchinson & their other inveterate Enemies have hinted to the Nation that they are Cowards. Administration may improve this Suggestion to promote their mad purposes, but when ever it is brought to the Test it will be found to be a fatal Delusion. The People are recollecting the Achievements of their Ancestors and whenever it shall be necessary for them to draw their Swords in the Defence of their Liberties, they will shew themselves to be worthy of such Ancestors. I ear-nestly wish that Lord North would no longer listen to the Voice of Faction. Interested Men whose very Being depends upon the Emoluments derivd to them from the American Revenue, have been artfully de ceiving him. Such Men as these, some of them, under a mere pretence of flying to the Army for Protection, have got themselves about General Gage. They are supposd to be perpetually filling his Ears with gross Misrepresentations. Hutchinson who is now in Eng-land has the Tongue & the Heart of a Courtier. His Letters to Whately show what his Designs have been and how much he has contributed towards bringing on the present Difficulties, America never will, Britain never ought to forgive him. I know, at least

I thought I knew his ambitious and avaritious De-signs long before he wrote those Letters. I know the part he bore in the several Administrations of Shirly of Pownal & of Bernard. Pownal⁵ Views were generous. I pitied him under his Embarrassments. Even Bernard I can forgive. If Administration are determind still to form their measures from the In formation of an inveterate Party, they must look to the Consequences. It will be in vain for others to attempt to undeceive them. If they are disposd to bring Matters to an Accommodation they know the Sense of the Colonies by the Measures of the Con tinental Congress. If our Claims are just & reason-able they ought to concede to them. To pretend that it is beneath the Dignity of the Nation for them to do that which Justice demands of them is worse than Folly. Let them repeal every American revenue Law—recall standing Armies—restore . . .

TO STEPHEN COLLINS.

[*Historical Magazine*, 2nd ser., vol. iv., p. 219.]

BOSTON Jany 31 1775

SIR

I received your kind letter some time ago, which should have been acknowledged before this time but I beg you would consider that our hands are full. Our "worthy citizen" Mr Paul Revere will explain to you the intelligence which we have just received from England. It puts me in mind of what I remember to have heard you observe, that we may all be soon under the necessity of keeping *Shooting Irons*. God grant that we may not be brought to extremity or otherwise prepare us for all events.

Mr Tudor has informed me that a report has pre vailed in Philadelphia of a Fracas between Mr Cushing and myself at our late Provincial Congress, he showed me your letter ; you may depend upon it there is not the least Foundation for the Report. Any Difference between Mr Cushing and me is of very little con sequence to the public cause. I take notice of it only as one of the many Falshoods which I know to have been propagated by the⌠Enemies of America.⌡ It is also a Misrepresentation that the sect taken notice of for opening their Shops on our late Thanksgiving Day, was that of the People called Quaquers. They were the Disciples of the late Mr Sanderman, who worship God here without the least Molestation ac cording to their own manner, and are in no other Light disregarded here but as it is said they are in general avowed Friends of the Ministerial Measures. This is what I am told, for my own part I know but little or nothing about them. The Different de nominations of Christians here (excepting those amongst them who Espouse the cause of our Ene mies) are in perfect peace and Harmony, as I trust they always will be.

I have written this letter in very great Haste, while in the Committee of Correspondence and con clude with due Regard to your Spouse, and all friends

Yours affectionately

TO EDWARD ARCHER AND OTHERS.[1]

[*Collections* of Massachusetts Historical Society, 4th ser., vol. iv., pp. 161, 162.]

BOSTON, Feb. 1, 1775.

GENTLEMEN,

The Committee appointed to receive and distribute the donations made for the relief and employment of the sufferers by the Port Bill, have received your letter of the 6th December last, inclosing a bill of lading for seven hundred and fifteen bushels corn, thirty-three barrels pork, fifty-eight barrels bread, and ten barrels flour. We are sorry to inform you that the vessel was cast away, but being timely advised of the dis aster by Capt. Rysam, we have, though not without considerable expense, the good fortune of saving the most part of the cargo.

The County and Borough of Norfolk, and Town of Portsmouth, who made this charitable donation for the sufferers above mentioned, have the due acknowl edgments of this Committee, and their hearty thanks, with assurance that it shall be applied agreeable to the benevolent design. The cheerful accession of the gentlemen of Virginia to the measures proposed by the late Continental Congress, is an instance of that zeal for, and attachment to the cause of America, in which that colony has ever distinguished herself.

This Town is suffering the severest strokes of min isterial vengeance, for their adherence to the same virtuous cause; and while the sister Colonies are testi fying their approbation of its conduct, and so liberally contributing for its support, we trust the inhabitants

---

[1] A committee for the county and borough of Norfolk and town of Ports-mouth, Virginia.

will continue to bear their suffering with a manly
fortitude, and preserve a superiority over their insult
ing enemies.

I am, in the name of the Committee, Gentlemen,
your sincere friend and fellow-countryman,

TO RICHARD RANDOLPH.[1]

[*Collections* of Massachusetts Historical Society, 4th ser., vol. iv., pp. 185, 186.]

BOSTON, February 1, 1775.

SIR,

Your letter of the 29th December last, directed to
Mr. Cushing, Mr. John Adams, Mr. Paine and myself,
inclosing bill of lading for three hundred twenty-nine
and a half bushels wheat, one hundred thirty-five
bushels corn, and twenty-three barrels flour, was de
livered to us by Capt. Tompkins, and we have laid
it before the Committee of this Town appointed to
receive and distribute Donations made for the relief
and employment of the sufferers by the Port Bill.   I
am, in the name of the Committee, to desire you to
return their hearty thanks to the worthy gentlemen
of Henrico County, who have so generously con
tributed for that charitable purpose, and to assure
them that their donations shall be applied so as duly
to answer their benevolent intention.

The Colony of Virginia made an early stand, by
their ever memorable Resolves, in 1765, against the
efforts of a corrupt British Administration to enslave
America, and has ever distinguished herself by her
exertions in support of our common rights.   The

[1] Of Henrico County, Virginia.

sister Colonies struggled separately, but the Minister himself has at length united them, and they have lately uttered language that will be heard.   It is the fate of this Town to drink deep of the cup of minis terial vengeance ;   but while America bears them witness that they suffer in *her* cause, they glory in their sufferings.   Being thus supported by *her* liberal ity, they will never ungratefully betray her rights. Inheriting the spirit of their virtuous ancestors, they will, after their example, endure hardships, and con fide in an all-gracious Providence.   Having been born to be free, they will never disgrace themselves by a mean submission to the injurious terms of slavery. These, Sir, I verily believe to be the sentiments of our inhabitants, and if I am not mistaken, such assist ances are to be expected from them, as you assure us are most sincerely and unanimously wished by every Virginian.

I am, in the name of the Committee, Sir, your sin cere friend and fellow-countryman,

TO BENJAMIN WATKINS AND ARCHIBALD CARY.[1]

[*Collections* of Massachusetts Historical Society, 4th ser., vol. iv., pp. 182, 183.]

February 1, 1775.

GENTLEMEN,

Capt. Tompkins duly delivered your letter, dated Virginia, Chesterfield County, Dec. 1774, directed to Mr. Cushing, Mr. John Adams, Mr. Paine and myself, with a bill of lading inclosed for 1,054 bushels of wheat, 376 1/2 bushels corn, and five bushels peas,

---

[1] Of Chesterfield County, Virginia.

of which 210 bushels wheat, and 12 1/2 corn we perceive comes from the people of Cumberland. As this Town have appointed a Committee to receive and distribute donations made for the relief and employment of the sufferers by the Boston Port Bill, for which charitable purpose these donations of your constituents are appropriated, your letter and the bill of lading are assigned to them, and in their name I am now to desire you to accept of their grateful acknowledgments for the benevolent part you have taken, and also to make their returns of gratitude to the worthy gentlemen of Chesterfield and Cumberland County, for the very generous assistance they have afforded for the relief of the inhabitants of Boston, yet suffering, as you express it, under cruel oppression for the common cause of America. It is a sense of the dignity of the cause which animates them to suffer with that fortitude which you are pleased candidly to attribute to them ; and while they are thus encouraged and supported by the sister Colonies, they will, by God's assistance, rather than injure or stain that righteous cause, endure the conflict to the utmost.

The Committee have received 192 1/2 bushels of wheat, mentioned in your letter, as a donation from the people of Goochland County. You will greatly oblige the Committee if you will return their hearty thanks to their generous friends in that County.

I am, with truth and sincerity, Gentlemen, your respectful friend and humble servant,

TO JONATHAN TABB, ROBERT BOLLING, AND
JONATHAN BANNISTER.[1]

[*Collections* of Massachusetts Historical Society, 4th ser., vol. iv., p. 174.]

BOSTON, February 7th, 1775.

GENTLEMEN,

I duly received your letter of the 16th December, 1774, directed to Mr. Jno. Adams, and myself, acquainting us of a donation made to the sufferers in this Town by the Boston Port Bill, and desiring us to order it into such a channel as that it may be productive of the end proposed. I have accordingly laid your letter before a Committee appointed by the Town to receive and distribute donations made for that benevolent purpose, and am now, in their name, to thank you for the care you have taken, and the gentlemen of Amelia and Dinwiddie Counties, for their generous donations, assuring them that it shall be applied for the benefit of those sufferers, agreeable to their design.

It affords great satisfaction to the Committee, to have your testimony that the spirited conduct which the people of Boston have maintained in a time of oppression, and their great perseverance in the cause of American liberty, has entitled them to the assistance of their fellow-subjects in the other Colonies. While the virtuous tradesmen and others in this Town are struggling under the hand of tyranny for their adherence to so great a cause, our friends in all the other Colonies have shown an equal attachment to the common liberty, by their liberal contributions to alleviate their sufferings. Thus united and resolved

---

[1] Of Amelia and Dinwiddie, Virginia.

to aid each other, may not the Colonies indulge a prospect that, under the influence of divine Provi dence, the plans of a corrupt and infatuated British Administration to enslave them, will soon be defeated, and that the restoration and establishment of the liberties of America may be the happy fruits of all our sufferings, is the ardent wish of the Committee, in whose behalf I subscribe,

Gentlemen, your affectionate friend, and obliged humble servant,

TO ARTHUR LEE.

[R. H. Lee, *Life of Arthur Lee*, vol. ii., pp. 223, 224; a text is also in Force, *American Archives*, 4th ser., vol. i., p. 1239, and a draft is in Samuel Adams Papers, Lenox Library.]

CAMBRIDGE, Feb. 14th, 1775.

My DEAR SIR,—A few days ago I received your letter of the 7th December, and was greatly pleased to find that you had returned from Rome at so critical a time. A sudden dissolution of the late parliament was a measure which I expected would take place. I must needs allow that the ministry have acted a politic part; for if they had suffered the election to be put off till the spring, it might have cost some of them their heads. The new parliament can with a very ill grace impeach them for their past conduct, after having so explicitly avowed it. The thunder of the late speech and the servile answers, I view as designed to serve the purposes of saving some men from the block. I cannot conclude that lord North is upon the retreat, though there seems to be some appear ance of it. A deception of this kind would prove fatal to us.   Our safety depends upon our being in readiness for the extreme event.   Of this the people here are thoroughly sensible, and from the preparations they are making I trust in God they will defend their liberties with dignity.   If the ministry have not abandoned themselves to folly and madness the firm union of the colonies must be an important objection. The claims of the colonies are consistent . . . . and necessary to their own existence as free subjects, and they will never recede from them.   The tools of power here are incessantly endeavouring to divide them, but in vain.   I wish the king's ministers would duly consider what appears to me a very momentous truth, that one regular attempt to subdue those in any other colony, whatever may be the first issue of the attempt, will open a quarrel, which will never be closed till what some of *them* affect to apprehend, and we sincerely deprecate, shall take effect.   Is it not then high time that they should hearken not to the clamours of passionate and interested men, but to the cool voice of impartial reason ?   No sensible minister will think that millions of free subjects, strengthened by such an union, will submit to be slaves; no honest minister would wish to see humanity thus disgraced.

My attendance on the provincial congress now sitting here will not admit of my enlarging at present.

I will write you again by the next opportunity, and till I have reason to suspect our adversaries have got some of my letters in their possession.   I yet venture to subscribe, yours affectionately,

TO JOSEPH NYE.[1]

[*Collections* of Massachusetts Historical Society, 4th ser., vol. iv., pp. 206, 207.]

BOSTON, Feb. 21, 1775.[2]

SIR,

Your letter of the 17th of January, written in behalf of the Committee of Correspondence for the Town of Sandwich, came duly to hand. Capt. Tobey, the bearer, was kind enough to deliver to the Committee of this Town, appointed to receive Donations for the relief and employment of the sufferers by the Boston Port Bill, a charitable collection from the Congregational societies in Sandwich, amounting to nineteen pounds and three pence, for which he has our Treasurer's receipt. I am to desire you, in the name of our Committee, to return their sincere thanks to our worthy brethren, for the kindness they have shown to those sufferers by so generous a contribution for their support under the cruel hand of oppression. It affords us abundant satisfaction to have the testimony of such respectable bodies of men, that the inhabitants of this Town are not sufferers as evil doers, but for "their steady adherence to the cause of liberty," and we cannot but persuade ourselves that the Supreme Being approves our conduct, by whose all powerful influence the British American continent hath been united, and thus far successful,

---

[1] Member of the committee of correspondence of Sandwich, Massachusetts.

[2] The actual date of this letter would appear to have been February 25, from a prior manuscript copy in the library of the Massachusetts Historical Society. All letters here printed from the *Collections*, 4th ser., vol. iv., are contained in a volume of manuscript copies, from which apparently the texts in the *Collections* were edited. The text of the *Collections* has been followed in the present volume.

in disappointing the enemies of our common liberty, in their hopes, that by reducing the people to want and hunger, they should force them to yield to their unrighteous demands.

I am, Sir, in the name of the Committee, with sincere good wishes, your friend and countryman,

---

THE COMMITTEE OF CORRESPONDENCE OF BOSTON TO JOHN BROWN.[1]

[MS., Committee of Correspondence Papers, Lenox Library.]

BOSTON Feb 21 1775

SIR/

Agreable to the Order of the Provincial Con gress, the Committee of Correspondence of this Town have written Letters to some Gentlemen of Montreal and Quebeck, which are herewith inclosd.   We have also sent you Twenty Pounds as directed by the Con gress.   We hope you will make the utmost Dispatch to Canada, as much depends upon it.   We are with sincere good Wishes.

Your humble Servants,

THE COMMITTEE OF CORRESPONDENCE OF BOSTON TO IN-HABITANTS OF THE PROVINCE OF QUEBEC.[2]

[MS., Committee of Correspondence Papers, Lenox Library.]

BOSTON Feb 21 1775

GENTLEMEN/

At a Time when the British Colonies in North

---

[1] Of Pittsfield, Mass.

[2] A similar letter was at the same time addressed to residents of Montreal ; their reply, dated, April 28, 1775, is in *Journals of each Provincial Congress of Massachusetts*, pp. 751, 752.   *Cf.*, W. V. Wells, *Life of Samuel Adams*, vol. ii., p. 273.

America are universally complaining of the Oppres
sion of a corrupt Administration, the Necessity and
Advantage of a free Communication of Sentiments
as well as Intelligence must be obvious to all. Hence
it is that the Committee of Correspondence appointed
by the Town of Boston, have long been sollicitous of
establishing a friendly Intercourse with their Breth
ren and Fellow Subjects in your Province. Having
receivd Direction for this important Purpose from our
Provincial Congress sitting at Cambridge on the first
of this Instant,[1] we take the Liberty of addressing a
Letter to you Gentlemen, begging you would be as
sured that we have our mutual Safety and Prosperity
at heart. It is notorious to all the Colonies, that at
the Conclusion of the last War, a System was formd
for the Destruction of our common Rights & Liber
ties. The Design of the British Ministry was to make
themselves Masters of the Property of the Colonists,
and to appropriate their Money in such a Manner as
effectually to enslave them. The Ministry had influ
ence enough in Parliament to procure an Act, declar
atory of a Right in the King Lords and Commons of
Great Britain to make Laws binding his Majestys
Subjects in America in all Cases whatsoever; and
also to pass other Acts for taxing the American Sub
jects with the express Purpose of raising a Revenue,
and appropriating the same for the Support of Civil
Government & defraying the Charges of the Admin
istration of Justice in such Colonies where his Majesty
should think proper. The Principle upon which these

---

[1] The session began February 1; the resolution referred to was adopted
February 15. *Journals of each Provincial Congress of Massachusetts,* p, 100.

Acts was grounded, is in our opinion totally incon
sistent with the Idea of a free Government ; for there
can be no Freedom where a People is governd by
the Laws of a Parliament, in which they have no
Share and over which they can have no Controul; and
if such a Legislature shall give and grant as much of
our Money as it pleases without our Consent in Per
son or by our Representatives what are we but Bond
Servants instead of free Subjects? These Revenue
Laws have in their operation been grievous to all the
Colonies & this in a particular Manner. Our own
property has been extorted from us, and applied to
the purpose of rendering our provincial & only Leg
islature an insignificant Body ; and by providing for
the Executive & judiciary Powers in the Province in
dependent of the People, to place them under the
absolute Power & Controul of a Minister of State.
Our righteous and stedfast opposition to this System
of Slavery, has been artfully held up to our fellow
Subjects in Britain as springing from a latent Design
to break off all political Connections with the Parent
Country and to set up an independent Government
among ourselves. The Letters of Bernard, Hutchinson and Oliver have been detected ; by which it
appears how great a Share they have had in misrep
resenting & calumniating this Country, and in plot
ting the total Ruin of its Liberties, for the Sake of
enriching & aggrandising themselves & their families.
The two last named were Natives of the Colony, of
ancient families in it, and having by Art & Intrigue
gaind a considerable Influence over an unsuspecting
People, and thereby a reputation in England, they

found Means to get themselves advancd to the high
est Seats in this Government; and they improvd
these Advantages, to put a period to our free Consti
tution, by procuring an Act of Parliament to disanul
the essential parts of our Charter & constitute an
absolute despotick Government in its Stead; fourteen
regiments are now assembled in this Capital, and Re
inforcements are expected, to put this Act into Exe
cution. The People are determined that this shall
not be done. They are united & firmly resolvd to
withstand it at the utmost Risque of Life and For
tune. A Scene therefore may open soon, unless the
Ministry hearken to the Voice of Reason & Justice,
which the Friends of Britain and America must
deprecate.

In the same Session of the British Parliament the
Act for establishing a Government in the Province of
Ouebeck was passed; whereby our Brethren & fel
low Subjects in that Province are deprived of the
most valueable Securities of the British Constitution,
for which they wisely stipulated, & which was sol
emnly guaranteed to them by the Royal Proclamation.
These new Governments of Quebeck and Massachu
setts Bay, of a kind nearly alike, though before un
heard of under a British King, are looked upon by the
other Colonies from Nova Scotia to Georgia, as Mod
els intended for them all; they all therefore consider
themselves as deeply concernd to have them abol-
ishd; and it is for this Reason, that, although the Ad
vantage of Delegates from your Province could not
be had at the late Continental Congress, the Quebeck
bill was considerd then not only as an intollerable

Injury to the Subjects in that Province but as a capi
tal Grievance on all.   It is an inexpressible Satisfac
tion to us to hear that our fellow Subjects in Canada,
of French as well as English Extract, behold the In
dignity of having such a Government obtruded upon
them with a resentment which discovers that they
have a just Idea of Freedom & a due regard for them
selves & their Posterity.   They were certainly mis
represented in the most shameful Manner, when, in
order to enslave them it was suggested that they were
too ignorant to enjoy Liberty.   We are greatly pleasd
to hear that Remonstrances are already sent to the
Court & Parliament of Britain against an Act so dis
graceful to human Nature, and Petitions for its repeal.
We pray God to succeed such noble Exertions, &
that the Blessing of a free Government may be establishd there & transmitted to their latest posterity.
The Enemies of American Liberty will surely be chagrind when they find, that the People of Quebeck
have in common with other Americans the true Sen
timents of Liberty.   How confounded must they be,
when they see those very Peoples upon whom they
depended to aid them in their flagitious Designs, lend
ing their Assistance to oppose them, chearfully adopt
ing the resolutions of the late Continental Congress
& joyning their own Delegates in another, to be held
at Philadelphia on the 10ᵗʰ of May next.   The Acces
sion of that Colony in particular will add great Repu
tation & Weight to the Common Cause.

 We rejoyce in the opportunity of informing you
that the Assembly of the Island of Jamaica have
warmly espousd our Interest.   We have seen a Copy

of their Petition to the King in which they declare
. . . .

We promise ourselves that great Good will be the
Effect of this ingenuous Application in Behalf of the
Northern Colonies.

As it is possible you may not have seen the Kings
Speech at the opening of the Parliament we inclose
it. Lord Dartmouth in a Circular Letter to the Gov
ernors in America, a Copy of which we have seen is
pleasd to say " The Resolutions of both Houses to
support the great *Constitutional* Principles by which
his Majestys Conduct hath been governd, and their
entire Approbation of the Steps his Majesty has taken
for carrying into Execution *the Laws passed in the
last Session*, will, I trust, have the Effect to remove
the *false Impressions* which have been made upon the
Minds of his Majestys Subjects in America, and put
an End to those *Expectations of Support* in their *unwarrantable Pretensions*, which have been held forth
by *artful & designing Men* " Dated Whitehall Dec^r
20 1774. What Ideas his Lordship has of the Con
sistency of the Quebec Act with constitutional Prin
ciples, which deprives the Subjects in Canada of those
darling Privileges of the British Constitution, *Jurors*
and the *habeas Corpus* Act, and in all Crown Causes,
consigns them over to Laws made without their Con
sent in person or by their Representatives, perhaps
by a Governor & Council dependent upon the Crown
for their Places & Support, & to be tryed by Judges
equally dependent, we will leave to your Considera
tion. The Boston Port Bill is another act passed the
last Session & it is executed with the utmost Rigour.

How consistent was it with the great Principles of the Constitution founded on the Laws of Nature & reason, to punish forty or fifty thousand Persons for what was done in all Probability by only forty or fifty. His Lordship may possibly find it very difficult with his superior understanding to prove that the Destruction of the Tea in Boston was, considering the Circumstances of the Action, morally or politically wrong, or, if he must needs think it was so, could his Lordship judge it inconsistent with the Laws of God for a Tribunal to proceed to try condemn and punish even the Individuals who might be chargd with doing it without giving them an opportunity of being heard or even calling them to answer! Such however is the Policy, the Justice of the British Councils. Such his Lordships Ideas of "great constitutional Principles"! Nothwithstanding the great Confidence of the Noble Lord, we still have the strongest "Expectations of Support," not as his Lordship would have it, in the "unwarrantable Pretensions held forth by artful & designing Men," but in the rational & just Claims of every unpensiond & disinterested Man in this extended Continent.

We beg that you will favor the Committee of Correspondence by the return of this Messenger with your own Sentiments and those of the respectable Inhabitants of your Colony; and shall be happy in uniting with you in the necessary Means of obtaining the Redress of our Common Grievances.

We are Gentlemen with sincere good Wishes,

Your Friends & Countrymen,

TO GEORGE READ.

[*Collections* of Massachusetts Historical Society, 4th ser., vol. iv., pp. 233, 234 ;
the text is also in W. T. Read, *Life and Correspondence of
George Read*, pp. 101, 102.]

BOSTON, Feb. 24, 1775.

SIR,

By your letter of the 6th instant, directed to Mr.
David Jeffries, the Committee of this Town appointed
to receive and distribute the donations made for the
employment and relief of the sufferers by the Boston
Port Bill, are informed that a very generous col
lection has been made by the inhabitants of the
County of New Castle on Delaware, and that there
is in your hands upwards of nine hundred dollars for
that charitable purpose. The care you have taken,
with our worthy friend Nicholas Vandyke, Esq., in
receiving these contributions, and your joint en
deavors to have them remitted in the safest and
most easy manner, is gratefully acknowledged by our
Committee ; and they have directed me to request
that you would return their sincere thanks to the
people of New Castle County, for their great lib
erality towards their fellow subjects in this place who
are still suffering under the hand of oppression and
tyranny. It will, I dare say, afford you abundant
satisfaction to be informed that the inhabitants of
this Town, with the exception only of a contemptible
few, appear to be animated with an inextinguishable
love of liberty. Having the approbation of all the
sister Colonies, and being thus supported by their
generous benefactions, they endure the most severe
trials, with a manly fortitude which disappoints and
perplexes our common enemies. While a great con-

tinent is thus anxious for them, and constantly ad
ministering to their relief, they can even smile with
contempt on the feeble efforts of the British ad
ministration to force them to submit to tyranny, by
depriving them of the usual means of subsistence.
The people of this Province, behold with indignation
a lawless army posted in its capital, with a professed
design to overturn their free constitution.   They restrain their just resentments, in hopes that the most
happy effects will flow from the united applications of
the Colonies for their relief.

May Heaven grant that the councils of our sover
eign may be guided by wisdom, that the liberties of
America may be established, and harmony restored
between the subjects in Britain and the Colonies,

I am, your very obliged friend and humble servant,

TO ISAAC VAN DAM.[1]

[*Collections* of Massachusetts Historical Society, 4th ser., vol. iv., pp. 191, 192.]

BOSTON, Feb. 28, 1775.

SIR,

Your letter of the 30th December, addressed to
John Hancock, Esq., has been laid before the Com
mittee appointed by this Town, to receive and dis
tribute the donations made for the employment and
relief of the sufferers by the Act of Parliament, com
monly called the Boston Port Bill.   I am directed by
the Committee to return you their hearty thanks for
the care you have generously taken in the disposal of
a parcel of corn, (free of charge,) which was shipped

---

1 At St. Eustatia.

for that charitable purpose, by our friends in Essex County, in Virginia, on board the schooner Sally, James Perkins, master, driven by stress of weather to St. Eustatia. An account of sales of the corn was inclosed in your letter, together with a bill of ex change drawn by Mr. Sampson Mears on Mr. Isaac Moses of New York, for one hundred seventy-one pounds, eight shillings, that currency, being the amount thereof.

The opinion you have formed of the inhabitants of this Town, as having so virtuously dared to oppose a wicked and corrupt ministry, in their tyrannical acts of despotism, must needs be very flattering to them. The testimony of our friends so fully in our favor, more especially of those who are not immediately interested in the unhappy contest between Britain and her Colonies, must strongly excite this people to a perseverance in so righteous a cause.

Be pleased, Sir, to accept of due acknowledgments for your kind wishes for our speedy relief, and be assured that I am, (in the name of the Committee,)

Your very obliged friend and humble servant,

TO WILLIAM BLACK.[1]

[*Collections* of Massachusetts Historical Society, 4th ser., vol. iv., pp. 188, 189 ; the text, dated March 2, 1775, is in Force, *American Archives*, 4th ser., vol. ii., p. 16.]

SIR,

Your letter of the 24th December last to Mr. Cushing and others, by Capt. Tompkins, of the schooner

---

[1] James River, Virginia.

Dunmore, in which was brought several valuable donations from our friends in Virginia, to the suf ferers in this Town by the Port Bill, was communi cated to the Committee appointed to receive such donations, and by their direction I am to acquaint you that they cheerfully consented, at your request, that the schooner should be discharged at Salem, thinking themselves under obligation to promote her dispatch, more especially as there was unexpected delay in her loading, and you have very generously declined receiving demurrage.

We have repeatedly had abundant evidence of the firmness of our brethren of Virginia in the American cause, and have reason to confide in them that they will struggle hard for the prize now contending for.

I am desired by the Committee to acquaint you that a ship has lately sailed from this place bound to James River, in Virginia ; the master's name is Crowel Hatch. When he was building his ship, a proposal was made to him by some of the Committee, to employ the tradesmen of this Town, for which he should receive a recompense by a discount of five per cent on their several bills, but he declined to accept of the proposal. This, you are sensible, would have been the means of his employing our sufferers at their usual rates, and at the same time as cheap to him as if he had got his vessel built by more ordinary work men from the country. There is also another circum stance which I must relate to you. Capt. Hatch proposed that the Committee should employ our smith, in making anchors for his vessel, at a price by which they could get nothing but their labor for

their pains, because he could purchase cast anchors
imported here, for the same price, which was refused.
At this he was very angry, and (perhaps in a gust of
passion) declared in the hearing of several persons of
credit, that he was used ill, threatening repeatedly
that he would stop all the donations he could, and
that no more should come from the place where he
was going to, meaning Virginia.   These facts the
Committee thought it necessary to communicate to
you, and to beg the favor of you to use your influence
that Capt. Hatch may not have it in his power, (if he
should be disposed,) to traduce the Committee and
injure the sufferers in this Town, for whose relief our
friends in Virginia have so generously contributed.

I am, in the name of the Committee, Sir, your
obliged friend and humble servant,

TO CHARLES DICK, CHARLES WASHINGTON, AND GEORGE
THORNTON.[1]

[*Collections* of Massachusetts Historical Society, 4th ser., vol. iv., p. 211.]

BOSTON, March—1775.

GENTLEMEN,

Your letter of the 23d of January last, directed to
the Overseers of the Poor of the Town of Boston,
has been laid before the Committee appointed to
receive and distribute Donations for the sufferers by
that cruel and unrighteous Act of the British Parlia
ment, commonly called the Boston Port Bill.   I am
now in behalf of this Committee to acknowledge the
receipt of seven hundred thirty-six and a quarter

---

[1] Of Spottsylvania County, Virginia.

bushels wheat, twenty-five bushels Indian corn, three barrels flour, and three barrels bread, shipped on board the schooner Betsey, Capt. John Foster, being a very generous contribution of Spotsylvania County, in Virginia, to those sufferers.

You will be pleased, gentlemen, to return the sincere thanks of the Committee to our friends of that County, for the warm sympathy they have in this instance discovered with their distressed brethren in this Capital. Encouraged by these liberal donations, the inhabitants of this Town still endure their com plicated sufferings with patience. As men, they feel the indignities which are offered to them. As citizens, they suppress their just resentment. But I trust in God, that this much injured Colony, when urged to it by extreme necessity, will exert itself at the utmost hazard in the defence of our common rights. I flatter myself that I am not mistaken, while they deprecate that necessity, they are very active in preparing for it.

I am, Gentlemen, in behalf of the Committee, your obliged and affectionate friend and countryman,

TO ARTHUR LEE.

[MS., Samuel Adams Papers, Lenox Library.]

BOSTON March 4 1775

My DEAR SIR

Till now I did not hear of this opportunity of writing to you. I have therefore only a few Moments before the Vessel sails to give you a short Account of Affairs here. General Gage is still at the head of his Troops with a professd Design to put the regulating

& the Murder Acts into Execution. I therefore consider this Man as void of a Spark of Humanity, who can deliberately be the Instrument of depriving our Country of its Liberty. or the people of their Lives in its Defence. We are not however dismayed ; believe me this People are prepared to give him a warm Re ception if he shall venture to make the bold Attack. I know very well the policy of great Men on your side the Water. They are backward to exert themselves in the Cause of America, lest we should desert our selves and leave them to the Contempt and Ridicule of a Ministry whom they heartily despise. But assure them that though from the Dictates of sound Policy we restrain our just Resentment at the Indignities already offered to us, we shall not fail to resist the Tyranny which threatens us at the utmost risque. The publick Liberty must be preservd though at the Expense of many Lives !

We had the last Lords Day a small Specimen of the military Spirit of our Countrymen in the Town of Salem an Account of which is in the inclosed paper. I am just now told by a Gentleman upon whose Veracity I depend that he knew that Coll L— — at the Governors Table had declared this Account in every part of it to be true, excepting his giving orders to fire.

Every Art has been practicd to intimidate our leading Men on the popular side, at the same time the General is held up by the Friends of Govern ment as a most humane Man, in order to induce the leading Men to behave in such a Manner as to be shelterd under his Banner in Case of Extremity—this

may have an Effect on Some, but very few—We keep
our Town Meeting alive[1] and to-morrow an oration
is to be deliverd by Dr Warren. It was thought
best to have an experiencd officer in the political
field on this occasion, as we may possibly be attackd
in our Trenches.

The Town of Marshfield, have lately applied to
G. Gage for *Leave* to have a Meeting, according to
the Act of Parliament, & have resolvd as you may
observe by the inclosd. They will be dealt with
according to the Law of the Continental Congress.
The Laws of which are more observd throughout this
Continent than any human Laws whatever.

Another Congress will meet at Philadelphia in
May next. Every Colony has appointed its Dele
gates (I mean those which did before) except N York,
whose Assembly I have just heard have resolvd not
to send any. The People of that City & Colony, are
infested with Court Scribblers who have labord, per
haps with some Success, to divide them ; they are how
ever in general firm, and have with regard to the
Arrival of a Ship from London since the first of
February, behaved well.—You know their Parliament
is septennial—and therefore must be corrupted. It
is best that the Tories in their house have acted
without Disguise. This is their last Session and the
house will, I hope, be purgd at the next Election.

There is a Combination in that Colony of high
Church Clergymen & great Landholders—of the
former, a certain D^r C is the head ; who knows an

---

[1] See Columbia University *Studies in History, Economics and Public Law*,
vol. vii., pp. 74, 75.

American Episcopate cannot be establishd and conse
quently he will not have the pleasure of strutting thro
the Colonies in Lawn Sleeves, until the Authority of
parliament to make Laws for us binding in all Cases
whatever is settled. The Latter are Lords over
many Slaves; and are afraid of the Consequences
that would follow, if a Spirit of Liberty should pre
vail among them. This however is so far the Case
yᵗ I doubt not the People will chuse Delegates for
the Congress, as they did before.—When that Con
gress meets, it is expected, that they will agree upon a
Mode of Opposition (unless our Grievances are
redressd) which will render the Union of the Colonies
more formidable than ever. Concordia res parvæ
crescunt.

We have lately opend a correspondence with
Canada [1] which, I dare say will be attended with
great and good Effects. Jonathan Philanthrop under
the Signature of Massachutensis, & other pensiond
Scribblers have been endeavoring to terrify the peo
ple with strange Ideas of Treason & Rebellion, but
in vain. The people hold the Invasion of their Rights
& Liberties the most horrid rebellion and a Neg
lect to defend them against any Power whatsoever
the highest Treason.

We have almost every Tory of Note in the prov
ince, in this Town ; to which they have fled for the
Generals protection. They affect the Stile of Rab-
shekeh, but the Language of the people is, " In the
Name of the Lord we will tread down our Enemies."

The Army has been very sickly thro the Winter

---

[1] Cf., page 182.

& continue so. Many have died. Many have deserted. Many I believe intend to desert. It is said
there are not in all 2200 effective Men. I have seen
a true List of the 65th & the Detachment of Royal
Irish, in both which there are only 167 of whom 102
are effective.

To—— ————.[1]

[MS., Samuel Adams Papers, Lenox Library.]

BOSTON March 12 1775

DEAR SIR

I receivd your favor of the 20 Jan[y] by Capt Hunt
via New York. I never had the least doubt in my
Mind but that the Colony of South Carolina, which
has distinguishd itself through all our Struggles for the
Establishment of American Liberty, would approve of
and support the proceedings of the Continental
Congress. I cannot but think that every sensible
Man (Whig or Tory) must see that they are well
adapted to induce the British Government to do us
Justice, and I still flatter my self they will operate
to that Effect. There are a Set of infamous & atro
ciously wicked Men, here & there in this Continent,
who have been endeavoring to make the Appear
ance of Divisions among us, in order that our Ene
mies in Britain may avail themselves of it, and thereby
prevent the good Effects of the Decisions of the
Congress; but every impartial Man who has gone
from America must be able to convince the Nation,
that no human Law has ever been more observd
than those resolutions.

---

[1] Endorsed as " To a Southern Friend."

The people of this Town have at length gone through the Winter with tollerable Comfort. Next to the gracious Interposition of Heaven we acknow ledge the unexampled Liberality of our Sister Colo nies. If I am called an Enthusiast for it, I cannot help thinking that this Union among the Colonies and Warmth of Affection, can be attributed to Nothing less than the Agency of the supreme Being. If we believe that he superintends & directs the great Af fairs of Empires, we have reason to expect the restora tion and Establishment of the publick Liberties, unless by our own Misconduct we have renderd ourselves unworthy of it; for he certainly wills the Happiness of those of his Creatures who deserve it, & without publick Liberty, we cannot be happy.

Last Monday an Oration was deliverd to a very crowded Audience in this Town in Commemoration of the Massacre perpetrated by Preston and his party on the 5 of March 1770—Many of the Officers of the Army attended. They behaved tollerably well till the Oration was ended, when some of them began a Dis turbance, which was soon suppressed & the remain ing Business of the Meeting went on as usual.[1]

---

[1] Hutchinson, in his diary for September 6, 1775, mentions a call from Colo nel James, who left Nantasket July 29, and continues : "He tells an odd story of the intention of the Officers the 5 March that 300 were in the Meeting to hear Dr Warrens oration—that if he had said anything against the King &c an Officer was prepared who stood near, with an Egg to have thrown in his face and that was to have been a signal to draw swords & they would have massacred Hancock Adams & hundreds more & he added he wished they had. I am glad they did not for I think it would have been an everlasting disgrace to attack a body of people without arms to defend themselves. He says one Officer cried Fy Fy. S. Adams immediately asked who dared say so and then said to the Officer he should mark him. The Officer answered and I will mark you. I

On Thursday following a simple Country man was inveigled by a Soldier to bargain with him for a Gun ; for this he was put under Guard and the next day was tarred & featherd by some of the Officers and Sol diers of the 47. I did not see this military parade, but am told & indeed it is generally said without any Contradiction that I have heard, that the Lt Coll headed the Procession. We are at a Loss to account for this Conduct of a part of the Army in the face of the Sun unless there were good Assurances that the General would connive at it. However he *says* he is very angry at it. You see what Indignities we suffer, rather than precipitate a Crisis.

I have not time to write any more, only to acquaint you that this Letter will be deliv^d to you by Mr Wm Savage a son of one of my most valueable Acquain tances. .Any Civilities which you may show him will be gratefully acknowledgd by

Your friend,

TO JONATHAN UPSHAW AND OTHERS.[1]

[*Collections* of Massachusetts Historical Society, 4th ser., vol. iv., pp. 84, 85.]

BOSTON, 14 March, 1775.

GENTLEMEN,

I am to acquaint you, that immediately after the arrival of the unrighteous and cruel edict for shutting up our harbor, the inhabitants of this Town

live at such a place & shall be ready to meet you. Adams said he would go to the General. The Officer said his General had nothing to do with it the Affair was between them two &c." Egerton MS. No. 2662, British Museum.

[1] Archibald Ritchie, Jonathan Lee, and Robert Beverly, of Essex County, Virginia.

appointed a Committee to receive and distribute such donations as our friends were making, for the employ ment and relief of those who would become sufferers thereby.

Your letter of the 19th of September last, directed to Jno. Hancock, Esq., or the Overseers of the Poor of the Town of Boston, was laid before the same Committee, inclosing a bill of lading for one thousand and eighty-seven bushels of corn, being part of a very valuable contribution, shipped on board the schooner Sally, James Perkins, master, for the sufferers, from our respectable friends in Essex County, in Virginia. The schooner was by contrary winds driven to the island of St. Eustatia.   Mr. Isaac Van Dam,[1] a repu table merchant of that place, generously took the care of the corn, and having made sale of it, remitted the amount of the proceeds, (free of all expense,) being one hundred seventy-one pounds 8/, New York cur rency, in a bill of exchange, drawn on Mr. Isaac Moses, of that city, which we doubt not will be duly honored.

The Committee very gratefully acknowledge their obligations to you, Gentlemen, for your trouble in transmitting this charitable donation, and they re quest that you would return their sincere thanks to the benevolent people of your County, for their great liberality towards the oppressed inhabitants of this devoted Town.

This is one among many testimonies afforded to us, that the Virginians are warmly disposed to assist their injured brethren and fellow-subjects in this place. This consideration has hitherto encouraged our in-

---

[1] Cf., page 190.

habitants to bear indignities with patience, and having the continual approbation of all the Colonies, with that of their own minds, as being sufferers in the common cause of their country, I am fully persuaded of their resolution, by God's assistance, to persevere in the virtuous struggle, disdaining to purchase an exemption from suffering by a tame surrender of any part of the righteous claim of America. May Heaven give wisdom and fortitude to each of the Colonies, and succeed their unremitted efforts, in the establish ment of public liberty on an immoveable foundation.

I am, in behalf of our Committee, Gentlemen, your affectionate friend and countryman,

TO SAMUEL PURVIANCE, JUNIOR.[1]

[*Collections* of Massachusetts Historical Society, 4th ser., vol. iv., p. 263.]

BOSTON, March 14th, 1775.

SIR,

I am directed by the Committee appointed by this Town, to acquaint you that your bill of exchange, drawn on Jeremiah Lee, Esq., for two hundred pounds Maryland currency, being the amount of a generous collection made by the respectable people of the middle division of Frederick County, for the relief of the sufferers by the Boston Port Bill, is duly received. Be pleased, Sir, to accept of the Commit tee's sincere acknowledgments of your kindness in transacting this affair; and if it be not too trouble some, permit me to ask the further favor of you, that

---

[1] At Baltimore, Maryland.

a collection which the Committee are advised is mak
ing by our friends in Cecil County, which will amount
to three or four hundred pounds, may in like manner
pass through your hands.

I am, Sir, with very great regard, in behalf of the
Committee, your obliged and affectionate friend and
countryman,

TO JONATHAN HANSON.[1]

[*Collections* of Massachusetts Historical Society, 4th ser., vol. iv., pp. 244,245.]

BOSTON, March 15th, 1775.

SIR,

I am to acknowledge your letter of the 17th of
February last, directed to Mr. Cushing, who is a
member of the Committee appointed by this Town to
receive and distribute the donations from our friends
to the sufferers by the Act of Parliament, commonly
called the Boston Port Bill, and to acquaint you that
agreeable to your directions, Mr. Sam'l Purviance, Jr.,
has remitted, in a bill of exchange, the sum of two
hundred pounds, your currency, being a contribution
from the gentlemen of the Middle Division of Fred
erick County, in Maryland, for that charitable pur
pose. You will be pleased to return the hearty
thanks of our Committee to those gentlemen for the
generous donation, and to assure them that it will be
applied to its proper use.

It will doubtless afford them satisfaction to be in
formed that their brethren in this place endure the
sufferings inflicted upon them by that unrighteous

---

[1] At Frederick Town, Maryland.

and barbarous edict, with patience and fortitude, and that they will continue to bear oppression, and count it all joy so to do, rather than stain their own reputa tion by a base compliance with the demands of arbi trary power.

With very great regard, I am, in behalf of the Committee, your obliged and affectionate friend and countryman,

---

TO JONATHAN VEAZEY AND OTHERS. [1]

[*Collections* of Massachusetts Historical Society, 4th ser., vol. iv., pp. 227, 228.]

BOSTON, March 15th, 1775.

GENTLEMEN,

The Committee appointed by this Town to receive and distribute Donations made for the relief and em ployment of the sufferers by the Boston Port Bill, have received your favor of the 2d of February, directed to the Committee of Correspondence of Boston, whereby you acquaint them that a collection is making by the gentlemen of Cecil County, in Maryland, for those sufferers, and desire to be in formed in what way it will be most agreeable to have it remitted to this place. As Mr. Sam'l Purviance, of Baltimore Town, has already obliged us by his kind offices of this kind, the Committee have asked the further favor of him, (if it be most agreeable to you,) that this generous donation may be remitted through his hands.

I am, with sincere regard for our sympathizing brethren in your County, in behalf of the Committee,

---

[1] The committee of correspondence for Cecil County, Virginia.

Gentlemen, your obliged and affectionate friend and countryman,

---

TO RICHARD HENRY LEE.

[MS., Samuel Adams Papers, Lenox Library ; a shorter text is in Force, *American Archives*, 4th ser., vol. ii., p. 176 ; portions of the letter are printed in W. V. Wells, *Life of Samuel Adams*, vol. ii., pp. 256, 257, 281.]

BOSTON Mar [21] 1775

SIR/

I am much obligd to you for your Favor of the 4th of Feb last by Cap Leighton. From the begining of this great Contest with the Mother Country Virginia has distinguishd herself in Sup port of American Liberty ; and we have abundant Testimony, in the liberal Donations receivd from all parts of that Colony, for the Sufferers in this Town, of their Zeal and Unanimity in the Support of that all important Cause. I have the pleasure to inform you, that the People of this Colony are also firm and united, excepting a few detestable Men most of whom are in this Town. General Gage is still here with Eleven Regiments besides a Detachment from the 59th & 65th, yet it is generally supposd there are not more than 2500 effective Men in all. They have been very sickly thro' the Winter past. Many of them have died and many others have deserted. I have lately seen a joynt List, which I believe to be a true one, of the Royal Irish and the Detachment from the 65th in which the whole Number was 167 & only 102 ef fective. But though the Number of the Troops are diminishd, the Insolence of the officers (at least some

of them) is increased. In private Rencounters I have
not heard of a single Instance of their coming off other
than second best. I will give you several Instances
of their Behavior in publick. On the 6th Instant there
was an Adjournment of our Town Meeting when
an Oration was deliverd in Commemoration of the
Massacre on the 5th of March 1770. I had long ex
pected they would take that Occasion to beat up a
Breeze, and therefore (having the Honor of being the
Moderator of the Meeting and seeing Many of the
Officers present before the Orator came in) I took
Care to have them treated with Civility, inviting them
into convenient Seats &c that they might have no
pretence to behave ill, for it is a good Maxim in
Politicks as well as War to put & keep the Enemy in
the wrong. They behaved tollerably well till the
oration was finishd when upon a Motion made for
the Appointm^t of another orator they began to hiss,
which irritated the Assembly to the greatest Degree,
and Confusion ensued. They however did not gain
their End, which was apparently to break up the
Meeting, for order was soon restored & we proceeded
regularly & finishd. I am perswaded that were it
not for the Danger of precipitating a Crisis, not a
Man of them would have been spared. It was pro
voking enough to the whole Core that while there
were so many Troops stationd here with the Design
of suppressing Town Meetings there should yet be a
Meeting, for the purpose of delivering an Oration to
commemorate a Massacre perpetrated by Soldiers &
to show the Danger of Standing Armies. They there
fore it seems a few days after vented their passion on

a poor simple Countryman the state of whose Case
is drawn up by himself and sworn to before a Magis
trate as you will see by the inclosd. Thus you see
that the practice of tarring & feathering which has so
often been exclaimd against by the Tories, & even
in the British House of Commons, as inhuman &
barbarous, is at length revivd by some of the polite
Gentlemen of the British Army, stationd in this
place, professedly to prevent Riots. Some Gentle·
men of the Town waited on the General on this
Occasion. He *appeard* to be angry at it & declared
that he knew Nothing about any such Design. He
said that he indeed heard an irregular beat of the
Drum (for they passed by his House) but thought
they were drumming a bad Woman through the
Streets ! This to be sure would not have been a Riot.
The Selectmen of Billerica an Inland town about
thirty Miles distant to which the poor abused Man
belongs, have since made a remonstrance to the Gen
eral a Copy of which is inclosd ; the General promised
them that he would enquire into the Matter, but we
hear nothing more about it. Some say that he is affraid
of displeasing his Officers & has no Command over
them. How this may be I cannot say. If he does
not soon punish the officers concernd in this dirty
Action, which was done in direct Defiance of their
own Articles, one would think it is so. If he does
not do it, he must look to his own Commission. Qui
non prohibet nec puniit fecit. This Town resents it
and have directed their Committee of Correspondence
to enquire into this and other Conduct and have
Depositions before Magistrates in perpetuam rei

Memoriam, to be improvd as Opportunity may offer. A Change of Ministers and proper representations may reduce a Tyrant, at least to the Condition of a private Subject. The People are universally enragd, but from the Motives of sound Policy their resentment is for the present restraind. Last Saturday a Waggon going from this Town into the Country was stopped by the Guards on the Neck, having Nine Boxes of Ball Cartridges which were seisd by the Troops. Application has been made to the General, by a private Gentleman who claimd them as his property. The General told him that he would order them to be markd as such, but they could not *then* be deliverd. The Gentleman told him that if they were not soon deliverd he should seek recompence elsewhere. I think you may be satisfied that though "the General has compleated his Fortification" at the only Entrance into the Town by Land, and our Harbour is still shut up, "our People are in good Spirits," and I dare say "the Business of Discipline goes on well."

I have just received Letters from our mutual Friends in London dated the 24, 26 & 28 Dec^r & 4 & 7 Jan^y, some Extracts from which I have thought it necessary to have inserted in our News papers, as youl see by the inclosd. One paragraph which alarms me I have not disclosd to any one, which is this "I have been in the Country with Lord Chatham to shew him the petition of the Congress of which he highly approvd. He is of Opinion that a solemn Renunciation of the Right to *tax* on the one side, and *an Acknowledgment of the Supremacy* on the other should accompany the repeal of all the obnoxious Acts. Without that, he

says, the Hearts of the two Countries will not openly
embrace each other with unfeigned Affection & Re
concilement." In this short Sentence I think it is
easy to see that his Lordships plan of reconciliation
is the same now with that which he held forth in his
Speech at the time of the repeal of the Stamp Act.
However highly I think of his Lordships *Integrity* I
confess I am chagrind to think that he expects an
Acknowledgment of the Supremacy in terms on our
part. I imagine that after such an Acknowledgment,
there may be a variety of Ways by which Great Brit-
tain may enslave us besides taxing us without our
Consent. The possibility of it should greatly awaken
our Apprehensions. Let us take Care lest America,
in Lieu of a Thorn in her foot should have a Dagger
in her heart. Our united Efforts have hitherto suc
ceeded. This is not a Time for us to relax our Meas
ures. Let us like prudent Generals improve upon our
Success, and push for perfect political Freedom.

Mr John Allston a young Gentleman in my Neigh
borhood who owns the Vessel in which Cap Leighton
returns is also a Passenger on board. His Views are
to form Commercial Connections in Virginia. You
will excuse me if I bespeak your favorable Notice of
him should he fall in your way.

I am with sincere regards
Your affectionate Friend & Countryman

TO JONATHAN AUGUSTINE WASHINGTON.

[*Collections* of Massachusetts Historical Society, 4th ser., vol. iv., pp, 239, 240.]

BOSTON, 21 March, 1775.

SIR,

I have before me your letter of the 10th of Febru ary, directed to Mr. Hancock, Mr. Cushing and myself, inclosing a bill of lading for one thousand and ninety- two bushels of grain, being a generous donation sent by the inhabitants of Westmoreland County, in Vir ginia, to the sufferers in this Town by the Boston Port Bill. Soon after that barbarous edict arrived, our in habitants had notice of the kind intentions of our brethren of the other Colonies, towards them, and they appointed a Committee to receive and distribute such donations as should be made. I have their di rection to request that you would be pleased to return their grateful acknowledgments to our worthy friends in your County, for this very liberal contribution, and to assure them that it will be disposed of agreeable to their benevolent design.

Your candid opinion of the inhabitants of this Town, as having some share in defending the common rights of British America, cannot but be very flattering to them, and it will excite in them a laudable ambition, by their future conduct, to merit the continuance of it. They are unjustly oppressed, but, by the smiles of Heaven and the united friendship and support of all North America, the designs of our enemies to oblige them to make base compliances, to the injury of our common cause, have been hitherto frustrated. They bear re peated insults of the grossest kind, not from want of the feelings of just resentment, or spirit enough to make ample returns, but from principles of sound policy and reason. Put your enemy in the wrong, and keep him so, is a wise maxim in politics, as well as in war. They consider themselves as connected with a great continent, deeply interested in their patient sufferings. They had rather, therefore, forego the gratification of revenging affronts and indignities, than prejudice that all important cause which they have so much at heart, by precipitating a crisis. When they are pushed by clear necessity for the defence of their liberties to the trial of arms, I trust in God, they will convince their friends and their enemies, of their mil itary skill and valor. Their constant prayer to God is, to prevent such necessity ; but they are daily pre paring for it. I rejoice with you, Sir, in most earnestly wishing for the speedy and full restoration of the rights of America, which are violated with so high and ar bitrary a hand, and am, in behalf of the Committee, with great respect,

Your obliged and affectionate friend and countryman,

P. S.—Our last accounts from Great Britain, are of the 19th December.

ADDRESS OF MASSACHUSETTS TO MOHAWK INDIANS.
[MARCH, 1775.]

[W. V. Wells, *Life of Samuel Adams*, vol. ii., pp. 282-284.[1]]

Brothers,—We, the delegates of the inhabitants of the Province of the Massachusetts Bay, being come together to consider what may be best for you and

---

[1] It is here stated that portions of the original draft in the autograph of Adams were in existence.

ourselves to do, in order to get ourselves rid of those hardships which we feel and fear, have thought it our duty to tell you, our good brothers, what our fathers in Great Britain have done and threaten to do with us.

Brothers,—You have heard how our fathers were obliged by the cruelty of their brethren to leave their country ; how they crossed the great lake and came here ; how they purchased this land with their own money ; and how, since that time, they and we, their sons and grandsons, have built our houses and cut down the trees, and cleared and improved the land at their and our own expense ; how we have fought for them, and conquered Canada and a great many other places which they have had and have not paid for ; after all which and many other troubles, we thought we had reason to hope that they would be kind to us, and allow us to enjoy ourselves, and sit in our own houses, and eat our own victuals in peace and quiet ; but alas ! our brothers, we are greatly distressed, and we will tell you our grief ; for you, as well as we, are in danger.

Brothers,—Our fathers in Great Britain tell us our land and houses and cattle and money are not our own ; that we ourselves are not our own men, but their servants ; they have endeavored to take away our money without our leave, and have sent their great vessels and a great many warriors for that purpose.

Brothers,—We used to send our vessels on the great lake, whereby we were able to get clothes and what we needed for ourselves and you ; but such has lately been their conduct that we cannot ; they have told us we shall have no more guns, no powder to use, and kill our wolves and other game, nor to send to you for you to kill your victuals with, and to get skins to trade with us, to buy your blankets and what you want. How can you live without powder and guns? But we hope to supply you soon with both, of our own making.

Brothers,—They have made a law to establish the religion of the Pope in Canada, which lies so near you. We much fear some of your children may be induced, instead of worshipping the only true God, to pay *his* dues to images made with their own hands.

Brothers,—These and many other hardships we are threatened with, which, no doubt, in the end will equally affect you; for the same reason they would get our lands, they would take away yours. All we want is, that we and you may enjoy that liberty and security which we have a right to enjoy, and that we may not lose that good land which enables us to feed our wives and children. We think it our duty to inform you of our danger, and desire you to give notice to all your kindred; and as we much fear they will attempt to cut our throats, and if you should allow them to do that, there will nobody remain to keep them from you, we therefore earnestly desire you to whet your hatchet, and be prepared with us to defend our liberties and lives.

Brothers,—We humbly beseech that God who lives above, and does what is right here below, to enlighten your minds to see that you ought to endeavor to prevent our fathers from bringing those miseries upon us; and to his good providence we commend you.

TO MRS. ADAMS.[1]

[MS., Samuel Adams Papers, Lenox Library.]

NEW YORK May 7 1775

MY DEAR BETSY

Having an opportunity by a Gentleman going to Braintree I acquaint you that I arrivd in this place yesterday in good Health and Spirits. The City of New York did great Honor to the Delegates of this Province and Connecticutt by raising their Militia to escort them into the City and we have each of us two Centinels at our respective Lodgings. We intend to proceed tomorrow for Philadelphia. My great Con cern is for your health and Safety. Pray take the advice of Friends with respect to removing further into the Country. I receivd your Letter of 26 of April & Hannahs of the 19th which gave me much Pleasure. Pray write to me as often as you can. Send me whatever you may hear of my dear imprisond Son. Make use of the Money in your hands for your Comfort. I have always been well satisfied in your Prudence. I shall do well enough. I have only time to add that I am my dearest Betsy most affectionately

Your,

---

[1] Addressed to her at Dedham, Massachusetts. Adams, in 1749, married Elizabeth Checkley (*cf.* Vol. ii., page 380), who died in 1757. He married, in 1764, Elizabeth Wells (*cf.* Vol. ii., page 337), who died in 1808.

[2] An army surgeon ; born, 1751 ; died 1788.

TO MRS. ADAMS.

[MS., Samuel Adams Papers, Lenox Library.]

PHILADELPHIA June 10 1775

MY DEAR BETSY

Your last Letter to me was dated the 26 of April. I fear you think too much of the Expence of Post age. I beg of you my dear not to regard that, for I shall with the utmost Chearfulness pay for as many Letters as you shall send to me. It was with very great Pleasure that I heard from D[r] Church that he met you on the Road and that you were well on the 20th of last Month—that your Mother had been releasd from the Prison Boston. I also have this day been told that you were at Cambridge on Saturday last in good health. It would afford me double Satis faction to have such Accounts under your own hand. D[r] Church[s] Servant assures me that he saw my Son at Cambridge the day before he left that place ; but the D[r] himself tells me that when he saw you (which was after he left Cambridge) you expressd great Concern that he was still in Boston. I am impatient to hear of him and the two Servants,—Pray do not omit writing to me by the next post which passes by your Door—you may inclose your Letter to our Brother Checkley [1] at Providence with your Request to him to forward it to me by the Constitutional Post, which he will readily comply with.

I have wrote you five or six Letters since my De parture from Worcester[2] the latter End of April. I

---

[1] *Cf* page 127.

[2] *Cf.* John Hancock to Committee of Safety, April 24, 1775. A. E. Brown, *Hancock, His Book*, p. 196.

wish you would inform me how many you have receivd and their Dates.

I have lately receivd a Letter from your Brother
Andrew and another from your Brother Sam[ll]—they
were both well in April last when their Letters were
dated and desire their due Regards to your Mother
and all friends. I am now my dear to inform you that
your Brother Sam[l] (who supposd I should receive his
Letter in Boston) desired me to communicate to your
Mother the sorrowful News of the Death of her Son
Billy on the 7th of April—he had been long ailing,
and was at length seizd with the bilious Cholick and
died in three days. May God support your Mother
and other Relations under this repeated Affliction.
Sam[l] writes me that he left no Will and that he will
take Care of his Effects—which I think by Law be
long to his Mother to whom they will be sent when the
Times will admit of it. I will write to your Brother
at S[t] Eustatia by the first Vessel from this place. I
beg you not to suffer your Mind to be overborn with
these Tydings. Open the Matter to your Mother
with your usual Discretion.

I am confident it will afford you Pleasure to be informd that I am in health. My Duty to your Mother
—tell my Daughter & Sister Polly, & Hannah (who
I hope is with you) that I love them, and be assured
my dear Betsy, that I am with the warmest Affection
Your,

TO MRS. ADAMS.

[MS., Samuel Adams Papers, Lenox Library.]

PHILADELPHIA June 16 1775

My DEAR

I have so often wrote to you, without having a single Line in Answer to one of my Letters, that I have doubted whether you have receivd any of them. Had I not heard that you dined with some of my Friends at Cambridge about a fortnight ago I should have suspected that you had changed your Place of Abode at Dedham and that therefore my Letters had not reached you, or I should have been very anxious lest by some bodily Indisposition you were renderd unable to write to me. It is painful to me to be absent from you. As your Letters would in some Measure afford me Reliefe, I beg you would omit no Opportunity of writing. Your Backwardness leads me to apprehend there has something happend which would be disagreable to me to hear. If any ill Accident has befallen my Son or any other person dear to me, I would chuse to hear it. Our Boston Friends are some of them confined in a Garrison, others dispersd I know not where. Pray, my dear, let me know as much about them as you can. I make no Doubt but it will be a pleasure to you to hear that I am in good Health and Spirits. I wish I could consistently inform you what is doing here. I can however tell you that Matters go on, though slower than one could wish, yet agreable to my Mind. My Love to all Friends. I earnestly recommend you and them to the Protection and Blessing of Heaven. The Bearer is waiting for this Letter, I must therefore conclude with assuring you that I am with the greatest Sincerity, my dear Betsy,

Your affectionate husband and Friend

June 17

We have had Occasion to detain the Bearer which gives me the Pleasure of acknowledging your very acceptable and obliging Letter of the 6th Instant. I am rejoycd to hear that you are recoverd from a late Indisposition of Body. I pray God to confirm your Health. I wonder that you have receivd but one Letter from me since I left Worcester. I wrote to you at Hartford and New York and I do not know how often since I came into this City.

It is a great Satisfaction to me to be assured from you that your Mother & Family are out of Boston, and also my boy Job. I commend him for his Contrivance in getting out. Tell him from me to be a good Boy. I wish to hear that my Son and honest Surry were releasd from their Confinement in that Town. I am much pleasd my dear with the good Sense and publick Spirit you discoverd in your Answer to Maj^{r} Kains Message—your Concern for my comfortable Subsistence here is very kind and obliging to me —when I am in Want of Money I will write to you.

Your,

TO ELBRIDGE GERRY.

[J. T. Austin, *Life of Elbridge Gerry*, vol. i., pp. 90, 91.]

PHILADELPHIA, June 22, 1775.

MY DEAR SIR,

Our patriotic general Washington will deliver this

letter to you. The Massachusetts delegates have jointly given to him a list of the names of certain gentlemen, in whom he may place the greatest con fidence. Among these you are one. Major-general Lee and major Mifflin accompany the general. They are a triumvirate which will please the circle of our friends. Mifflin is aid-de-camp to the general. I re gret his leaving this city; but have the satisfaction of believing that he will add great spirit to our army. Time will not admit of my adding at present more than that I am

Your affectionate friend,

TO JAMES WARREN.

[MS., Collection of John Boyd Thacher, Esq.]

PHIL^D June 22 1775

MY DEAR SIR,

Our patriotick General Washington will deliver this Letter to you. The Massachusetts Delegates have joyntly given to him a List of the Names of certain Gentlemen in whom he may place the greatest Confidence. Among these you are one. We have assurd him that he may rely upon such others as you may recommend to him. Excuse my writing to you so short a letter and believe me to be

Your affectionate friend,

Major General Lee and Major Mifflin accompany the General. A Triumvirate you will be pleased with. Cannot our friend Joseph Greenleaf be employd to his own & his Countrys Benefit?

TO MRS. ADAMS.

[MS., Samuel Adams Papers, Lenox Library.]

PHILADᴬ June 28 1775

MY DEAREST BETSY,

Yesterday I receivd Letters from some of our Friends at the Camp informing me of the Engagement between the American Troops and the Rebel Army, in Charlestown. \ I cannot but be greatly rejoycd at the tryed Valor of our Countrymen, who by all Accounts behavd with an Intrepidity becoming those who fought for their Liberties against the mercenary Soldiers of a Tyrant. It is painful to me to reflect upon the Terror I must suppose you were under on hearing the Noise of War so near you. Favor me, my dear, with an Account of your Apprehensions at that time, under your own hand. I pray God to cover the heads of our Countrymen in every day of Battle, and ever to protect you from Injury in these distracted Times. The Death of our truly amiable and worthy Friend Dʳ Warren is greatly afflicting. The Language of Friendship is, how shall we resign him! But it is our Duty to submit to the Dispensations of Heaven, "Whose Ways are ever gracious, ever just." He fell in the glorious Struggle for the publick Liberty.

Mʳ Pitts and Dʳ Church inform me that my dear Son has at length escapd from the Prison of Boston. I have inclosd a Letter to him, which I desire you would seal and deliver to him, or send it to him if he is not with you. Remember me to my dear Hannah and Sister Polly and to all Friends. Let me know where good old Surry is.

Gage has made me respectable by naming me first
among those who are to receive no favor from him. ʼ
I thoroughly despise him and his Proclamation. It
is the Subject of Ridicule here, as you may see by
the inclosd which I have taken from this days paper.
I am in good health and Spirits. Pray my dear let
me have your Letters more frequently—by every
opportunity. The Clock is now striking twelve. I
therefore wish you a good Night.

Yours most affectionately,

TO MRS. ADAMS.[1]

[MS., Samuel Adams Papers, Lenox Library.]

PHILADELPHIA July 30 1775

MY DEAR BETSY

As I have no doubt but the Congress will adjourn
in a few days, perhaps tomorrow, I do not expect to
have another opportunity of writing to you before I set
off for New England. The arduous Business that has
been before the Congress and the close Application of
the Members, added to the Necessity and Importance
of their visiting their several Colonies & attending
their respective Conventions, have inducd them to
make a Recess during the sultry Month of August.
My Stay with you must be short, for I suppose the
Congress will meet again early in September. I have
long ago learnd to deny my self many of the sweetest
Gratifications in ɾe for the Sake of my Country.

[1] Addressed '' To Mʳˢ. Elizabeth Adams at Dedham, near the Hon Mʳ
Dexters Favord by Mʳ Barrell.''

This I may venture to say to you, though it might be thought Vanity in me to say it to others. I hear that my Constituents have given me the Choice of a Seat in either House of our new Assembly—that is, that Boston have chosen me again one of their Members, and the House have chosen me one of the Council— you know better than I do, whetner there be a founda tion for the Report. My Constituents do as they please, and so they ought. I never intrigud for their Suffrages, and I never will. I am intimately conscious that I have servd them as well as I could, and I believe tney think so themselves. I heartily wish I could serve them better—but the Testimony of my own Conscience and their Approbation, makes me feel my self superior to the Threats of a Tyrant, either at S* James* or in the Garrison of Boston.

I have receivd a Letter from my Friend M* Dexter dated the 18 Instant. Present my due Regards to him. He informd me that you had been at his house a few Evenings before and was well, and that you deliverd a Letter to a young Gentleman present, to carry to Cambridge for Conveyance to me. I am greatly mortified in not having receivd it by the Express that brought me his Letter.

M* Adams[1] of Roxbury also wrote me that he had often met with you and was surprised at your Steadiness & Calmness under Tryal. I am always pleasd to hear you well spoken of, because I know it is doing you Justice.

I pray God that at my Return I may find you and the rest of my dear Friends in good health. The

[1] Amos Adams ; under date of July 18, 1775.

Treatment which those who are still in Boston meet with fills me with Grief and Indignation. What Punishment is due to General Gage for his Perfidy!

Pay my proper Respects to your Mother & Family, M^r & Mrs Henshaw, my Son & Daughter, Sister Polly &^c. Tell Job and Surry that I do not forget them. I conclude, my dear, with the warmest Affection

Your

P. S. Mr William Barrell will deliver you this Letter—he was kind enough to tell me he would go out of his way rather than not oblige me in carrying it— he boards with us at Mrs Yards, and is a reputable Merchant in this City. Richard Checkley is his Apprentice—you know his Sister Mrs Eliot. I know you will t[re]at him with due respect.

MOSES GILL TO SAMUEL ADAMS.   RECEIPT.[1]

[MS., Samuel Adams Papers, Lenox Library.]

DEDHAM Septmb^r 4 1775.

Receivd of Samuel Adams the following Sums of Money which were deliverd to him by several Gentlemen in Philadelphia for the Benefit of the Poor of Boston, viz

One thousand Dollars delivered to him by . . . Reed Esqr being the Donation of the County of Newcastle on Delaware.

One second Bill of Exchange drawn by Samuel & Robert Purviance on Mess Geyer and Burgess Merchants in Boston for the Sum of £228. 2. 11 and

---

[1] Wholly in the autograph of Adams, except the signature.

another second Bill, drawn by the said Saml & Robt Purviance on Stephen Hooper, Esqr Merch^t in New-bury Port for £78. 2. 1, both payable to the said Adams and amounting to three hundred and Six pounds Penn sylvania Currency, the Donation of Cecil County in Maryland.[1]

Three hundred and fifty Eight pounds ten shillings and four pence Pennsylvania Currency, being the pro duce of two sterling Bills of Exchange deliverd to said Adams by Peyton Randolph Esqr the Donations of the City of Williamsburgh and the County of James River in Virginia, viz £239. n. 2p. sterling sold in Philadelphia at 50 p cent and one hundred and fifty pounds Pennsylvania Currency being the produce of a Bill of Exchange for £100 sterling deliv erd to said Adams by Patrick Henry Esqr and the Donation of the County of Hannover in Virginia.

Seventy pounds Pennsylvania Currency deliverd to said Adams by Mr Moor Fyrman and the Donation of the County of Hunterdon in New Jersey.

Thirteen ounces fourteen pennyweight and twenty Grains of Gold deliverd to the said Adams by . . . Jefferson Esqr and is the Donation of the County of Lancaster in Virginia.

Four ounces and Nineteen pennyweight of Gold and two pistarenes being the Donation of the County of Amherst in Virginia.

Four ounces two pennyweight and five Grains of Gold, five ounces ten pennyweight and six Grains of Silver, and fifty-seven Dollars, the Donation of King

---

[1] Cf. page 204.

William County in Virginia—Contain^g 51. 5. 4 Phil^a Currency.

Fifty-one pounds fifteen Shillings & nine pence Pennsylvania Currency deliverd to him by Mr Winccoop and is the Donation of the County of Bucks in Pennsylvania.

One hundred and seventy Eight pounds fourteen shillings and Nine pence deliverd to said Adams by James Willson Esqr, being Pennsylvania Currency and the Donation of the County of Cumberland in Pennsylvania.

Also a Bill drawn by Eliezer Callander on William Shattuck, Merchant in Watertown for forty Eight pounds Sixteen Shillings and nine pence Virginia Currency payable to Charles Dick[1] Charles Washington and George Thornton Esq^{rs} and by them indorsd, being the Donation of the County of Augusta, in Virginia.

All which Sums of Money and Bills as aforesaid I have receivd of the said Samuel Adams in behalf of the Committee appointed by the General Assembly of this Colony at the last Session, to receive Donations that are or have been made, for the Reliefe of the poor Sufferers by the Boston Port bill and others in the Town of Boston and Colony of the Massachusetts Bay.

MOSES GILL, Treasurer to s^d Committee.

---

[1] *Cf.* page 193.

TO ELBRIDGE GERRY.

[J. T. Austin, *Life of Elbridge Gerry*, vol. i., pp. 113, 114 ; the text is in Force, *American Archives*, 4th ser., vol. iii., p. 806.]

PHILADELPHIA, Sept. 26, 1775.

MY DEAR SIR,

I arrived in this city on the 12th instant, having rode full three hundred miles on horseback, an exer cise which I have not used for many years past. I think it has contributed to the establishment of my health, for which I am obliged to my friend Mr. John Adams, who kindly offered me one of his horses the day after we sat off from Watertown.

I write you this letter, principally to put you in mind of the promise you made me to give me intelli gence of what is doing in our assembly and the camp. Believe me, sir, it is of great importance that we should be informed of every circumstance of our affairs. The eyes of friends and foes are attentively fixed on our province, and if jealousy or envy can sully its reputation, you may depend upon it they will not miss the opportunity. It behoves our friends, therefore, to be very circumspect, and in all their public conduct to convince the world, that they are influenced not by partial or private motives, but alto gether with a view of promoting the public welfare.

Some of our military gentlemen have, I fear, dis graced us ; it is then important that every anecdote that concerns a man of real merit among them, and such I know there are, be improved, as far as decency will admit of it, to their advantage and to the honour of a colony, which, for its zeal in the great cause, as well as its sufferings, deserves so much of America.

Until I visited head quarters at Cambridge, I had never heard of the valour of Prescott at Bunker's hill, nor the ingenuity of Knox and Waters in plan ning the celebrated works at Roxbury. We were told here that there were none in our camp who understood the business of an engineer, or any thing more than the manual exercise of the gun. This we had from great authority, and for want of more cer tain intelligence were obliged at least to be silent. There are many military geniuses at present unem ployed and overlooked, who I hope, when the army is new modelled, will be sought after and invited into the service of their country. They must be sought after, for modest merit declines pushing itself into public view. I know your disinterested zeal, and therefore need add no more than to assure you that I am with cordial esteem,

Your friend,

TO MRS. ADAMS.

[MS., Samuel Adams Papers, Lenox Library.]

PHILADELPHIA Octob^r 20th 1775.[1]

MY DEAR BETSY

I have not yet receivd a Letter from you, altho' it is more than seven Weeks since I left you. I do not mean to chide you, for I am satisfied it is not your Fault. Your Want of Leisure or opportunity to write to me, or perhaps the Miscarriage of your

---

[1] A letter by Adams, on the same date, to William Heath has recently been printed in *Collections* of Massachusetts Historical Society, 7th ser., vol. iv., pp. 6, 7.

Letters, is certainly a Misfortune to me, for the Receipt of them would serve to alleviate my Cares.   I have wrote you several times since my Arrival here. In my last I gave you a particular Account of our latest Intelligence from England, which I [rely upon ;] it came from a Correspondent whose [Connections] have always afforded him the Opportunity of giving me the earliest and best Advice.

The Affairs of our Country are at this Moment in the most critical Scituation.   Every Wheel seems now to be in Motion.   I am so fully satisfied in the Justice of our Cause, that I can confidently as well as de voutly pray, that the righteous Disposer of all things would succeed our Enterprises.   If he suffers us to be defeated in any or all of them I shall believe it to be for the most wise and gracious Purposes and shall heartily acquiesce in the Divine Disposal.   It is an unspeakable Consolation to an Actor upon the publick Stage, when, after the most careful Retrospect, he can satisfy himself that he has had in his View no private or selfish Considerations, but has ever been [guided] by the pure Motive of serving his Country, and delivering it from the rapacious Hand of a Tyrant.

I am exceedingly anxious to hear from our Northern and Eastern Armies.   Much, I was going to say, All depends upon the military Virtue of Schuyler and Arnold.   If they do what they can, it will be all in Reason their Country ought to expect from them. Mortals cannot command Success.   Should they succeed, (God grant they may !) the plan which our Enemies have laid for the Destruction of the New

England Colonies, and in the Event of all the rest, will be defeated.

Pray, my dear, let me hear from you soon. I am greatly concernd for your Security & happiness, and that of my Family. I wrote to my Daughter yesterday. Pay my particular Regards to Sister Polly. Tell my Domesticks individually that I re member them. I pray God to bless you all.

TO ELBRIDGE GERRY.

[J. T. Austin, *Life of Elbridge Gerry*, vol. i., pp. 119-122 ; the text is in Force, *American Archives*, 4th ser., vol. iii., p. 1248.]

PHILADELPHIA, Oct. 29, 1775.

MY DEAR SIR,

I wrote to you a few days ago by young Mr. Brown, and then acknowledged your favour of the 9th instant.

You tell me that a committee of both houses of as sembly is appointed to bring in a militia bill. I am of your opinion, that this matter requires great atten tion, and I wish with you to see our militia formed not only into battalions, but also brigades. But should we not be cautious of putting them under the direction of the generals of the continent, at least until such a legislative shall be established over all America, as every colony shall consent to?

The continental army is very properly under the direction of the continental congress. Possibly, if ever such a legislative should be formed, it may be proper that the whole military power in every Colony should be under its absolute direction.

Be that as it may, will it not till then be pru
dent that the militia of each colony should be
and remain under the sole direction of its own
legislative, which is and ought to be the sover
eign and uncontrollable power within its own lim
its or territory? I hope our militia will always be
prepared to aid the forces of the continent in this
righteous opposition to tyranny. But this ought to
be done upon an application to the government of
the colony. Your militia is your natural strength,
which ought under your own direction to be em
ployed for your own safety and protection. It is a
misfortune to a colony to become the seat of war. It
is always dangerous to the liberties of the people to
have an army stationed among them, over which they
have no control. There is at present a necessity for
it; the continental army is kept up within our colony,
most evidently for our immediate security. But it
should be remembered that history affords abundant
instances of established armies making themselves the
masters of those countries, which they were designed
to protect. There may be no danger of this at pre
sent, but it should be a caution not to trust the whole
military strength of a colony in the hands of com
manders independent of its established legislative.

It is now in the power of our assembly to establish
many wholesome laws and regulations, which could
not be done under the former administration of gov
ernment. Corrupt men may be kept out of places of
public trust; the utmost circumspection I hope will be
used in the choice of men for public officers. It is to
be expected that some who are void of the least

regard to the public, will put on the appearance and even speak boldly the language of patriots, with the sole purpose of gaining the confidence of the public, and securing the loaves and fishes for themselves or their sons or other connexions. Men who stand candidates for public posts, should be critically traced in their views and pretensions, and though we would despise mean and base suspicion, there is a degree of jealousy which is absolutely necessary in this degen erate state of mankind, and is indeed at all times to be considered as a political virtue. It is in your power also to prevent a plurality of places incom· patible with each other being vested in the same per· sons. This our patriots have loudly and very justly complained of in time past, and it will be an everlast· ing disgrace to them if they suffer the practice to con· tinue. Care I am informed is taking to prevent the evil with as little inconvenience as possible, but it is my opinion that the remedy ought to be deep and thorough.

After all, virtue is the surest means of securing the public liberty. I hope you will improve the golden opportunity of restoring the ancient purity of princi ples and manners in our country. Every thing that we do, or ought to esteem valuable, depends upon it. For freedom or slavery, says an admired writer, will prevail in a country according as the disposition and manners of the inhabitants render them fit for the one or the other.

P.S. Nov. 4th. Yesterday the colours of the 7th regiment were presented to the Congress. They

were taken at Fort Chamblee ; the garrison surren
dered prisoners of war to Major Brown of the Massa
chusetts forces, with one hundred and twenty-four
barrels of gunpowder ! May heaven grant us further
success.[1]

TO JAMES WARREN.

[MS., Samuel Adams Papers, Lenox Library.]

PHILAD[a] Novr 4 1775

MY DEAR SIR

I thank you heartily for your acceptable Letter
of the 23[d] of Octob by Fessenden. It is very
afflicting to hear the universal Complaint of the Want
of that necessary Article Gun powder especially in the

---

[1] In the Samuel Adams Papers, Lenox Library, is the draft of a letter, en
dorsed as to James Warren, the body of which is almost identical with the
foregoing. The postscript, however, is as follows :

Nov, 4th

My Time is so little at my own Disposal that I am obligd to improve a
Moment as I can catch it to write to a Friend. I wish I was at Liberty to
communicate to you some of our Proceedings, but I am restraind, and though
it is painful to me to keep Secrets from a few confidential Friends, I am resolvd that I will not violate my Honor. I may venture to tell you one of our
Resolutions which in the Nature of it must be immediately made publick, and
that it is to recommend to our Sister Colony of N Hampshire to exercise Gov
ernment in such a form as they shall judge necessary for the preservation of
peace and good order, during the continuance of the present Contest with
Britain. This I would not have you mention abroad till you see it published
or hear it publickly talkd of. The Government of the N England Colonies I
suppose will soon be nearly on the same Footing, and I am of opinion that it
will not be long before every Colony will see the Necessity of setting up
Government within themselves for reasons that appear to me to be obvious.

Yesterday the Congress was presented with the Colors of the 7th Regiment
taken at Fort Chamblee which was a few days ago surrendered to Major
Brown—*One hundred & twenty four Barrils of Gun powder*—May Heaven
grant us further success. I am

Your affectionate Friend,

Camp before Boston. I hope however that this Want will be soon supplied, and God grant that a good Use may be made of it.

The Congress yesterday was presented with the Colours of the 7th Regiment taken in Fort Chamblee, which is surrenderd to Major Brown. The Acquisi tion of 124 Barrils of powder gives a happy Turn to our Affairs in that Quarter, the Success of which I almost began to despair of.

The Gentlemen who have lately returnd from the Camp, may, *perhaps all* of them entertain a more favorable Opinion of our Colony. I may possibly be partial in saying, not more favorable than it deserves.

In Addition to the Continental Army four new Battalions are to be raisd viz three for the Defence of So Carolina & one for Georgia. These, with 1000 men before orderd for No Carolina, with the Assist ance of provincial Forces, it is hoped will be sufficient to defend the three southermost Colonies.

It is recommended to N Hampshire to form a Governmt to their liking during this Contest;[1] and So Carolina is allowd to do the same if they judge it necessary.[2] I believe the Time is near when the most timid will see the absolute Necessity of every one of the Colonies setting up a Governmt within it self.

No Provisions or Produce is to be exported from any of the united Colonies to any part of the World till the 1st of March next, except for the Importation of Arms and Ammunition, and for Supplys from one Colony to another under the Direction of Committees ;

---

[1] Vote of November 3, 1775 ; *Journals* (1904 edit.) vol. iii., p. 319.
[2] Vote of November 4, 1775 ; *ibid.*, vol. iii., p. 326.

and a further Exception of live Stock under the first head, and Horses are allowd to be sent to the foreign West Indies. We shall by the Spring know the full Effects of our Non exportation Agreement in the West Indies. Perhaps Alliances may be formd with foreign Powers and Trade opend to all the World, Great Britain excepted.

You will possibly think I have set my self down to furnish a few Paragraphs for Edes & Gills News Paper[1]; and what is still more that I am betraying the Secrets of the Congress. I confess I am giving my Friend as much Information as I dare, of things which are of such a Nature as that they cannot long be kept secret, and therefore I suppose it never was intended they should be. I mention them however in Confidence that you will not publish them. I wish I was at Liberty to tell you many of the Transactions of this Body; but I am restraind by the Ties of Honor and tho' it is painful to me, you know, to keep Secrets, I will not violate my Honor to relieve my self or please my Friend.

We live my Friend in a most important Age, wch demands that every Moment should be improvd to some serious Purpose. It is the Age of George the Third, and to do Justice to our *most gracious King*, I will affirm it as my opinion, that his Councils and Administration will necessarily produce the grandest Revolutions the World has ever seen. The Wheels of Providence seem to be in their swiftest Motion. Events succeed each other so rapidly, that the most industrious and able politicians can scarcely im-

---

[1] The *Boston Gazette.*

prove them to the full Purposes for which they seem to
be designd. You must send your best Men here;
therefore recall me from this Service. Men of moderate Abilities, especially when weakned with Age are
not fit to be employd in *founding Empires.*

Let me talk with you a little about the Affairs
of our own Colony. I perswade my self, my dear
Friend, that the greatest Care and Circumspection
will be used to conduct its internal Police with
Wisdom and Integrity. The Eyes of Mankind will
be upon you to see whether the Government, which
is now more popular than it has been for many years
past, will be productive of more Virtue moral and
political. We may look up to Armies for our Defence,
but Virtue is our best Security. It is not possible
that any State sh^d long remain free, where Virtue
is not supremely honord. This is as seasonably as
it is justly said by one of the most celebrated
Writers of the present time. Perhaps the Form of
Governm^t now adopted & set up in the Colony may
be permanent. Should it be only temporary the
golden opportunity of recovering the Virtue & reform
ing the Manners of our Country should be indus
triously improvd. Our Ancestors in the most early
Times laid an excellent Foundation for the security
of Liberty by setting up in a few years after their
Arrival a publick Seminary of Learning; and by
their Laws they obligd every Town consisting of a
certain Number of Families to keep and maintain
a Grammar School. I shall be very sorry, if it be
true as I have been informd, that some of our
Towns have dismissd their Schoolmasters, alledging

that the extraordinary Expence of defending the Country renders them unable to support them. I hope this Inattention to the Principles of our Fore fathers does not prevail. If there should be any Danger of it, would not the leading Gentlemen do eminent Service to the Publick, by impressing upon the Minds of the People, the Necessity & Importance of encouraging that System of Education, which in my opinion is so well calculated to diffuse among the Individuals of the Community the Principles of Morality, so essentially necessary to the Preserva tion of publick Liberty.

There are Virtues & vices which are properly called *political.* "Corruption, Dishonesty to ones Country Luxury and Extravagance tend to the Ruin of States." The opposite Virtues tend to their Establishment. But "there is a Connection between Vices as well as Virtues and one opens the Door for the Entrance of another." Therefore " Wise and able Politicians will guard against other Vices," and be attentive to promote every Virtue. He who is void of virtuous Attachments in private Life, is, or very soon will be void of all Regard for his Country. There is seldom an Instance of a Man guilty of betraying his Country, who had not before lost the Feeling of moral Obligations in his private Connections. Before — — was detected of holding a criminal Correspondence with the Enemies of his Country, his Infidelity to his Wife had been notorious. Since private and publick Vices, are in Reality, though not always apparently, so nearly connected, of how much Importance, how necessary is it, that the utmost

Pains be taken by the Publick, to have the Princi
ples of Virtue early inculcated on the Minds even
of Children, and the moral Sense kept alive, and
that the wise Institutions of our Ancestors for these
great Purposes be encouragd by the Government.
For no People will tamely surrender their Liberties,
nor can any be easily subdued, when Knowledge
is diffusd and Virtue is preservd. On the Contrary,
when People are universally ignorant, and debauchd
in their Manners, they will sink under their own
Weight without the Aid of foreign Invaders.

There are other things which I humbly conceive
require and therefore I trust will have the most seri
ous Consideration of the Government. We have here
tofore complaind, and I think justly, that bad Men
have too often found their Way into places of publick
Trust. " Nothing is more essential to the Estab
lishment of Manners in a State than that all Persons
employd in Places of Power and Trust be Men of
unexceptionable Characters. The Publick cannot be
too curious concerning the Characters of publick
Men "——We have also complaind that a Plurality
of Places incompatible with each other have sometimes been given to one Person. If under the former
Administration, there was no Danger to be appre
hended from vesting the different Powers of Governm^t
in the same Persons, why did the Patriots object to it ?
If Danger is always to be apprehended from it, should
we not, by continuing the Practice, too much imitate
the degenerate Romans, who upon the Fall of Julius
set up Augustus. " They changd indeed their Mas
ters, and when they had destroyd the Tyrant sufferd

the Tyranny to continue"—Tell me if you can, how a Judge of Probate can consistently sit at the Council Board and joyn in a Determination there upon an Appeal from *his own* Judgment. Perhaps I may view another Appointment, being personally inter-rested in it, with a more partial Eye. But you may well remember that the Secretary of the Colony declind taking a Seat at the Council Board to which he had been elected *prior* to his Appointment until in the House of Representatives he had publickly requested their opinion of the Propriety of it ; and an eminent and truly patriotick Member had explicitly declared it as his opinion, that as the Place was not then as it formerly had been the Gift of the Crown but of the People, there was no Impropriety in his holding it. Major H———[1] has as much of the stern Virtue and Spirit of a Roman Censor as any Gentleman I ever conversd with. The Rest of the Members were silent. The Appointment of the Sec retary and his Election to a Seat at the Board were both made in the Time of his Absence from the Colony, and without the Sollicitation of any of his Friends that he knows of. Most assuredly with out his own. As he is resolvd never wittingly to disgrace himself or his Country, he still employs his Mind on the Subject, and wishes for your candid and impartial Sentiments.

I fear I have greatly trespassd on your Leisure, and therefore conclude with my best Regards to the Circle of Friends to our Country in Watertown, as suring you that I am very affectionately,

Yours,

[1] Joseph Hawley.

TO MRS. ADAMS.

[MS., Samuel Adams Papers, Lenox Library.]

PHILAD^A Novr 7th 1775

MY DEAR

My last Letter to you I sent by young Mr Gowen Brown who left this place about a fortnight ago. I know not how many I have written. I wish you would send me the Dates of those you have receivd, in your next.

My Son informs me in a late Letter, that you were about removing to little Cambridge. I am exceed ingly pleasd with it, because I am sure you could not be comfortable in your house at Dedham in the cold Season. When we shall return to our Habita· tion in Boston, if ever, is uncertain. The Barbarit· of our Enemies in the Desolations they have wantonly made at Falmouth and elsewhere, is a Presage of what will probably befall that Town which has so long endur'd the Rage of a merciless Tyrant. It ha; disgracd the Name of Britain, and added to the Character of the Ministry, another indelible Mark of Infamy. We must be content to suffer the Loss of all things in this Life, rather than tamely surrender the publick Liberty. The Eyes of the People of Britain seem to be fast closed; if they should ever be opened they will rejoyce, and thank the Americans for resisting a Tyranny which is manifestly intended to overwhelm them and the whole British Empire. Righteous Heaven will surely smile on a Cause so righteous as ours is, and our Country, if it does its Duty will see an End to its Oppressions. Whether I shall live to rejoyce with the Friends of Liberty and Virtue, my fellow Laborers in the Common Cause, is a Matter of no Consequence. I will endeavor by Gods Assistance, to act my little part well —to approve my self to Him, and trust every thing which concerns me to his all-gracious Providence.

The Newspapers will give you an Account of the Surrender of the Garrison at Fort Chambly to Major Brown of the Massachusetts. The Colors of the 7th Regiment were taken there and were brought to the Congress on Fryday last.

I wrote to my Daughter not long ago. I hope she has receivd the Letter. Remember me to her and to Sister Polly and all the other Friends.

You will believe, my dear Betsy, without the Formality of my repeating it to you, that I am, most affectionately,

Your,

———————

TO JAMES BOWDOIN.

[*Proceedings* of Massachusetts Historical Society, 1st ser., vol. xii., pp. 226, 227.]

PHILADELPHIA. Nov. 16. 1775.

SIR,—I embrace this opportunity of writing to you by your son, whose unexpected arrival from London the last week gave me much pleasure. He seems in a great degree to have recovered his health; & I dare say it will be still more satisfactory to you to find, that he is warmly attached to the Rights of his Country & of mankind. Give me leave to con gratulate you, & also to express to you the joy I feel on another occasion : which is, that your own health is so far restored to you, as to enable you again, & at so important a crisis, to aid our Country with your council. For my own part, I had even buried you, though I had not forgot you. I thank God who had disappointed our fears ; & it is my ardent prayer that your health may be perfectly restored & your eminent usefulness long continued.

We live, my Dear Sir, in an important age—an age in which we are called to struggle hard in sup port of the public Liberty. The conflict, I am satis fied, will the next spring be more severe than ever. The Petition of Congress has been treated with in solent contempt. I cannot conceive that there is any room to hope from the virtuous efforts of the people of Britain. They seem to be generally unprincipled and fitted for the yoke of arbitrary power. The op position of the few is feeble and languid—while the Tyrant is flushed with expectations from his fleets & armies, & has, I am told, explicitly declared, that "Let the consequences be what they may, it is his *unalterable* determination, to *compel* the colonists to *absolute* obedience."

The plan of the British Court, as I was well in formed the last winter, was, to take possession of New York, make themselves masters of Hudson's River & the Lakes, cut off all communication between the Northern & Southern Colonies, & employ the Canadians upon whom they greatly relied, in dis tressing the frontiers of New England. Providence has smiled upon our northern expedition. Already St. Johns is reduced, & if we gain the possession of all Canada this winter, of which there is a fair pros pect, their design, so far as it respects this part of their plan, will be totally frustrated.

I will not further trespass upon your time. If you
can find leisure, a letter from you will exceedingly
oblige me, for you may believe me when I assure you
that I am with the greatest esteem—
       Your Friend and very humble Servant,

TO JAMES OTIS.[1]

[MS., Samuel Adams Papers, Lenox Library ; a certified copy is in the Mas
sachusetts Archives, 194 : 160 ; and a text is in Force, *American Archives*, 4th
ser., vol. iii, p. 1654, and in *Acts and Resolves of the Province of Massachusetts
Bay*, vol, v., pp. 524, 525.]

                                    PHILADELPHIA NOV 23 1775
SIR/
Having maturely considerd your Letter of the 11th
of Nov[r] written in the Name & by order of the Hon[b]
the Council of the Massachusetts Bay & directed to
the Delegates of that Colony,[2] and consulted with my
Colleagues[3] thereon, I beg Leave to offer it as my
opinion, that the Resolve of Congress passed on the 9th
of June last relative to establishing Civil Government
must be superseeded by the subsequent resolve of the
3 of July following so far as they appear to militate
with each other. By the last of these Resolves the
Conventions, or Assemblies of the several Colonies
annually elective are at their Discretion either to adopt
the Method pointed out for the regulation of their
Militia in whole or in part or to continue their former
Regulations as they on Consideration of all Circum
stances shall think fit ; It seems manifest therefore

---

[1] Addressed as President of the Council of Massachusetts Bay.
[2] The words " in the Continental Congress " were here stricken from the draft.
[3] Originally " Brethren."

that the Hon^{bl} Council are under no restraint from yielding to the Hon^{bl} House a Voice . . . . them in the Choice of the Militia officers in the Colony.

I am prevaild upon to believe that this is the Sense of the Congress because they have lately recommended to the Colony of New Hampshire to set up & exercise Government in such form as they shall judge most conducive to the promotion of peace & good order among themselves — without Restriction of any kind.

As the Hon Board have been pleasd to direct us to give our opinion either with or without consulting our Brethren of the Congress as we shall judge best, I hope I shall be justified in declining on my part to have the Matter laid before Congress for Reasons which were of Weight in my own Mind ; and indeed I am of opinion that the Congress would not chuse to take any order of that kind, they having constantly declind to determine on any Matter which concerns the internal Police of either of the united Colonies.

It is my most ardent Wish that a cordial Agreement between the two Houses may ever take place, and more especially in the Establishment of the Militia, upon which the Safety of the Colony so greatly depends.

I am with all due regards to the Hon^{bl} Board,

Sir, your most humble Servant,

TO JAMES WARREN.

[MS., Samuel Adams Papers, Lenox Library.]

PHILADELPHIA Decr 26 1775

My dear Sir/

I have receivd your obliging Letter of the 5th Inst^t by Fessenden for which I am very thankful to you.

The present Government of our Colony, you tell me, is not considerd as permanent. This affords the strong est Motive to improve the Advantages of it, while it continues. May not Laws be made and Regulations establishd under this Government, the salutary Ef- fects of which the People shall be so convincd of from their own Experience, as never hereafter to suffer them to be repeald or alterd. But what other Change is expected? Certainly the People do not already hanker after the Onions & the Garlick! They cannot have so soon forgot the Tyranny of their late Gov ernors, who, being dependent upon and the mere Creatures of a Minister of State, and subservient to his Inclinations, have *forbid* them to make such Laws as would have been beneficial to them or to repeal those that were not. But, I find *every where* some Men, who are affraid of a free Government, lest it should be perverted, and made Use of as a Cloke for Licenciousness. The fear of the Peoples abusing their Liberty is made an Argument against their having the Enjoyment of it ; as if any thing were so much to be dreaded by Mankind as Slavery. But the Bearer Mr Bromfield, of whose Departure I did not know, till a few Minutes past, is waiting. I can therefore say no more at present but that I am,

Your affectionate Friend,

Mr Bromfield who went in a Stage Coach, set off before I could close my Letter. I shall therefore for ward it by the Post or any other Conveyance that may next offer. Your last Letter informd |me that "the

late Conduct of the ------ had weakned that Confidence & Reverence necessary to give a well disposd
Government its full operation and Effect." I am sorry
for it; and presume it is not to be imputed to a fault
in the Institution of that order but a Mistake in the
Persons of whom it is composd. All Men are fond of
Power. It is difficult for us to be prevaild upon to
believe that we possess more than belongs to us. Even
publick Bodies of men legally constituted are too prone
to covet more Power than the Publick hath judgd it
safe to entrust them with. It is happy when their
Power is not only subject to Controul while it is exercisd, but frequently reverts into the hands of the
People from whom it is derivd, and to whom Men in
Power ought for ever to be accountable. That ven
erable Assembly, the Senate of Areopagus in Athens,
whose Proceedings were so eminently upright and im
partial that we are told, even "foreign States, when
any Controversies happend among them, would vol
untarily submit to their Decisions," "not only their
Determinations might be called into Question and if
need was, retracted by an Assembly of the People, but
themselves too, if they exceeded the due Bounds of
Moderation were liable to account for it." At present
our Council as well as our House of Representatives
are annually elective. Thus far they are accountable
to the people, as they are lyable for Misbehavior to
be discarded; but this is not a sufficient Security
to the People unless they are themselves *virtuous.* If
we wish for "another Change," must it not be a Change
of Manners? If the youth are carefully educated—If
the Princi les of Moralit ai stron l inculcated on

the Minds of the People — the End and Design of
Government clearly understood and the Love of our
Country the ruling Passion, uncorrupted Men will
then be chosen for the representatives of the People.
These will elect Men of distinguishd Worth to sit at
the Council Board, and in time we may hope, that in
the purity of their Manners, the Wisdom of their Coun
cils, and the Justice of their Determinations our Senate
may equal that of Athens, which was said to be "the
most sacred and venerable Assembly in all Greece."
I confess, I have a strong desire that our Colony
should excell in Wisdom and Virtue.   If this proceeds
from Pride, is it not . . . . . . Pride?   I am willing
that the same Spirit of Emulation may pervade every
one of the Confederated Colonies.   But I am calld
off and must conclude with again assuring you that
I am, with the most friendly Regards to Mrs Warren,
very affectionately,

Yours,

TO ELBRIDGE GERRY.

[J. T. Austin, *Life of Elbridge Gerry*, vol. i., pp. 125–127 ; a text is in
Force, *American Archives*, 4th ser., vol. iv., p. 541 ; and a draft is in the
Samuel Adams Papers, Lenox Library.]

PHILADELPHIA, Jan. 2, 1776.

MY DEAR SIR,
    Your very acceptable letter of the 13th of De
cember is now before me.   Our opinions of the
necessity of keeping the military power under the
direction and control of the legislative, I always
thought were alike.   It was far from my intention in
my letter to you on the subject, to attempt the cor-

recting any imagined errour in your judgment, but
rather shortly to express my own apprehensions at
this time, when it is become necessary to tolerate that
power, which is always formidable, and has so often
proved fatal to the liberties of mankind.

It gives me great satisfaction to be informed, that
the members of the house of representatives are
possessed of so warm a spirit of patriotism, as that
" an enemy to America may as well attempt to scale
the regions of bliss, as to insinuate himself into their
favour." Whatever kind of men may be denominated
enemies to their country, certainly he is a very inju
dicious friend to it, who gives his suffrage for any
man to fill a public office, merely because he is rich ;
and yet you tell me there are recent instances of this
in our government. I confess it mortifies me greatly.
The giving such a preference to riches is both dis
honourable and dangerous to a government. It is
indeed equally dangerous to promote a man to a
place of public trust only because he wants bread, but
I think it is not so dishonourable ; for men may be
influenced to the latter from the feelings of humanity,
but the other argues a base, degenerate, servile
temper of mind. I hope our country will never see
the time, when either riches or the want of them will
be the leading considerations in the choice of public
officers. Whenever riches shall be deemed a necessary qualification, ambition as well as avarice will
prompt men most earnestly to thirst for them, and it
will be commonly said, as in ancient times of de
generacy,

> Quærenda pecunia primum est,
> Virtus post nummos.

"Get money, money still,
And then let virtue follow if she will."

I am greatly honoured, if my late letter has been acceptable to the house. I hope the militia bill, to which that letter referred, is completed to the satisfaction of both houses of the assembly.

The account you give me of the success our people meet with in the manufacture of salt-petre is highly pleasing to me. I procured of a gentleman in the colony of New-York, the plan of a powder mill, which I lately sent to Mr. Revere. I hope it may be of some use.

I have time at present only to request you to write to me by the post, and to assure that I am

Your affectionate friend,

RESOLUTIONS OF THE CONTINENTAL CONGRESS.
JANUARY 5, 1776.[1]

[W. V. Wells, *Life of Samuel Adams*, vol. ii., pp. 342, 343; a text is in *Journals* of the Continental Congress (Library of Congress edition), vol. iv., pp. 32, 33.]

The committee appointed to consider the letter of General Washington, dated the 18th of December, and the enclosed papers, brought in a report upon that part which relates to James Lovell, who has long been, and still is, detained a close prisoner in Boston, by order of General Howe, which, being taken into consideration, was agreed to, and is as follows :—

That it appears to your committee that the said

---

[1] See below, page 254. Wells, at vol. ii., pp. 364-366, prints certain resolutions of the Continental Congress of January 2, 1776, attributing them to Adams.

Mr. Lovell hath for years past been an able advocate for the liberties of America and mankind ; that by his letter to General Washington, which is a part of said enclosed papers, he exhibits so striking an instance of disinterested patriotism, as strongly recommends him to the particular notice of this continent.

Whereupon, *Resolved*, That Mr. James Lovell, an inhabitant of Boston, now held a close prisoner there by order of General Howe, has discovered under the severest trials the warmest attachment to public lib erty, and an inflexible fidelity to his country; that by his late letter to General Washington he has given the strongest evidence of disinterested public affec tion, in refusing to listen to terms offered for his relief, till he could be informed by his countrymen that they were compatible with their safety and honor.

Resolved, That it is deeply to be regretted that a British general can be found degenerate enough, so ignominiously and cruelly to treat a citizen who is so eminently virtuous.

Resolved, That it be an instruction to General Washington to make an offer of Governor Skene in exchange for the said Mr. Lovell and his family.

Resolved, That General Washington be desired to embrace the first opportunity which may offer of giving some office to Mr. Lovell equal to his abilities, and which the public service may require.

Ordered, That a copy of the foregoing resolutions be transmitted to the General as speedily as possible.

TO JAMES WARREN.

[MS., Samuel Adams Papers, Lenox Library; *Cf.* R. Frothingham, *Rise of the Republic*, p. 470.]

PHILAD^A Jany 7 1776

My Dear Sir—

I verily believe the Letters I write to you are three, to one I receive from you—however I consider the Multiplicity of Affairs you must attend to in your various Departments, and am willing to make due Allowance. Your last is dated the 19th of December. It contains a List of very important Matters lying before the General Assembly. I am much pleased to find that there is an End to the Contest between the two Houses concerning the Establishment of the Militia—and that you are in hopes of making an effectual Law for that Purpose. It is certainly of the last Consequence to a free Country that the Militia, which is its natural Strength, should be kept upon the most advantageous Footing. A standing Army, however necessary it may be at some times, is always dangerous to the Liberties of the People. Soldiers are apt to consider themselves as a Body distinct from the rest of the Citizens. They have their Arms always in their hands. Their Rules and their Discipline is severe. They soon become attachd to their officers and disposd to yield implicit Obedience to their Commands. Such a Power should be watchd with a jealous Eye. I have a good Opinion of the principal officers of our Army. I esteem them as Patriots as well as Soldiers. But if this War contin- ues, as it may for years yet to come, we know not who may succeed them. Men who have been long subject to military Laws and inured to military Customs and Habits, may lose the Spirit and Feeling of Citizens. And even Citizens, having been used to admire the Heroism which the Commanders of their own Army have displayd, and to look up to them as their Saviors may be prevaild upon to surrender to them those Rights for the protection of which against Invaders they had employd and paid them. We have seen too much of this Disposition among some of our Countrymen. The Militia is composd of free Citizens. There is therefore no Danger of their making use of their Power to the destruction of their own Rights, or suffering others to invade them. I earnestly wish that young Gentlemen of a military Genius (& many such I am satisfied there are in our Colony) might be instructed in the Art of War, and at the same time taught the Principles of a free Gov ernment, and deeply impressd with a Sense of the indispensible Obligation which every member is under to the whole Society. These might be in time fit for officers in the Militia, and being thorowly acquainted with the Duties of Citizens as well as Soldiers, might be entrusted with a Share in the Command of our Army at such times as Neces sity might require so dangerous a Body to exist.

I am glad that your Attention is turnd so much to the Importation of Powder & that the manufacture of Salt-petre is in so flourishing a way. I cannot think you are restraind from exporting fish to Spain, by the resolve of Congress. I will make myself more certain by recurring to our Records when the Sec retary returns tomorrow, he being at this time (6 o'clock P. M.) at his House three miles from Town ;

and I will inform you by a Postscript to this Letter, or by another Letter p Post. I have the Pleasure to acquaint you that five Tons of Powder *certainly* arrivd at Egg harbour the Night before last besides two Tons in this River—a part of it is consignd to the Congress—the rest is private property, partly belonging to Mr Thos Boylston and partly to a Gentleman in this City. Congress has orderd the whole to be purchasd for publick Use. We are also informd that 6 Tons more arrivd a few days ago in New York which I believe to be true. But better still—a Vessel is certainly arrivd in this River with between 50 & 60 Tons of Salt petre. This I suppose will give you more Satisfaction for the present than telling you Congress News as you request.

You ask me "When you are to hear of our Confederation?" I answer, when some Gentlemen (to use an Expression of a Tory) shall "feel more bold." You know it was formerly a Complaint in our Colony, that there was a timid kind of Men who perpetually hinderd the progress of those who would fain run in the path of Virtue and Glory. I find wherever I am that Mankind are alike variously classd. I can discern the Magnanimity of the Lyon the Generosity of the Horse the Fearfulness of the Deer and the *Cunning of the Fox*—I had almost overlookd the Fidelity of the Dog. But I forbear to indulge my rambling Pen in this Way lest I should be thought chargeable with a Design to degrade the Dignity of our nature by comparing Men with Beasts. Let me just observe that I have mentiond only the more excellent Properties that are to [be] found among Quadrupeds. Had I suggested an Idea of the Vanity of the Ape the Tameness of the Ox or the stupid Ser vility of the Ass I might have been lyable to Censure.

Are you sollicitous to hear of our Confederation? I will tell you. It is not dead but sleepeth. A Gen- tleman of this City told me the other day, that he could not believe the People without doors would follow the Congress *passibus æquis* if such Measures as *some* called spirited were pursued. It put me in mind of a Fable of the high mettled horse and the dull horse. My excellent Colleague Mr J. A. can repeat this fable to you ; and if the Improvement had been made of it which our very valueable Friend Coll M—— proposd, you would have seen that Confed- eration compleated long before this time. I do not despair of it—since our Enemies themselves are hastening it. While I am writing an Express has come in from Baltimore in Maryland with the Depo sition of Cap Horn of the Snow bird belonging to Providence. The Deponent says that on Monday the first Instant, he being at Hampton in Virginia heard a constant firing of Cannon—that he was in- formd a Messenger had been sent to enquire where the firing was who reported that the ships of War were cannonading the Town of Norfolk—that about the Middle of the Afternoon they saw the smoke ascending from Norfolk as they supposd—that he saild [from] Hampton the Evening of the same day and the firing continued till the following afternoon. This will prevail more than a long train of Reason ing to accomplish a Confederation and other Matters which I know your heart as well as mine is much set upon.

I forgot to tell you that a Vessel is arrivd in Maryland having four thousand yards of Sail Cloth —an Article which I hope will be much in Demand in America.

Adieu my Friend,

TO JAMES WARREN.

[MS., Samuel Adams Papers, Lenox Library.]

PHILADELPHIA January 10 1776

My dear Sir/

I wrote to you the 7th Instant by Mr Anthony by the way of Providence, and should not so soon have trou bled you with another Letter, but to inform you that upon looking over the Journals of Congress I find that the Recommendation of the 26th of October to export Produce for a certain Purpose is confind to the foreign West Indies—and the Resolution to stop all Trade till the first of March is subsequent to it. This last Resolution prevents your exporting mer chantable Fish to Spain, for the purpose mentiond, which I am satisfied was not intended, because I am very certain the Congress means to encourage the Im portation of those necessary Articles under the Direc tion of proper Persons, from every part of the World. I design to propose to my Colleagues to joyn with me in a Motion, to extend the Recommendation so as to admit of exporting fish to any Place besides the for eign West Indies.

A few days ago, being one of a Committee to con sider General Washington's last Letter to Congress,

---

² See above, page 248.

I proposd to the Committee and they readily con
sented to report the Inclosd Resolution[1] which were
unanimously agreed to in Congress. The Committee
reported that a certain sum should be paid to M^r
[Lovell] out of the military Chest towards enabling
him to remove himself & his Family from Boston, but
the Precedent was objected to and the last Resolve
was substituted in its stead. The Gentlemen present
however contributed and put into my hands Eighty-
two Dollars for the Benefit of M^{rs} [Lovell], which I
shall remit either in Cash or a good Bill. I hope I
shall soon be so happy as to hear that he is releasd
from Bondage. I feel very tenderly for the rest of my
fellow Citizens who are detaind in that worst of
Prisons. Methinks there is one Way speedily to re-
lease them all.

Adieu,

TO JOHN PITTS.[1]

[MS., Samuel Adams Papers, Lenox Library.]

PHILAD^e Jany 21 1776

My dear Sir

It is a long time since I had the pleasure of receiving a Letter from you. I flatter myself that you still
place me among your Friends. I am not conscious of
having done any thing to forfeit your Regards for me
and therefore I will attribute your Omission not to a
designd Neglect, but to a more probable Cause, the
constant Attention you are called upon to give to the
publick Affairs of our Colony. It is for this Reason

---

[1] Of Boston. In the preceding year he had been a member of the second
and third provincial congresses of Massachusetts.

that I make myself easy, though one post arrives and one Express after another without a Line from you; assuring myself that your Time is employd to much better purpose than writing to or thinking of me. I speak Truth when I tell you, that I shall be exceed ingly gratified in receiving your Favors, whenever your Leisure may admit of your suspending your Atten tion to Matters of greater Importance. I will add that your Letters will certainly be profitable to me; for I shall gain that Intelligence and Instruction from them which will enable me the better to serve the Publick in the Station I am placed in here. Give me Leave to tell you therefore, that I think it is a part of the Duty you owe to our Country to write to me as often as you can.

You have seen the *most gracious* Speech—Most Gracious! How strangely will the Tools of a Tyrant pervert the plain Meaning of Words! It discovers, to be sure, the most *benevolent* & *humane* Feelings of its Author. I have heard that he is his own Minister —that he follows the Dictates of his own Heart. If so, why should we cast the odium of distressing Mankind upon his Minions & Flatterers only. Guilt must lie at his Door. Divine Vengeance will fall on his head; for all-gracious Heaven cannot be an indifferent Spec· tator of the virtuous Struggles of this people.

In a former Letter I desired you to acquaint me of your Father's health and the Circumstances of the Family. I have a very great Regard for them and repeat the Request.   Adieu,

TO JAMES SULLIVAN.[1]

[MS., Samuel Adams Papers, Lenox Library.]

PHILADᴇ Janʸ 12 1776

My dear Sir

Your very acceptable Letter of the 3ᵈ Insᵗ duly came to hand. I thank you heartily for the favor and shall be much obligd to you if you will write to me as often as your Leisure will admit of it.

It gave me pain to be informd by you, that by an unlucky Circumstance you were prevented from executing a plan, the Success of which would have afforded you Laurels, and probably in its immediate Effects turnd the present Crisis in favor of our Coun try. We are indebted to you for your laudable Endeavor; Another Tryal will, I hope, crown your utmost Wish.

I have seen the Speech which is falsly & shame-fully called *most gracious.* It breathes the most malevolent Spirit, wantonly proposes Measures cal culated to distress Mankind, and determines my Opinion of the Author of it as a Man of a wicked Heart. What a pity it is, that Men are become so degenerate and servile, as to bestow Epithets which can be appropriated to the Supreme Being alone, upon Speeches & Actions which will hereafter be read & spoken of by every Man who shall profess to have a spark of Virtue & Honor, with the utmost Con tempt and Detestation.—What have we to expect from Britain, but Chains & Slavery? I hope we shall act the part which the great Law of Nature points out. It is high time that we should assume

---

[1] Of Biddeford; a member of each provincial congress of Massachusetts.

that Character, which I am sorry to find the Capital of your Colony has publickly and expressly disavowd. It is my most fervent prayer to Almighty God, that he would direct and prosper the Councils of America, inspire her Armies with true Courage, shield them in every Instance of Danger and lead them on to Victory & Tryumph.

I am y^r affectionate Friend,

TO JOHN ADAMS.

[MS., Adams Papers, Quincy ; a modified text is in John Adams, *Works*, vol. ix., pp. 371-373, and a draft is in the Lenox Library.]

PHILAD^E Jany 15 1776.

My dear sir

Altho I have at present but little Leisure, I can not omit writing you a few Lines by this Express.

I have seen certain Instructions which were given by the Capital of the Colony of New Hampshire to its Delegates in their provincial Convention,[1] the Spirit of which I am not altogether pleasd with. There is one part of them at least, which I think discovers a Timidity which is unbecoming a People oppressd and insulted as they are, and who at their own request have been advisd & authorizd by Con-/gress to set up and exercise Government in such form as they should judge most conducive to their own Happiness.   It is easy to understand what they mean when they speak of "perfecting a form of Gov^t *stable* and *permanent*" –They indeed explain them selves by saying that they "*should prefer the Gov^t of*

---

[1] *Cf.* New Hampshire *Provincial Papers*, vol. vii., pp. 701, 702.

Congress, (their provincial Convention) till quieter times." The Reason they assign for it, I fear, will be considerd as showing a Readiness to condescend to the Humours of their Enemies, and their publickly expressly & totally disavowing Independency either on the Nation or *the Man* who insolently & perseveringly demands the Surrender of their Liberties with the Bayonet pointed at their Breasts may be construed to argue a Servility & Baseness of Soul for which Language doth not afford an Epithet. It is by indiscrete Resolutions and Publications that the Friends of America have too often given occasion to their Enemies to injure her Cause. I hope however that the Town of Portsmouth doth not in this In stance speak the Sense of that Colony. I wish, if it be not too late, that you would write your Senti ments of the Subject to our worthy Friend M^r L—— who I suppose is now in Portsmouth.—If that Colony should take a wrong Step, I fear it would wholly defeat a Design which, I confess I have much at heart.

A motion was made in Congress the other Day to the following purpose—that whereas we had been chargd with aiming at Independency, a Com^te should be appointed to explain to the People at large the Principles & Grounds of our Opposition &c. The Motion alarmd me. I thought Congress had already been explicit enough, & was apprehensive that we might get our selves upon dangerous Ground. Some of us prevaild so far as to have the Matter postpond but could not prevent the assigning a Day to con sider it.—I may perhaps have been wrong in opposing this Motion, and I ought the rather to suspect it, be cause the Majority of your Colony as well as of the Congress were of a different Opinion.

I had lately some free Conversation with an emi nent Gentleman whom you well know, and whom your Portia, in one of her Letters, admired if I recol lect right, for his *expressive Silence*, about a Con federation—A Matter which our much valued Friend Col¹ W– · is very sollicitous to have compleated. We agreed that it must soon be brought on, & that if all the Colonies could not come into it, it had better be done by those of them that inclind to it. I told him that I would endeavor to unite the New England Colonies in confederating, if *none* of the rest would joyn in it. He approvd of it, and said, if I succeeded, he would cast in his Lot among us.

Adieu.

Jany 16th

As this Express did not sett off yesterday, accord ing to my Expectation, I have the Opportunity of acquainting you that Congress has just receivd a Letter from General Washington inclosing the Copy of an Application of our General Assembly to him to order payment to four Companies stationd at Brain tree Weymouth & Hingham. The General says they were never regimented, & he can not comply with the Request of the Assembly without the Direc tion of Congress. A Com^e is appointed to consider the Letter, of which I am one. I fear there will be a Difficulty, and therefore I shall endeavor to prevent a Report on this part of the Letter, unless I shall see a prospect of Justice being done to the Colony, till I can receive from you authentick Evidence of those Companies having been actually employed by the continental officers, as I conceive they have been, in the Service of the Continent. I wish you w^d inform me whether the two Companies stationd at Chelsea & Malden were paid out of the Continents Chest. I suppose they were, and if so, I cannot see Reason for any Hesitation about the paym^t of these. I wish also to know how many Men our Colony is at the Expence of maintaining for the Defence of its Sea Coasts. Pray let me have some Intelligence from you, of the Colony which we represent. You are sensible of the Danger it has frequently been in of suffering greatly for Want of regular information.

ARTICLE SIGNED "CANDIDUS."

[W. V. Wells, *Life of Samuel Adams*,[1] vol. ii., pp. 360-363.]

[February 3, 1776.]

When the little pamphlet, entitled "Common Sense," first made its appearance in favor of that so often abjured idea of independence upon Great Britain, I was informed that no less than three gentle men of respectable abilities were engaged to answer it. As yet, I have seen nothing which directly pre tends to dispute a single position of the author. The oblique essay in Humphrey's paper, and solemn "Testimony of the Quakers," however intended, hav ing offered nothing to the purpose, I shall take leave to examine this important question with all candor and attention, and submit the result to my much interested country.

---

[1] Wells, at vol. ii., pp. 349–352, prints an article entitled "An Earnest Appeal to the People," and signed "Sincerus," attributing the authorship to Adams.

Dependence of one man or state upon another is either absolute or limited by some certain terms of agreement. The dependence of these Colonies, which Great Britain calls constitutional, as declared by acts of Parliament, is absolute. If the contrary of this be the bugbear so many have been disclaiming against, I could wish my countrymen would consider the con sequence of so stupid a profession. If a limited de- pendence is intended, I would be much obliged to any one who will show me the Britannico-American Magna Charta, wherein the terms of our limited dependence are precisely stated. If no such thing can be found, and absolute dependence be accounted inadmissible, the sound we are squabbling about has certainly no determinate meaning. If we say we mean that kind of dependence we acknowledged at and before the year 1763, I answer, vague and uncertain laws, and more especially constitutions, are the very instru ments of slavery. The Magna Charta of England was very explicit, considering the time it was formed, and yet much blood was spilled in disputes concerning its meaning.

Besides the danger of an indefinite dependence upon an undetermined power, it might be worth while to consider what the characters are on whom we are so ready to acknowledge ourselves dependent. The votaries of this idol tell us, upon the good people of our mother country, whom they represent as the most just, humane, and affectionate friends we can have in the world. Were this true, it were some encourage ment ; but who can pretend ignorance, that these just and humane friends are as much under the tyranny

of men of a reverse character as we should be, could
these miscreants gain their ends? I disclaim any
more than a mutual dependence on any man or
number of men on earth; but an indefinite depen
dence upon a combination of men who have, in the
face of the sun, broken through the most solemn cove
nants, debauched the hereditary, and corrupted the
elective guardians of the people's rights; who have,
in fact, established an absolute tyranny in Great
Britain and Ireland, and openly declared themselves
competent to bind the Colonies in all cases whatso
ever,—I say, indefinite dependence on such a combina
tion of usurping innovators is evidently as dangerous
to liberty, as fatal to civil and social happiness, as any
one step that could be proposed even by the destroyer
of men. The utmost that the honest party in Great
Britain can do is to warn us to avoid this dependence
at all hazards. Does not even a Duke of Grafton
declare the ministerial measures illegal and dan
gerous? And shall America, no way connected with
this Administration, press our submission to such
measures and reconciliation to the authors of them?
Would not such pigeon-hearted wretches equally for
ward the recall of the Stuart family and establishment
of Popery throughout Christendom, did they consider
the party in favor of those loyal measures the strong
est? Shame on the men who can court exemption
from present trouble and expense at the price of their
own posterity's liberty! The honest party in Eng
land cannot wish for the reconciliation proposed. It
is as unsafe to them as to us, and they thoroughly
apprehend it. What check have they now upon the

Crown, and what shadow of control can they pretend, when the Crown can command fifteen or twenty millions a year which they have nothing to say to? A proper proportion of our commerce is all that can benefit any good man in Britain or Ireland; and God forbid we should be so cruel as to furnish bad men with the power to enslave both Britain and America. Administration has now fairly dissevered the danger ous tie. Execrated will he be by the latest posterity who again joins the fatal cord!

"But," say the puling, pusillanimous cowards, "we shall be subject to a long and bloody war, if we de clare independence." On the contrary, I affirm it the only step that can bring the contest to a speedy and happy issue. By declaring independence we put our selves on a footing for an equal negotiation. Now we are called a pack of villainous rebels, who, like the St. Vincent's Indians, can expect nothing more than a pardon for our lives, and the sovereign favor respect ing freedom, and property to be at the King's will. Grant, Almighty God, that I may be numbered with the dead before that sable day dawns on North America.

All Europe knows the illegal and inhuman treat ment we have received from Britons. All Europe wishes the haughty Empress of the Main reduced to a more humble deportment. After herself has thrust her Colonies from her, the maritime powers cannot be such idiots as to suffer her to reduce them to a more absolute obedience of her dictates than they were heretofore obliged to yield. Does not the most superficial politician know, that while we profess our-

selves the subjects of Great Britain, and yet hold
arms against her, they have a right to treat us as
rebels, and that, according to the laws of nature
and nations, no other state has a right to interfere in
the dispute? But, on the other hand, on our declara
tion of independence, the maritime states, at least, will
find it their interest (which always secures the ques
tion of inclination) to protect a people who can be so
advantageous to them. So that those shortsighted poli
ticians, who conclude that this step will involve us in
slaughter and devastation, may plainly perceive that
no measure in our power will so naturally and effectu
ally work our deliverance. The motion of a finger of
the Grand Monarch would produce as gentle a temper
in the omnipotent British minister as appeared in the
Manilla ransom and Falkland Island affairs. From
without, certainly, we have everything to hope, nothing
to fear. From within, some tell us that the Presby·
terians, if freed from the restraining power of Great
Britain, would overrun the peaceable Quakers in this
government. For my own part, I despise and detest
the bickerings of sectaries, and am apprehensive of
no trouble from that quarter, especially while no
peculiar honors or emoluments are annexed to either.
I heartily wish too many of the Quakers did not give
cause of complaint, by endeavoring to counteract
the measures of their fellow-citizens for the common
safety. If they profess themselves only pilgrims here,
let them walk through the men of this world without
interfering with their actions on either side. If they
would not pull down kings, let them not support
tyrants ; for, whether they understand it or not, there

is, and ever has been, an essential difference in the characters.

Finally, with M. de Vattel, I account a state a moral person, having an interest and will of its own ; and I think that state a monster whose prime mover has an interest and will in direct opposition to its prosperity and security. This position has been so clearly demonstrated in the pamphlet first mentioned in this essay, that I shall only add, if there are any argu ments in favor of returning to a state of dependence on Great Britain, that is, on the present Adminis tration of Great Britain, I could wish they were timely offered, that they may be soberly considered before the cunning proposals of the Cabinet set all the timid, lazy, and irresolute members of the com munity into a clamor for peace at any rate.

CANDIDUS.

TO MRS. ADAMS.

[MS., Samuel Adams Papers, Lenox Library.]

PHILAD^A Feby 26 1776

MY DEAR

I have been impatiently waiting for a Letter from you. I think your last was dated the 21st of January— you cannot do me a greater Pleasure than by writing to me often. It is my Intention to make you a Visit as soon as the Roads which are now excessively bad shall be settled. Perhaps it may be not before April. I have tarried through the Winter, because I thought my self indispensibly oblig'd so greatly to deny my self. Some of my Friends here tell me that I ought

not to think of leaving this City at so critical a Season
as the Opening of the Spring, but I am happy in the
Return of Mr Adams with Mr Gerry and in being
assured that my Absence from Duty for a short time
may be dispensd with and though I am at present in
a good State of Health, the Jaunt may be necessary
for the Preservation of it.   Whenever I shall have
the pleasure of seeing you, to me it will be inexpres
sible, and I dare say our Meeting, after so long an
Absense, will not be disagreeable to you.

I have nothing new to write to you.   In one of
your Letters you told me that D^r C had requested
that I would sometimes write you on the Politicks of
this place, and that he might see my Letters of that
kind.   Pay my due Regards to the Doctor when you
see him & tell him that I can scarsely find time to
write you even a Love Letter.   I will however for
once give you a political Anecdote.   Dr Smith Provost
of the College here, by the Invitation of the Conti
nental Congress, lately deliverd a funeral Oration on
the gallant General Montgomery who fell at the
Walls of Quebec.   Certain political Principles were
thought to be interwoven with every part of the
Oration which were displeasing to the Auditory.   It
was remarkd that he could not even keep their Atten
tion.   A Circle of Ladies, who had seated themselves
in a convenient place on purpose to see as well as
hear the Orator, that they might take every Advan
tage for the Indulgence of Griefe on so melancholly
an Occasion, were observd to look much disappointed
and chagrind.   The next day a Motion was made
in Congress for requesting a Copy for the Press.

The Motion was opposd from every Quarter, and with so many Reasons that the Gentleman who made the Motion desired Leave to withdraw it. Such was the fate of that Oration which is celebrated in the *Newspapers* of this City, perhaps by some one of the Orators Friends for I will not presume that *he* was privy to the Compliment paid to it as " *very animated and pathetick.*"

TO JAMES WARREN.

[MS., Samuel Adams Papers, Lenox Library.]

PHILAD^E March 8 1776

MY DEAR SIR

I now sit down just to acknowledge the Receipt of your favor of the 14th of Feb^y, and to mention to you a Matter which considerd in it self may appear to be of small Moment but in its Effects may be mischiev ous. I believe I may safely appeal to all the Letters which I have written to my Friends since I have been in this City to vindicate my self in affirming that I have never mentiond M^r C or referrd to his Con duct in any of them, excepting one to my worthy Colleague M^r A when he was at Watertown a few Weeks ago, in which I informd him of the side M^r C had taken in a very interresting Debate; and then I only observd that he had a Right to give his opinion whenever he was prepard to form one. Yet I have been told that it has been industriously reported that M^r J A & my self have been secretly writing to his Prejudice and that our Letters had operated to his

being superceded. So fully perswaded were Gentle
men of the Truth of this Report, and M^r D of N Y
in particular whom I have heard express a warm
Affection for M^r C, that he seemd scarcely willing to
credit me when I contradicted it. Whether the re
port and a Beliefe of it engagd the confidential
Friends of M^r C to open a charitable Subscription in
Support of his Character, I am not able to say. If it
was so, they ought in Justice to him to have made
themselves certain of the Truth of it ; for to offer Aid
to the Reputation of a Gentleman without a real Ne
cessity is surely no Advantage to it. A Letter was
handed about addressed to Mr C. The Contents I
never saw—his Friends signd it. Other Gentlemen at
their request also set their hands to it, perhaps with
as much Indifference as a Man of Business would give
a shilling to get rid of the Importunity of a Beggar.
I hear it is supposd in Watertown to be an Address
of Thanks from the Congress to M^r C for his eminent
Services, in which his recall from Business here is
mentiond with Regret—but this is most certainly a
Mistake. The Gentlemen signd it in their private
Capacity. With Submission they should not have addressd it to another Person or publishd it to the
World after the Manner of other Addressers ; for if
they intended it to recommend M^r C to his own Con
stituents, was it not hard to oblige him to blow the
Trumpet himself which they had prepared to sound
his Praise. But Maj^r Osgood is in haste. I must
therefore drop this Subject *for the present* and con
clude with assuring you that I am affectionately yours,

TO MRS. ADAMS.

[MS., Samuel Adams Papers, Lenox Library.]

PHILADELPHIA March 10ᵗʰ 1776

MY DEAR BETSY

I arrivd in this City from Baltimore last Saturday. Having been indisposd there so as to be obligd to keep my Chamber ten days, I was unable to travel with my Friends, but through the Goodness of God I have got rid of my Disorder and am in good Health. Mʳˢ Ross, at whose House I took Lodging in Balti more treated me with great Civility and Kindness and was particularly attentive to me in my Sickness, and Wadsworth is as clever a young Man, as I ever met with. Tell Mʳ Collson, if you see him, he more than answers my Expectation even from the good Charac ter he gave me of him.

I hope, my dear, that you and my Family enjoy a good Share of Health. It is my constant & ardent Prayer that the best of Heavens Blessings may rest on you and on them. I lately receivd a Letter from my Son, and since I came to this Place, General Mor ris of New York tells me he frequently saw him at Peeks Kill, and that he behavd well. Nothing gives me greater Satisfaction than to hear that he sup ports a good Reputation. I hope my Friends do not flatter me.

I am greatly disappointed in not receiving your last Letter. It was owing to the Friendship of Mʳ Han- cock who took it up in this place, and not expecting my Return from Baltimore so soon, he forwarded it by a careful hand who promisd him to deliver it to me there. I shall receive it in a day or two by the Post. Pray write to me by every opportunity and believe me to be,

Your affectionate,

P. S.

Just as I was going to close this Letter I receivd from Baltimore your kind Letter of the 26th of Janu ary. The Post being now ready to set off I have only time to acknowledge the favor.

March 12th

TO JOSEPH PALMER.[1]

[MS., Samuel Adams Papers, Lenox Library; a part of the letter is in *New England Historical and Genealogical Register*, vol. xxx., p. 310; a portion of the text is in W. C. Ford, *Writings of George Washington*, vol. iii., p. 103, from MS. owned by Mrs. J. S. H. Fogg.]

PHILAD April 2 1776

My dear Sir/

I am yet indebted to you for the obliging Letter I received from you some Months ago. The Subject of it was principally concerning a young Gentleman whom I personally know, and whose Merit in my opinion intitles him to singular Notice from his Country. This may seem like Flattery—you may be assured it is not—nor indeed do I know how to flatter. Words however are oftentimes, though spoken in Sincerity, but Wind. If I had had it in my Power substantially to have servd that young Gentle man you would have long ago heard from me. The Want of that opportunity causd me to lay down my

---

[1] Of Braintree. A member of each provincial congress of Massachusetts.

pen divers times after I had even begun to write to you—you will not therefore, I hope, construe my long Delay as the least Want of that just Regard which I owe to you.

Many Advantages arose to our Colony by the Congress adopting the Army raisd in N Eng^d the last Spring but among the Misfortunes attending it this was one, namely that it being now a Continental Army, the Gentlemen of all Colonies had a Right to and put in for a Share in behalf of their Friends in filling up the various offices. By this means it was thought that military knowledge and Experience as well as the military Spirit would spread thro the Colonies and besides that they would all consider themselves the more interrested in the Success of our Army and in providing for its support. But then there was the less Room for Persons who were well worthy of Notice in the Colonies which had first raisd the Army. This was the Cause why many of our Friends were discontented who did not advert to it. When the Quarter Master was appointed, I question whether any of your Friends knew, I am sure I did not, that the Gentleman I have referrd to sustaind that office ; there was therefore no designd Neglect of him here. Mr M^s Character stood so high that no Gentleman could hesitate to put him into a place which was understood to be vacant & which he was so well qualified to fill. The Truth is, we have never had that Information from our Friends at Watertown of the State of things which we have thought we had good reason to expect from them. I do assure you I have often been made acquainted with the State of

Affairs in our Colony, as well as I could from Letters shown to me by Gentlemen of other Colonies. I do not mention this without duly considering that the Attention of our Friends must have been turnd to a great Variety of Business.

I heartily congratulate you upon the sudden and important Change of our Affairs in the Removal of the Barbarians from the Capital. ⸤We owe our grate ful Acknowledgments to him who is, as he is fre quently stiled in sacred Writ "The Lord of Hosts" "The God of Armies"—We have not yet been informd with Certainty what Course the Enemy have steerd.⸥I hope we shall be upon our Guard against future Attempts. Will not Care be taken immedi ately to fortify the Harbour & thereby prevent the Entrance of Ships of War ever hereafter? But I am called to Duty and must break off abruptly.

Adieu my Friend and be assured I am affection ately yours,

TO SAMUEL COOPER.

[MS., Samuel Adams Papers, Lenox Library.]

PHILADᴬ April 3 1776.

MY DEAR FRIEND

I lately recᵈ a very obliging Letter from you for which I now return you my hearty Thanks. I wish your Leisure would admit of your frequently favoring me with your Thoughts of our publick Affairs. I do assure you I shall make use of them, as far as my Ability shall extend, to the Advantage of our Coun try. If you please, I will employ a few Minutes in giving you my own Ideas, grounded on the best In telligence I have been able to obtain.

Notwithstanding Shame and Loss attended the Measures of the British Court the last Summer and Fall, yet by the latest Accounts rec^d from our Friends in that Country, it appears that they are determind to persevere. They then reckond (in December) upon having 20,000 Troops in America for the next Campaign. Their Estimate was thus— 6000 in Boston—7000 to go from Ireland—3000 Highlanders raising under General Frazier and the rest to be in Recruits—of the 7000 from Ireland, we are told, that 3000 were to sail for Virginia and North Carolina & were expected to be on that Coast in March or the Beginning of April. It is probable then that the Ministry have not quitted the Plan which they had agreed upon above a twelvemonth ago; which was, to take Possession of New York—make themselves Masters of Hudsons River & the Lakes, thereby securing Canada and the Indians—cut off all Communication between the Colonies Northward & Southward of Hudsons River, and thus to subdue the former in hopes by instigating the Negroes to make the others an easy Prey. Our Success, a great Part of which they had not then heard of, it is to be hoped has renderd this Plan impracticable; yet it is probable that the main Body of these Troops is designd to carry it into Execution, while the rest are to make a Diversion in the Southern Colonies. Those Colonies, I think, are sufficiently provided for. Our Safety very much depends upon our Vigilance & Success in N York & Canada. Our Enemies did not neglect Hudsons River the last year. We know that one of their Transports arrivd at N York, but

Gage, seizd with a Panick orderd that & the other Transports destind for that Place, to Boston. I have ever thought it to be their favorite Plan; not only because it appeard to me to be dictated by sound Policy, but because from good Intelligence which I receivd from England the last Winter, they revivd it after it had been broken in upon by Gage, and sent Tryon to New York to remove every obstacle in the Way of landing the Troops there, and to cooperate with Carleton in the Execution of it.—

The Kings Troops have now abandond Boston, on which I sincerely congratulate you. We have not yet heard what Course they have steerd. I judge for Hallifax. They may return if they hear that you are off your Guard. Or probably they may go up St Lawrence River as early as the Season will admit of it. Does it not behove N England to secure her self from future Invasions, while the Attention of Congress is turnd to N York & Canada. We seem to have the Game in our own hands; if we do not play it well, Misfortune will be the Effect of our Negligence and Folly. The British Court sollicited the Assistance of Russia; but we are informd that they faild of it through the Interposition of France by the Means of Sweden. The ostensible Reason on the Part of Russia was, that there was no Cartel settled between Great Britain and America; the Want of which will make every Power reluctant in lending their Troops. France is attentive to this Struggle and wishes for a Separation of the two Countries. I am in no Doubt that she would with Chearfulness openly lend her Aid to promote it, if

America would declare herself free and independent; for I think it is easy to see what great though differ ent Effects it would have in both those Nations. Britain would no longer have it in her Power to oppress.

Is not America already independent? Why then not declare it? Upon whom was she ever supposd to be dependent, but upon that Nation whose most barbarous Usage of her, & that in multiplied Instan ces and for a long time has renderd it absurd ever to put Confidence in it, & with which she is at this time in open War. Can Nations at War be said to be dependent either upon the other? I ask then again, why not declare for Independence? Because say some, it will forever shut the Door of Reconciliation. Upon what Terms will Britain be reconciled with America? If we may take the confiscating Act of Parliam' or the Kings last Proclamation for our Rule to judge by, she will be reconciled upon our abjectly submitting to Tyranny, and asking and receiving Pardon for resisting it. Will this redound to the Honor or the Safety of America? Surely no. By such a Reconciliation she would not only in the most shameful Manner acknowledge the Tyranny, but most wickedly, as far as would be in her Power, prevent her Posterity from ever hereafter resisting it.

But the Express now waits for this Letter. I must therefore break off. I will write to you again by an other opportunity. Pay my Respects to the Speaker pro Temp. and tell him that I have never receivd a

Line from him since I have been in this City. My
Respects are also due to M[r] S P S,[1] from whom I
yesterday receivd a kind Letter, which I shall duly
acknowledge to him when I have Leisure to write.
Give me Leave to assure you that I am with the
most friendly Regards for your Lady & Family very
affectionately,

Yours.

TO JOSEPH HAWLEY.

[MS., Samuel Adams Papers, Lenox Library.]

PHILADE April 15 1776

MY DEAR SIR

Your obliging Letter of the 1st Inst[t] came duly to
my hand. So early as the last Winter was a twelve
month past I was informd by a worthy and very intel
ligent Friend in London, that the Subduction of the
New England Colonies was the *first* Object of our
Enemies. This was to be effected, in a Manner coin
cident with your Ideas, by establishing themselves on
Hudsons River. They were thereby at once to se
cure Canada and the Indians, give Support and Pro
tection to the numerous Tories in New York, supply
their Army at Boston with Provisions from that
Colony and intirely prevent the southern from afford
ing any Aid to those invaded Colonies. This Plan
was in my opinion undoubtedly dictated by sound
Policy ; and it would have been put in Execution the
last Summer, had not the necessities to which Gage
was reducd & his Apprehensions from our having a

---

[1] Samuel P. Savage.

formidable Army before Boston, obligd him to break in upon it. They did not neglect Hudsons River the last year; for we know that two of their Transports actually arrivd at New York; But these were im mediately orderd by Gage, together with the rest of the Fleet to Boston. My Friend in London whose Intelligence I have never yet found to fail, informd me the last Fall, that our Enemies did not quit this Plan. Upon hearing that it had been thus inter· rupted, they revivd it, and sent Tryon to New York to keep the People there in good Humour and coop erate with Carleton in the Execution of it. They reckond the last Winter upon having 20,000 Troops in America for the ensuing Campaign, of which 3000 were to go to Virginia or one of the Carolinas. These last I suppose are designd for a Diversion, while the main Body of all the Troops they will be able to send, will be employd in executing their original & favorite Plan. Thus, my Friend, I am yet happy in concurring with you in Sentiments; and I shall persevere in using the small Influence I have here, agreable to your repeated Advice, "to prevent the Enemies establishing themselves & making Advances on Hudson & St Lawrence Rivers."

The Mercenary Troops have at length abandond Boston on which, I perceive, you will not allow me *yet* to give you Joy. May I not however advise, that the favorable opportunity which this important Event, added to the Season of the year has offerd, be improvd in fortifying the Harbour so as to render it impracticable for the Enemies Ships to enter it here after. I hope this fortunate Change of Affairs has

not put you off your Guard. Should you not im
mediately prepare against future Invasions, which
may be made upon you before you are aware ? Your
Sea Coasts must still be defended. We shall soon
realize the Destination of the Enemies Forces.
Those under the Command of General Howe will
probably remain at Hallifax till the Season of the
year will admit of their going up St Lawrence River.
The Troops coming from Ireland may be destind to
New York & will expect to get Possession there.
At least they will attempt it. A failure may lead
their Views back to Boston ; for I am in no Appre
hensions that they will think of subduing the Southern
Colonies till they shall have first subdued those of
the North. The Southern Colonies, I think, are
sufficiently provided for, to enable them to repell any
Force that may come against them the ensuing
Summer. Our Safety therefore much depends upon
the Care which New England shall take for her own
Preservation and our Vigilance and Success in New
York and Canada. There are Forces enough already
orderd to answer all our Purposes. Our business is,
to imitate our Enemies in Zeal Application & Perse·
verance in carrying our own Plans into Execution.

I am perfectly satisfied with the Reasons you offer
to show the Necessity of a publick & explicit Declara
tion of Independency. I cannot conceive what good
Reason can be assignd against it. Will it widen the
Breach ? This would be a strange Question after we
have raised Armies and fought Battles with the British
Troops, set up an American Navy, permitted the In
habitants of these Colonies to fit out armed Vessels

to cruize on all Ships &c belonging to any of the In
habitants of Great Britain declaring them the Enemies
of the united Colonies, and torn into Shivers their
Acts of Trade, by allowing Commerce subject to Reg
ulations to be made by *our selves* with the People of
all Countries but such as are Subjects of the British
King.   It cannot surely after all this be imagind that
we consider our selves or mean to be considerd by
others in any State but that of Independence.   But
moderate Whigs are disgusted with our mentioning
the Word! Sensible Tories are better Politicians.
They know, that no foreign Power can consistently
yield Comfort to Rebels, or enter into any kind of
Treaty with these Colonies till they declare them
selves free and independent.   They are in hopes that
by our protracting this decisive Step we shall grow
weary of War; and that for want of foreign Connec
tions and Assistance we shall be driven to the Neces
sity of acknowledging the Tyrant and submitting to
the Tyranny.   These are the Hopes and Expecta
tions of Tories, while moderate Gentlemen are
flattering themselves with the Prospect of Recon
ciliation when the Commissioners that are talked of
shall arrive. A mere Amusement indeed!   When
are these Commissioners to arrive? Or what Terms
of Reconciliation are we to expect from them that
will be acceptable to the People of America?   Will
the King of Great Britain empower his Commis
sioners even to promise the Repeal of all or any of
their obnoxious and oppressive Acts?   Can he do it?
Or if he could, has he ever yet discoverd a Disposi
tion which shew the least Degree of that princely

Virtue, Clemency? I scruple not to affirm it as my Opinion that his heart is more obdurate, and his Disposition towards the People of America is more unrelenting and malignant than was that of Pharaoh towards the Israelites in Egypt. But let us not be impatient. It requires Time to convince the doubting and inspire the timid. Many great Events have taken place "since the stopping the Courts in Berkshire"—Events at that time unforeseen. Whether we shall ever see the Commissioners is Matter of Uncertainty. I do not, I never did expect them. If they do come the Budget must open and it will be soon known to all whether Reconciliation is practicable or not. If they do not come speedily, the hopes which some Men entertain of reconciliation must vanish. I am my dear Sir very respectfully,

Yours,

TO SAMUEL COOPER.

[MS., Samuel Adams Papers, Lenox Library.]

PHILAD^A April 30 1776

My dear Sir

I am to acknowledge the Receipt of your Favor of the 18th Instant by the Post. The Ideas of Independence spread far and wide among the Colonies. Many of the leading Men see the absurdity of supposing that Allegiance is due to a Sovereign who has already thrown us out of his Protection. South Carolina has lately assumd a new Government. The Convention of North Carolina have unanimously agreed to do the same & appointed a Committee to prepare & lay before them a proper Form. They have also revokd certain Instructions which tied the Hands of their Delegates here. Virginia whose Convention is to meet on the third of next month will follow the lead. The Body of the People of Maryland are firm. Some of the principal Members of their Convention, I am inclind to believe, are timid or lukewarm but an occurrence has lately fallen out in that Colony which will probably give an agreable Turn to their affairs. Of this I will inform you at a future time when I may be more particularly instructed concerning it. The lower Counties on Delaware are a small People but well affected to the Common Cause. In this populous and wealthy Colony political Parties run high. The News papers are full of the Matter but I think I may assure you that Com mon Sense, prevails among the people—a Law has lately passed in the Assembly here for increasing the Number of Representatives and tomorrow they are to come to a Choice in this City & diverse of the Coun ties—by this Means it is said the representation of the Colony will be more equal. I am told that a very popular Gentleman who is a Candidate for one of the back Counties has been in danger of losing his Election because it was reported among the Electors that he had declared his Mind in this City against Independence. I know the political Creed of that Gentleman. It is, so far as relates to a Right of the British Parliament to make Laws binding the Colo nies in any Case whatever, exactly correspondent with your own. I mention this Anecdote to give you an Idea of the Jealousy of the People & their Attention to this Point. The Jerseys are agitating the great Question. It is with them rather a Matter of Prudence whether to determine till some others have done it before them. A Gentleman of that Colony tells me that at least one half of them have N Eng^d Blood running in their Veins—be this as it may their Sentiments & Manners are I believe similar to those of N England. I forbear to say any thing of New York, for I confess I am not able to form any opinion of them. I lately rec^d a Letter from a Friend in that Colony informing me that they would soon come to a Question of the Expediency of taking up Government; but to me it is uncertain what they will do. I think they are at least as unenlightned in the Nature & Importance of our political Disputes as any one of the united Colonies. I have not mentiond our little Sister Georgia; but I believe she is as warmly engagd in the Cause as any of us, & will do as much as can be reasonably expected of her. I was very sollicitous the last Fall to have Governments set up by the people in every Colony. It appears to me to be necessary for many reasons. When this is done, and I am inclind to think it will be soon, the Colonies will feel their Independence—the Way will be prepared for a Confederation, and one Government may be formd with the Consent of the whole—a distinct State composd of all the Colonies with a common Legislature for great & General Purposes. This I was in hopes would have been the Work of the last Winter. I am disappointed but I bear it tollerably well. I am disposd to believe that every thing is orderd for the best, and if I do not find my self chargeable with Neglect I am not greatly chagrind when things do not go on exactly according to my mind. Indeed I have the Happiness of believing that what I most earnestly wish for will in due time be effected. We cannot make Events. Our Business is wisely to improve them. There has been much to do to confirm doubting Friends & fortify the Timid. It requires time to bring honest Men to think & determine alike even in important Matters. Mankind are governed more by their feelings than by reason. Events which excite those feelings will produce wonderful Effects. The Boston Port bill suddenly wrought a Union of the Colonies which could not be brot about by the Industry of years in reasoning on the necessity of it for the Common Safety. Since the memorable 19th of April one Event has brot another on, till Boston sees her Deliverance from those more than savage Troops upon which the exe crable Tyrant so much relyed for the Completion of his horrid Conspiracys and America has furnishd her self with more than seventy Battalions for her Defence. The burning of Norfolk & the Hostilities committed in North Carolina have kindled the resent ment of our Southern Brethren who once thought their Eastern Friends hot headed & rash ; now indeed the Tone is alterd & it is said that the Coolness & Moderation of the one is necessary to allay the heat of the other. There is a reason that w^{d} induce one even to wish for the speedy arrival of the British Troops that are expected at the Southward. I think our friends are well prepared for them, & one Battle would do more towards a Declaration of Indepen dency than a long chain of conclusive Arguments in a provincial Convention or the Continental Congress. I am very affectionately yours,

TO JOHN SCOLLAY.

[MS., Samuel Adams Papers, Lenox Library.]

PHILADELPHIA Apr 30 1776

MY DEAR SIR

While I was sitting down to write you a friendly Letter I had the pleasure of receiving your Favor of the 22 Instant by the Post. My Intention was to congratulate you and your Brethren the Selectmen, upon the precipitate Flight of the British Army & its Adherents from the Town of Boston, and to urge on you the Necessity of fortifying the Harbour so as that the Enemies Ships might never approach it here after. Our grateful Acknowledgments are due to the Supreme Being who has not been regardless of the multiplied Oppressions which the Inhabitants of that City have sufferd under the Hand of an execrable Tyrant. Their Magnanimity & Perseverance during the severe Conflict has afforded a great Example to the World, and will be recorded by the impartial His torian to their immortal Honor. They are now restored to their Habitations & Privileges; and as they are purgd of those Wretches a Part of whose Policy has been to corrupt the Morals of the People, I am perswaded they will improve the happy oppor tunity of reestablishing ancient Principles and Purity of Manners—I mention this in the first place because

I fully agree in Opinion with a very celebrated Author, that " Freedom or Slavery will prevail in a (City or) Country according as the Disposition & Manners of the People render them fit for the one or the other"; and I have long been convincd that our Enemies have made it an Object, to eradicate from the Minds of the People in general a Sense of true Religion & Virtue, in hopes thereby the more easily to carry their Point of enslaving them. Indeed my Friend, this is a Subject so important in my Mind, that I know not how to leave it. Revelation assures us that " Righteousness exalteth a Nation"—Com munities are dealt with in this World by the wise and just Ruler of the Universe. He rewards or punishes them according to their general Character. The dim-inution of publick Virtue is usually attended with that of publick Happiness, and the publick Liberty will not long survive the total Extinction of Morals. " The Roman Empire, says the Historian, *must* have sunk, though the Goths had not invaded it. Why? Because the Roman Virtue was sunk." Could I be assured that America would remain virtuous, I would venture to defy the utmost Efforts of Enemies to subjugate her. You will allow me to remind you, that the Morals of that City which has born so great a Share in the American Contest, depend much upon / the Vigilance of the respectable Body of Magistrates ' of which you are a Member.

I am greatly concernd at the present defenceless State of Boston, & indeed of the whole Eastern Dis trict which comprehends New England. We have applied for and obtaind a Committee of Congress to

consider the State of that District. In the mean
time I hope the General Assembly and the Town are
exerting themselves for the Security of the Harbour.
I could indeed earnestly wish that the Inhabitants of
Boston, who have so long born the Heat & Burden
of the Day might now have some Respite. But this
is uncertain. Their generous Exertions in the Amer
ican Cause, have renderd them particularly obnoxious
to the Vengeance of the British Tyrant. It is there
fore incumbent on them to be on their Guard, and to
use the utmost Activity in putting themselves in a
Posture of Defence.

I trust their Spirits are not depressd by the Injuries
they have sustaind. The large Experience they have
had of military Tyranny should rather heighten their
Ideas of the Blessings of civil Liberty and a free
Government. While *their own* Troops are posted
among them for their Protection, they surely will not
lose the Feelings and resign the Honor of Citizens to
the military; but remember always that standing
Armies are formidable Bodies in civil Society, & the
Suffering them to exist at any time is from Necessity,
& ought never to be of Choice.

It is with heartfelt Pleasure that I recollect the
Meetings I have had with my much esteemd Fellow
Citizens in Faneuil Hall, and I am animated with
the Prospect of seeing them again in that Place
which has long been sacred to Freedom. There I
have seen the Cause of Liberty & of Mankind
warmly espousd & ably vindicated; and that, at Times
when to speak with Freedom had become so dan
gerous, that other Citizens possessd of less Ardour,

would have thought themselves excusable in not speaking at all.

Be so kind as to pay my due Respects to my Friends & be assured that I am with the most friendly Regards for Mrs. Scollay & Family,

Very affectionately,

Yours,

TO JAMES WARREN.

[MS., Samuel Adams Papers, Lenox Library.]

PHILAD^A May 12 1776

My dear Sir

I had the pleasure of receiving your very friendly Letter of the 2^d Instant by a Mr Parks. I can readily excuse your not writing to me so often as I could wish to receive your Letters, when I consider how much you are engagd in the publick Affairs; and so you must be while your Life is spared to your Country. I am exceedingly concernd to find by your Letter as well as those of my other Friends that so little attention has been given to a Matter of such weighty Importance as the fortifying the Harbour of Boston. To what can this be attributed? Is it not wise to prevent the Enemies making Use of every Avenue especially those which lead into the Capital of our Country. I hope no little party Animosities even exist much less prevail in our Councils to obstruct so necessary a Measure. Such Contentions you well remember that Fiend Hutchinson & his Confederates made it their constant Study to stir up between the friends of the Colony in the different parts of it, in order to prevent their joynt Exertions for the Common Good. Let us with great Care avoid such Snares as our Enemies have hereto fore laid for our ruin, and which we have found by former Experience have provd too successfull to their wicked purposes. This will, I think be an important Summer to America ; I confide therefore in the Wis dom of our Colony, and that they will lay aside the Consideration of smaller Matters for the present, and bend their whole Attention to the necessary Means for the common Safety. I hope the late Situation of Boston is by this time very much alterd for the better ; if not, it must needs be a strong Inducement to the Enemy to reenter it, and whether we ought not by all means in our Power to prevent it, I will leave to you and others to judge.

Yesterday the Congress resolvd into a Committee of the whole to take under Consideration the report of a former Committee appointed to consider the State of the Eastern District which comprehends New Eng^d. It was then agreed that the Troops in Boston be augmented [to] Six Thousand. The Question lies before the Congress and will be considerd tomorrow. I am inclind to think the Vote will obtain. [But] what will avail the ordering additional Regiments if Men will not inlist ? Do our Countrymen want animation at a time when [all] is at Stake ! Your Presses have been too long silent. What are your Committees of Correspondence about ? I hear Noth ing of circular Letters—of joynt Committees, &c. Such Methods have in times past raised [the] Spirits of the people—drawn off their Attention from *pick-*

ing up Pins, & directed their Views to great objects—
But, not having had timely Notice of the Return of
this Express, I must conclude (with my earnest prayers
for the recovery of your Health,) very affectionately,

Your,

TO GEORGE WASHINGTON.

[MS., Samuel Adams Papers, Lenox Library.]

PHILAD^A May 15 1776

SIR/

It was not till the Beginning of this Month that I
had the Honor of receiving your Favor of the 22^d of
March, respecting a Proposition of Coll Baillie for
opening a Road from Connecticutt River to Montreal.
The President, soon after, laid before Congress your
Letter of the 5th, a Paragraph of which referrs to the
same Subject. The Resolution of Congress thereon
has, I presume, before this Time been transmitted to
you by him; by which it appears that they have fully
concurrd with you in Opinion of the Utility of the
Measure proposd.

I beg Leave by this Opportunity to acquaint your
Excellency, that the Letters I have receivd from
some Gentlemen of the Colony of Massachusetts Bay
express great Concern at the present defenceless state
of the Town of Boston, while they are not without
Apprehension of another Visit from the Enemy.
They thought themselves extremely happy in your
Presense there, and regretted very much the Neces
sity of your Departure, to which Nothing reconciles
them, but their earnest Desire that the general

Service may be promoted. Congress have resolvd
that the five Battalions in that Colony be filled up,
and new ones raisd for the Defence of the Eastern
District. As two General Officers will be sent
thither, it would, I am perswaded, give great Satis
faction to the People, if Generals Gates and Mifflin
might be fixed upon. This however, I chearfully
submit to your Excellencys Judgment and Deter
mination ; being well assurd, that the Safety of that
distressd City will have as full a Share of your Atten
tion as shall be consistent with the good of the whole.
I have the Honor to be with very great Esteem and
Affection,

Your Excellencys most humb^e serv^t,

TO HORATIO GATES.

[MS., Lenox Library.]

PHILAD^E June 10 1776

My dear Sir

Your Favor of the 8th Instant was brought to me
by Express. I am exceedingly concernd that a Gen·
eral Officer is not yet fixed upon to take the Com
mand of the Troops in Boston—ever since the Enemy
abandond that place I have been apprehensive that
a renewed attack would probably be made on some
part of Massachusetts Bay. Your Reasons clearly
show that it will be the Interest of the Enemy to
make a grand push there if they are not properly pro
vided for a Defence. Congress judgd it necessary
that a Major & Brig^r Genl should be sent to Boston
or they would not have orderd it three Weeks ago.
The Wish of the Colony with regard to particular

Gentlemen has been repeatedly urgd, and I thought
that an appointment which has been made since you
left us would have given a favorable Issue to our re
quest. The Necessity of *your* taking the Command
in the Eastern District immediately, has been in my
mind most pressing since I have been informd by
your Letter that your Intelligence in respect to the
Attack on the Massachusetts is direct & positive.

It will be a great Disappointment to me if General
Mifflin does not go with you to Boston. I believe
that to prevent the apparent necessity for this, Gen¹
Whitcomb was thrown into View. He is indeed in
many respects a good Man, but to the other I think
the preference must be given.

The Hint you gave me when I last saw you re
specting the Enemies offering to treat, I have revolvd
in my Mind. It is my opinion that no such offers
will be made but with a Design to take Advantage
by the Delay they may occasion. We know how
easily our people, too many of them, are still amusd
with vain hopes of reconciliation. Such Ideas will,
no doubt, be thrown out to them, to embarrass the
Army as others have been; but I conceive that the
General in whose Wisdom & Valor I confide, will,
without Hesitation employ all his Force to annoy &
conquer immediately upon the Enemies Approach.
We want our most stable Councellors here. To send
Gentlemen of *indecisive* Judgments to assist as field
Deputies would answer a very ill purpose. The sole
Design of the Enemy is to subjugate America. I
have therefore no Conception that any terms can be
offerd but such as must be manifestly affrontive.

Should those of a different Complexion be proposd, under the hand of their Commanding officer, the Gen eral will have the opp^{ty} of giving them in to Congress in the space of a Day.   This I imagine he will think it prudent to do—at the same time, I am very sure, he will give no Advantage to the Enemy, and that he will conduct our affairs in so critical a Moment in a Manner worthy of himself.

I am affectionately yours,

TO PEREZ MOULTON.[1]

[MS., Samuel Adams Papers, Lenox Library.]

PHILAD^A June 1776

My dear Sir

When I was at Watertown in August last the Gen eral Assembly being then sitting, a Crowd of Business prevented our coming to an Agreement respecting an Allowance adequate to your Services in the Secre taries Office, or even conversing upon the Subject. I have been very easy about it, because I have never had the least Doubt of your Integrity and Honor. Publick Affairs have demanded so much of my Atten tion here that I have scarcely had Time to spend a Thought on my domestick Concerns.   But I am apprehensive that M^{rs} A—— will soon be in Want of Money for her Support, if that is not already her Case.   I shall therefore be much obligd to you if you will let her have such a part of the Fees you may have receivd as you can conveniently spare. Her Receipt shall be acknowledgd by me.   And as I

---

[1] *Cf.*, page 109.   His name appears as " Morton " in *Acts and Resolves of the Province of Massachusetts*, vol. v.   He was deputy secretary under Adams.

foresee that I shall not have the opportunity of visit
ing my Friends in New England so soon as I have
intended, you will further oblige me by sending me
an Account of the Monies paid into the office to
gether with your own opinion of what may be a
reasonable and generous Allowance for your Service.
I am with great Esteem & Affection,
Your Friend & hbl Servt

TO JOSEPH HAWLEY.

[MS., Samuel Adams Papers, Lenox Library.]

PHILAD^E July 9 1776 —

MY DEAR SIR/
I should sooner have acknowledgd the Receipt of
your Letters dated at Northampton & Springfield the
17th and 22^d of May, had I not expected that before
this Time I should have had the pleasure of seeing
and conversing with you—but Business here has been
so pressing and important, that I have not thought it
consistent with my Duty as yet to absent myself.
Our repeated Misfortunes in Canada have greatly
chagrind every Man who wishes well to America. I
dare not at present communicate to you what I take to
have been the real Causes of these Disasters. Some
of them indeed must be obvious to any Man who has
been attentive to that Department. Our secret Ene
mies have found Means to sow the Seeds of Discord
& Faction there and Heaven has sufferd the small
Pox to prevail among our Troops. It is our Duty to
try all Means to restore our Affairs to a good Footing
but I despair of that being effected till next Winter.

To be acting merely on the defensive at the Time
when we should have been in full possession of that
Country is mortifying indeed.   The Subject is disgust
ing to me.   I will dismiss it.

How[e] is arrivd, as you have heard, with his
Troops at New York.   The People in this Colony
& the Jerseys are in Motion and if the New England
Militia joyn our Army with their usual Alertness &
Spirit, I have no doubt but the Enemy will meet with
a warm Reception.   A few days may probably bring
on an Event which will give a favorable Turn to our
Affairs.

The Congress has at length declared the Colonies ↳
free and independent States.   Upon this I congratulate you, for I know your heart has long been set
upon it.   Much I am affraid has been lost by delaying
to take this decisive Step.   It is my opinion that
if it had been done Nine months ago we might have
been justified in the Sight of God and Man, three
Months ago.[1]   If we had done it then, in my opinion
Canada would [by] this time have been one of the
united Colonies ; but " Much is to be endurd for the
hardness of Mens hearts."   We shall now see the Way
clear to form a Confederation, contract Alliances &
send Embassadors to foreign Powers & do other Acts
becoming the Character we have assumd.   Adieu my
Friend.   Write to me soon.

---

[1] The first thirteen words of this sentence are crossed out in the draft.

TO RICHARD HENRY LEE.

[MS., American Philosophical Society ; a draft is in the Samuel Adams Papers, Lenox Library ; and a text is in R. H. Lee, *Life of R. H. Lee*, vol. i., pp. 182-184.]

PHILAD^A July 15 1776

MY DEAR SIR

I must acknowledge that when you left Congress I gave you Reason to expect a Letter from me before this Time. You will not, I am very certain, attribute my omission to the Want of a most cordial Esteem for you. The Truth is, I hardly knew how to write with out saying something of our Canadian Affairs ; and this is a Subject so thoroughly mortifying to me, that I could wish totally to forget all that has past in that Country. Let me however just mention to you that Schuyler & Gates are to command the Troops to be employ'd there ; the former, while they are without, and the latter, while they are within the Bounds of Canada.—Admitting both these Generals to have the military Accomplishments of Marlborough and Eu gene, I cannot conceive that such a Disposition of them can be attended with any happy Effects, unless Harmony subsists between them.—Alass ! I fear this is not the Case—Already Disputes have arisen, which they have referrd to Congress ! And though they ap pear to treat each other with a Politeness becoming their Rank, in my Mind, Altercations between Com manders who have Pretensions so nearly equal, I mean in Point of *Command*, forebode a Repetition of Misfortunes—I sincerely wish my Apprehensions may prove to be groundless.

General Howe, as you have heard, is arrivd at New

York.   He has brought with him from 8 to 10,000 Troops.   Lord Howe arrivd the last Week, and the whole Fleet is hourly expected.   The Enemy landed on Staten Island.   Nothing of Importance has been done, saving that last Friday at about three in the Afternoon a 40 and a 20 Gun Ship with several Ten ders, taking the Advantage of a fair and fresh Gale and flowing Tide, passd by our Forts as far as the Encampment at Kings bridge.   General Mifflin who commands there in a Letter of the 5 Instant informd us he had twenty one Cannon planted and hoped in a Week to be formidable.   Reinforcements are arrivd from N England, and our Army are in high Spirits. I am exceedingly pleasd with the calm & determind Spirit, which our Commander in Chiefe has discoverd in all his Letters to Congress.   May Heaven guide and prosper Him!   The Militia of the Jerseys—Penn sylvania & Maryland are all in Motion—General Mercer commands the flying Camp in the Jerseys. We have just now appointed a Committee to bring in a Plan for Reinforcement to compleat the Number of 20,000 Men to be posted in that Colony.

Our Declaration of Independency has given Vigor to the Spirits of the People.   Had this decisive Meas ure been taken Nine Months ago, it is my opinion that Canada would at this time have been in our hands. But what does it avail to find fault with what is past. Let us do better for the future.   We were more for tunate than expected in having 12 of the 13 Colonies in favor of the all important Question.   The Dele· gates of N York were not impowered to give their Voice on either Side.   Their Convention has since acceeded to the Declaration & publishd it even before they receivd it from Congress. So mighty a Change in so short a Time! N Jersey has finishd their Form of Government, a Copy of which I inclose. They have sent us five new Delegates, among whom are Dr Witherspoon & Judge Stockden.[1] All of them appear to be attachd to the American Cause. A Con vention is now meeting in this City to form a Consti tution for this Colony. They are empowerd by their Constituents to appoint a new Committee of Safety to act for the present & to chuse new Delegates for Congress. I am told there will be a Change of Men, and if so, I hope for the better.

A Plan for Confederation has been brot into Congress wch I hope will be speedily digested and made ready to be laid before the several States for their approbation. A Committee has now under Consideration the Business of foreign Alliance.

It is high time for us to have Ambassadors in for- eign Courts. I fear we have already sufferd too much by Delay. You know upon whom our Thoughts were turnd when you was with us.

I am greatly obligd to you for favoring me with the Form of Govern^t agreed upon by your Countrymen. I have not yet had time to peruse it, but dare say it will be a Feast to our little Circle. The Device on your great Seal pleases me much.

Pray hasten your Journey hither. Your Country most pressingly sollicits, or will you allow me to say, *demands* your Assistance here. I have written in

---

[1] Stockton.

great haste. Adieu to my dear Sir, and be assured
that I am very Affectionately,

Your Friend,

TO JAMES WARREN.

[MS., Samuel Adams Papers, Lenox Library.]

PHILAD July 16—76

MY DEAR FRIEND

There is no Necessity of my troubling you with a
long Epistle at present, for my very worthy Friend
and Colleague[1] who kindly takes the Charge of this
will fully inform you of the State of Affairs here. He
will tell you some things which I have often wishd
to communicate to you, but have not thought it
prudent to commit to writing.

Our Declaration of Independence has already been
attended with good Effects. It is fortunate beyond
our Expectation to have the Voice of every Colony
in favor of so important a Question.

I inclose you the Form of a Constitution which the
Convention of Virginia have agreed upon for that
Colony. It came to my hand yesterday by the Post,
and I spare it to you, although I have not had time
to peruse it. I suppose there are other Copies in
Town. Adieu.

---

[1] John Adams.

TO JAMES WARREN.

[MS., Samuel Adams Papers, Lenox Library.]

PHILAD^A July 17 1776

My dear Sir

By this Express the General Assembly will receive the most earnest Recommendation of Congress to raise & send with all possible Speed the 2000 Men requested of them for New York above a Month ago. There never was a more pressing Necessity for their Exertions than at present. Our Army in N. Y. con sists of not more than half the number of those which we have reason to expect will in a very short Time be ready to attack them—and to this let me add that when we consider how many disaffected Men there are in that Colony, it is but little better than an Ene mies Country. I am sensible this is a busy Season of the year, but I beg of you to prevail on the People to lay aside every private Concern and devote them selves to the Service of their Country. If we can gain the Advantage of the Enemy this Campaign we may promise ourselves Success against every Effort they will be able to make hereafter. But I need not multiply words. I am sure *your* Mind is fully im-pressd with the Importance of this Measure. Adieu my Friend, the Express waits—-

TO JOHN PITTS.

[MS., Samuel Adams Papers, Lenox Library.]

[PHILADELPHIA, July 17, 1776]

My dear Sir

You were informd by the last Post that Congress

had declared the thirteen united Colonies free & independent States. It must be allowd by the im-partial World that this Declaration has not been made rashly. The inclosd Catalogue of Crimes of the deepest Dye, which have been repeatedly perpe trated by the King will justify us in the Eyes of honest & good Men. By multiplied Acts of Oppres sion & Tyranny he has long since forfeited his Right to govern. The Patience of the Colonies in endur-ing the most provoking Injuries so often repeated will be Matter of Astonishm'. Too Much I fear has been lost by Delay, but an accession of several Col onies has been gaind by it. The Delegates of every Colony were present & concurrd in this important Act; except those of N. Y. who were not authorizd to give their Voice on the Question, but they have since publickly said that a new Convention was soon to meet in that Colony & they had not the least Doubt of their acceeding to it. Our Path is now open to form a plan of Confederation & propose Alliances with foreign States. I hope our Affairs will now wear a more agreable Aspect than they have of late.

TO SAMUEL COOPER.

[MS., Samuel Adams Papers, Lenox Library.]

PHILADA July 20 1776

MY DEAR SIR/

I have the Pleasure of informing you, that the Continental Troops under the Command of Major Gen' Lee, have tryumphd over the British Forces in South Carolina, the particulars of which you have in the inclosd Paper. I trust this Blow has given so great a Check to the Power of the Enemy as to prevent their doing us any material Injury in that part of America. We look towards New York, and earnestly Pray that God would order a decisive Event in our Favor there—you must have earlier Intelligence from time to time of the Circum stances of our Affairs in that Department than you can have from this place. Yesterday Circular Let ters with inclosd Declarations from Lord Howe to the late Governors of New Jersey & the Colonies Southward as far as Georgia, were laid before Con gress. As they were orderd to be publishd, I have the Opportunity of transmitting a printed Copy of them for your Amusement. There were also Letters from London to private Persons probably procured if not dictated by the British Ministry and written with a manifest Intention to form a Party here in favor of his Lordship, to induce People to believe that he is a cordial Friend to America, and that he is empowerd to offer Terms of Accommodation acceptable to the Colonists. But it is now too late for that insidious Court to play such Tricks with any reasonable Hopes of Success. The American States have declard themselves no longer the Subjects of the British King. But if they had remaind such, the Budget is now opened to the World, and the People see with their own Eyes, with how much *Magnanimity* the Prince offers them Pardon on Condition that they will submit to be his abject Slaves.

I was informd in a Letter I rec^d from London last

March, that this very Nobleman declind to accept
the Commission until he should be vested with Au
thority to offer to us honorable Terms—that he made
a Merit of it.   And yet he now comes with Terms
disgraceful to human Nature.   If he is a good kind
of Man, as these Letters import, I am mistaken if he
is not weak & ductile.   He has always voted, as I am
told, in favor of the Kings Measures in Parliament,
and at the same time professd himself a Friend to
the Liberties of America!   He seems to me, either
never to have had any good Principles at all, or not
to have had Presence of Mind openly and uniformly
to avow them.   I have an Anecdote which I will com
municate to you at another Time—at present I have
not Leisure.

Pray let me have a Letter from you soon.   You
cannot do me a greater Act of Kindness or more substantially serve me than by writing often.

I am affectionately,

Your Friend,

Will you be kind enough to let my Family know
that I am in health.   I wish you w^d present my
most respectful Comp^{ts} to my very venerable Friend
D C– —y.[1]   I hope the worthy old Gentleman is
yet in Health & Spirits.

TO BENJAMIN KENT.

[MS., Samuel Adams Papers, Lenox Library.]

PHILAD July 27 1776

MY DEAR FRIEND

I must beg you to impute to the true Reason my

---
[1] *Cf.*, page 155.

not having yet acknowledgd & answerd your very
obliging Letter of the 24 May. The *Want of Leisure*
often prevents my indulging the natural Inclination
of my Mind to converse with my distant Friends by
familiar Epistles ; for however unequal I feel my self
to the Station in which our Country has placed me
here, I am indispensibly obligd to attend the Duties
of it with Diligence.

It has been difficult for a Number of persons sent
from all parts of so extensive a Territory and repre
senting Colonies (or as I must now call them *States*)
which in many Respects have had different Interests
& Views, to unite in Measures materially to affect
them all. Hence our Determinations have been
necessarily slow. We have however gone on from
Step to Step, till at length we are arrivd to per
fection, as you have heard, in a Declaration of In
dependence. Was there ever a Revolution brot
about, especially so important as this without great
internal Tumults & violent Convulsions ! The Dele
gates of every Colony in Congress have given their
Voices in favor of the great Question, & the People
I am told, recognize the Resolution as though it were
a Decree promulgated from Heaven. I have thot
that if this decisive Measure had been taken six
months earlier, it would have given Vigor to our
Northern Army & a different Issue to our military
Exertions in Canada. But probably I was mistaken.
The Colonies were not then all ripe for so momentous
a Change. It was necessary that they sh^d be united,
& it required Time & patience to remove old pre
judices, to instruct the unenlightend, convince the

doubting and fortify the timid. Perhaps if our Friends had considerd how much was to be pre viously done they w^d not have been, as you tell me some of them were, "impatient under our Delay."

New Gov^{ts} are now erecting in the several Amer ican States under the Authority of the people. Mon archy seems to be generally exploded. And it is not a little surprizing to me, that the Aristocratick Spirit which appeard to have taken deep Root in some of them, now gives place to that of Democracy, You justly observe that "the Soul or Spirit of Democracy is *Virtue*" No State can long preserve its Liberty "where Virtue is not supremely honord." I flatter my self you are mistaken in thinking ours is so very deficient, and I do assure you, I find reliefe in sup posing your Colouring is too high. But if I deceive my self in this most essential point, I conjure you and every Man of Influence by Example and by all Means to stem the Torrent of Vice, which, as a cele brated Author tells us, "prevailing would destroy, not only a Kingdom or an Empire, but the whole moral Dominion of the Almighty throughout the Infinitude of Space." I have Time only to add that I am very affectionately,

Yours,

TO JOSEPH TRUMBULL.[1]

[MS., Samuel Adams Papers, Lenox Library.]

PHILAD^E Augt 3 1776[2]

My dear Sir

Our Friend Coll W brought & deliverd to me your Letter of the—July directed to Mr J. A. and myself. The Inclosures clearly show the deplorable State of our Affairs in the Northern Department and it is easy to see the Source of them. I am fully of opinion that *one Man* must be removd to some other Department, to put an End to our Misfortunes there but this has hitherto been impracticable, though it has been attempted and urgd. A little Time may perhaps unravel Mysteries and convince Gentlemen that they have been under certain Prejudices to which the wisest Men are lyable. It appears to me very extraordinary that Mr L. should insist upon acting after being apprizd of the Resolve of Congress, and it is still more extraordinary that he

---

[1] Addressed to him at New York; commissary-general of the continental army.

[2] At this point reference should be made to the pamphlet entitled "An Oration delivered at the State House in Philadelphia . . . on Thursday, the 1st of August, 1776, by Samuel Adams." This was "reprinted" at London, and the text is given in W. V. Wells, *Life of Samuel Adams*, vol. iii., pp. 405–422. Wells, at vol. ii., p. 440, states briefly the reasons why he does not credit the production to Adams. See also, against its authenticity, *Proceedings* of Massachusetts Historical Society, 1st ser., vol. xiii., p. 451. The text has been published, with no allusion to its doubtful origin, as recently as 1900, in *The World's Orators*, edited by Guy C. Lee, vol. viii., pp. 239–265. John Eliot of Boston apparently had the matter in mind when he wrote to Jeremy Belknap, June 17, 1777: "Mr S. Adams is a gentleman who hath sacrificed an immense fortune in the service of his country. He is an orator likewise, & there is a famous oration upon the independance of America, which, it is said, he delivered at Philadelphia, January, 1776, but which was never seen in America before." *Collections* of Massachusetts Historical Society, 6th ser., vol. iv., pp. 124, 125. *Cf.*, Sabin, *Bibliotheca Americana*, No. 344.

meets with the Support of . . . . in such Conduct.
I am very sure that our Affairs must greatly suffer if
he is allowd to persist in so doing, and your Reputa
tion as well as the Good of the Service may be at
Stake. I think it would not be amiss for you to State
the Matter to the General by which means it might
be laid before Congress. You are the best Judge of
the part proper for you to act on this occasion in your
own Department but I shall certainly do all in my
Power to have the Evils you mention corrected. I
have communicated your Letter to several Gentlemen
who will joyn with me in every practicable Method for
this purpose. Congress have this day passd several
Resolutions which I hope tend to this good Effect.
Paymasters & Deputy Paymasters are to make weekly
Returns to Congress of the State of the Military
Chests under their Direction. Jon^n Trumble Esqr
Pay Master in the Northern Department is to transmit
as soon as possible an Acc^t of all the Monies which
have passed through his Hands. Commissaries &
Dep^y Comss^{rs} Genl in the several Departments are to
transmit to Congress weekly Acco^{ts} of Monies they
receive of Pay Masters or their Deputies—Quarter
Masters & Deputy Q^r Masters to do the same—and
the Commanding Officers in Each Departm^t are to
make monthly returns to Congress of the Drafts they
make on the respective Paymasters. Com^{ry} General,
Q^r Masters Genl & their Deputies to make monthly
Returns at least of Stores in their Possession & the
Distribution of them. These Resolutions perhaps may
not please *every Body*, but if they are duly executed,
they may detect Mistakes or Frauds if any should

happen.   As to what has happend in Canada & near it, some person is in my opinion most egregiously to blame, and, to use a homely Proverb, the Saddle has been laid, or attempted to be laid on the wrong horse. I hope that by strict Scrutiny the Causes will be found out and the guilty Man made to suffer.   My Regards to Gen¹ Mifflin & all Friends.

I am respectfully,

Yours,

Since writing the foregoing I have turnd to the printed Journals of Congress and find that on the 17th of July 1775 Walter Livingston Esq was appointed "Commissary of Stores & provisions for the New York Departmᵗ during the *present* Campaign." Upon what Grounds then does he speak of himself as vested by Congress with full powers to act *till revok'd?* The last Campaign wᶜʰ limitted his power to act, is finishd. Under what pretence can he be supported by his Patron, especially since by the Resolution of Congress of the 8th of July last, you have "full Power to supply both Armies, that upon the Lakes as well as that at N Y, & also to appoint & employ such persons under you & to remove any Deputy Commissary as you shall think proper & expedient,"[1] and for this express Reason "it being absolutely necessary that the Supply of *both* Armies shᵈ be under *one* Direction." Has not Gen¹ S— – seen this Resolution? or if he has seen it, Does he judge that the Supply of the two Armies shᵈ be under different Directions, & undertake to order accordingly?   If the Persons whom you send to act

¹ *Journals* of the Continental Congress (Library of Congress edition), vol. v., p. 527.

under you in the Northern Army are confined & limitted by *any* other Person after they arrive there, unless
by order of Congress, & without giving you Notice in
Case such order sh^d be made, we must expect a
Repetition of the most mortifying Disappointments.
Upon my Word I think it your Duty to remonstrate
this, either to the Commander in Chief or to the
Congress. The former I should suppose you would
prefer.

Adieu,

TO JOHN ADAMS.

[MS., Adams Papers, Quincy; a text is in W. V. Wells, *Life of Samuel
Adams*, vol. ii., p. 441.]

PRINCETOWN Augt 13 1776

DEAR SIR

Before this reaches you,[1] you will have heard of
the Arrival of near an hundred more of the Enemies
ships. There are too many Soldiers now in Philad^a
waiting for Arms. Is it not of the utmost Impor
tance that they should march even without Arms,
especially as they may be furnishd with the Arms of
those who are sick at N York. Would it not be do
ing great Service to the Cause at this time if you w^d
speak to some of the Com^e of Safety of Pennsylva
nia relative to this matter. I write in haste. The
Bearer will inform you of the State of things.

Your Friend,

---

[1] Addressed to John Adams at Philadelphia.

TO JOHN ADAMS.

[MS., Adams Papers, Quincy ; a portion of the text is in W. V. Wells,
Life of Samuel Adams, vol. ii., p. 442.]

N York Augt 16 1776

My dear Sir

I sit down to write in great Haste as the post is just going. I reachd P. Ferry on Tuesday Six Clock P M & passd over the next morning—found the Genl & his family in Health & spirits. Indeed every Officer & Soldier appears to be determind. I have not had Opp^ty to view the Works here, but I am told they are strong & will be well defended whenever an Attack is made which is expected daily. I see now more than I ever did the Importance of Congress attending immediately to Inlistments for the next Campaign. It would be a pity to lose your old Soldiers. I am of Opinion that a more generous Bounty sh^d be given, 20 Dollars & 100 Acres of Land for three years at least—but enough of this—

The State of our Northern Army mends apace. The Number of invalids decreases. Harmony prevails. They carry on all kinds of Business within themselves. Smiths Armourers Carpenters Turners Carriage Makers Rope Makers &c &c they are well provided with. There were at Tyconderoga Augt 12 2,668 Rank & file fit for Duty at Crown Point & Skeensborough 750, in Hospital 1,110—Lt Whittemore returnd from his Discoveries—he left St Johns July 30 saw 2000 or 2500 at that place & Chamblee. Stores coming on from Montreal—counted 30 Batteaus. No Vessell built or building. This Acco^t may I think be depended upon. In my opinion we are happy to have G Gates there. The Man who has the Superintendency of Indian Affairs —the nominal Command of the Army—is the *real* Contractor & Quarter Master Genl &c &c has too many Employm^{ts} to attend to the reform of such an Army—besides the Army can confide in the *Valor &* *military* Skill & Accomplishments of *Gates—Sat Verbum Sapienti;* pray write me & let me know how the Confed. &c goes on. Major Meigs a brave officer & a Prisoner taken at Quebeck is at this time, as I suppose, at Philadelphia—he wishes to be ex changed—such an Officer would be very usefull here. I wish you w^d give him your Assistance. I propose to sett off tomorrow for the Eastward.

Adieu,

Cap Palmer is in this City waiting for inlisting orders. I wish the Rank of the Navy officers was settled & the Commissions made out. Capt Dear- borne of N Hampshire is in the same Predicament with Major Meigs. Coll Whipple who now sends his Regards to you, is very desirous that he may also be exchangd—his Character is remarkeably good as Maj Meigs can inform y,ou.

TO JOHN ADAMS.

[MS., Adams Papers, Quincy; a text is in John Adams, *Works*, vol. ix., pp. 441-443.]

Boston Sept 16 1776

MY DEAR SIR/

I very gratefully acknowledge the Receipt of your Letter dated the of August. I should have written to you from this place before, but I have not had Leisure. My Time is divided between Boston & Watertown, and though we are not engagd in Mat ters of such Magnitude as now employ your Mind, there are a thousand things which call the Attention of every Man who is concernd for his Country. Our Assembly have appointed a Committee to prepare a Form of Government—they have not yet reported. I believe they will agree in two legislative Branches —their great Difficulty seems to be to determine upon a free and adequate Representative,—they are at pre sent an unwieldy Body. I will inform you more of this when I shall have the Materials. The Defence of this Town you know has lain much upon our Minds. Fortifications are erected upon several of the Islands, which I am told require at least 8000 Men. You shall have a particular Account when I am at Leisure,—by my Manner of writing you may conclude that I am now in haste. I have receivd no Letter from Philad^e or New York since I was favord with yours, nor can I find that any other Person has. It might be of Advan· tage to the common Cause for us to know what is do ing at both those important places. We have a Report that a Committee is appointed (as the expression is) "to meet the Howes," and that you are one. This, without Flattery gave me pleasure. I am indeed at a Loss to conclude how such a Movement could be made consistent with the Honor of the Congress, but I have such an Opinion of the Wisdom of that Body, that I must not doubt of the Rectitude of the Meas ure. I hope they will be vigilant and firm, for I am told that Lord Howe is, though not a great man, an

artful Courtier. May God give us Wisdom Fortitude Perseverance and every other virtue necessary for us to maintain that Independence which we have as serted. It would be ridiculous indeed if we were to return to a State of Slavery in a few Weeks after we had thrown off the Yoke and asserted our Indepen dence. The Body of the people of America, I am per- swaded, would resent it—but why do I write in this Stile—I rely upon the Congress & the committee. I wish however to know a little about this Mat ter, for I confess I cannot account for it to my own Mind. I will write to you soon—in the mean time,
Adieu,

What has been the Issue of the Debates upon a weighty Subject when I left you, and another Matter (you know what I mean) of great Importance? Is it not high time they were finishd?

Pay my due Regards to the President Mess Paine [1] & Gerry [2] Coll Lees and other Friends.

TO JOHN ADAMS.

[MS., Adams Papers, Quincy; a text is in John Adams, *Works*, vol. ix., pp. 446, 447.]

BOSTON Sept 30 1776

MY DEAR SIR/

I am much obligd to you for your two Letters of the 8th & 14th of this Month, which I receivd, to gether, by the last Post. The Caution given in the first of these Letters was well designd; and had it

---

[1] Robert Treat Paine.

[2] A portion of a letter by Samuel Adams to Gerry, dated September 23, 1776, is printed in W. V. Wells, *Life of Samuel Adams*, vol. ii., pp. 447, 448.

come to me as early as you had Reason to expect it
would, I should have been relievd of a full fortnights
Anxiety of Mind. I was indeed greatly "concernd"
for the Event of the proposd Conference with Lord
Howe. It is no Compliment when I tell you, that I
fully confided in the Understanding and Integrity of
the Gentlemen appointed by Congress; but being
totally ignorant of the Motives which inducd such a
Measure, I was fearful lest we might be bro't into a
Situation of great Delicacy and Embarrassment. I
perceive that his Lordship would not converse with
you as Members of Congress or a Committee of that
Body ; from whence I concluded that the Conference
did not take its Rise on his part. As I am unac
quainted with its Origination and the Powers of the
Committee, I must contemplate the whole Affair as a
Refinement in Policy beyond my Reach, and content
myself with remaining in the Dark, till I have the Pleas
ure of seeing you, when, I trust, the Mystery will be
fully explaind to me. Indeed I am not so sollicitous to
know the Motives from whence this Conference
sprang, or the Manner in which it was brought up,
as I am pleasd with its Conclusion. The Sentiments
and Language of the Committee, as they are related
to me, were becoming the Character they bore. They
mannagd with great Dexterity. They maintaind the
Dignity of Congress, and in my Opinion, the Inde
pendence of America stands now on a better footing
than it did befóre. It affords me abundant Satisfaction, that the Minister of the British King, commis-
siond to require and fondly nourishing the Hopes of
receiving the Submission of America, was explicitly

and authoritatively assured, that neither the Commit
tee nor that Congress which sent them had Authority
to treat in any other Capacity than as *Independent
States.* His Lordship, it seems, "has no Instruction
on that Subject." We must therefore fight it out, and
trust in God for Success. I dare assure my self, that
the most effectual Care has before this time been
taken, for the Continuance and Support of our
Armies, not only for the Remainder of the present,
but for a future year. The People will chearfully sup
port their Independence to the utmost. Their Spirits
will rise upon their knowing the Result of the late
Conference. It has, you may depend upon it, been a
Matter of great Expectation. Would it not be at
tended with a good Effect, if an Account of it was
publishd by Authority of Congress? It would, I should
think, at least put it out of the Power of disaffected
Men (and there are some of this Character even here)
to amuse their honest Neighbors with vain hopes of
Reconciliation.

I wish that Congress would give the earliest Notice
to this State, of what may be further expected to be
done here for the Support of the Army. The Season
is advancing or rather passing fast. I intended when
I sat down to have written you a long Epistle, but I
am interrupted. I have a thousand Avocations which
require my Attention. Many of them are too trifling
to merit your Notice. Adieu, my Friend. I hope to
see you soon.

TO SAMUEL MATHER.

[MS., Dreer Collection, Historical Society of Pennsylvania ; a text is in the Emmet Collection, Lenox Library ; and a draft is in the Samuel Adams Papers, Lenox Library.]

PHILAD^A Octob 26 1776

My dear Sir,

On the Evening of the 24th Instant I arrivd in good health in this City—I give you this Information in Compliance with my Word, and flattering my self that I shall very soon be favord with a Letter from you— I will promise to give you hereafter as much Intelli gence as the Secrecy to which I am in honour bound will allow.

I met with Nothing disagreable in my Journey, saving my being prevented from passing through the direct Road in East Chester, the Enemy having taken Possession of the Ground there—Our Army is ex tended in several Encampments from Kings Bridge to White Plains which is 12 or 15 Miles Northward, commanded by the Generals Lord Sterling, Bell (of Maryland) Lincoln, McDougal, Lee, Heath & Putnam —I mention them, I think, in the order as they are posted from the Plains to the Bridge—The Generals Head Quarters are now at Valentine Hill about the Center of the Encampments. The Army is in high Spirits and wish for Action. There have been sev eral Skirmishes ; one on Fryday the 18th in which the Massachusetts Regiment commanded by Coll Glover distinguishd their Bravery and they have receivd the Thanks of the General. In this Rencounter the Enemy sustaind a considerable Loss, it is said not less than 700 Men—Another on the Night of the 21st. The infamous Major Rogers with about 400 Tories of Long Island, having advancd towards Mareneck[1] on the Main, was defeated by a Party of ours with the Loss of 36 Prisoners besides killed & wounded. This valiant Hero was the first off the Field—Such Skirmishes, if successful on our Part, will give Spirit to our Soldiers and fit them for more important and decisive Action, which I confess I impatiently wish for.—I have said that our Soldiers are in high Spirits; I add, that so far as I can learn the Character of the General officers of the Enemys Army, we at least equal them in this Instance, we have an excellent Commissary & Quarter Master General, officers of great Importance—Mifflin, who servd so much to our Advantage in the latter of these Employments, has condescended to take it again though he had been promoted to the Rank & Pay of a Brigadier General—The Enemy is posted in a rough hilly Country, the Advantages of which Americans have convincd them they know how to improve— Under all these Circumstances I should think that the sooner a General Battle was brot on, the better; but I am no Judge in military Matters.

An interresting Affair, about which a Circle of Friends whom I had the Pleasure of meeting at D[r] Chauncys, is finishd, I think, agreably to their Wishes —I can only add at present that I am with the most cordial Esteem,

Sir your assured Friend

& very humble Servant

---

[1] Mamaroneck.

TO MRS. ADAMS.

[MS., Samuel Adams Papers, Lenox Library.]

PHILAD^A Novr 14th 1776

My dear Betsy

I wrote to you within a Day or two after my Arrival here by an Express. I cannot say that I was not disappointed in not receiving a Line from you by the last Post, as I thought I had Reason to expect. While I am absent from you I am continually anxious to know the State of your Health. I must therefore beg you to write to me often. I have not for many years enjoyd a greater Share of that invalueable Blessing than I have since I left Boston. I believe the Journey on Horseback has been greatly beneficial to me.

We have lately receivd Intelligence from the Northern Army of certain Movements of the Enemy in that Quarter, of which you will see an Account in the inclosd News Paper. This day we have further Intelligence that they have totally abandond Crown Point & retreated into Canada. We have also just receivd a Letter from a Gentleman living on the Sea Coasts of New Jersey informing us that near 100 Sail of the Enemies Ships with two Frigates & a fifty Gun Ship were seen steering to the Eastward. It is supposd they are bound to England. We had before heard that the whole Force of the Enemy had marchd unexpectedly & precipitately into the City of New York. This evening an Express is come in from General Greene who commands on this Side the North River in the Jersys with Advice that ten thousand of the Enemies Troops were embarkd, and that it was given out that they were destind to South Carolina. This may be a Feint. Possibly they may be coming to this City, which in my Opinion is rather to be desired, because the People of this State are more numerous than that of South Carolina. In either Case however I dare say that a good Account will be given of them. It is said that Lord Dunmore is to take the Command. If this be true, it looks as if they were going to Virginia. Be it as it may, the withdrawing so great a Part of their Troops from New York, it is hoped, will make it an easy matter for our Army to conquer the Remainder.

It has not been usual for me to write to you of War or Politicks,—but I know how deeply you have always interrested yourself in the Welfare of our Country and I am disposd to gratify your Curiosity. Besides you will hope that from these Movements of our Enemies a Communication between Boston and Philadelphia will be more safe and we may the more frequently hear from each other.

Novr 17th I wish you would acquaint your Brother Sammy that General Mifflin is now Quartermaster General in Room of Coll Moylan—that when I was at Head Quarters I mentiond to the General the treatment your Brother had met with. He told me that he would have him state the Matter to him in Writing and that he would endeavor to have Justice done to him. The Letter your Brother formerly wrote to me I left at Boston. If he will give me a full Account of the Matter in another Letter, I will state it to General Mifflin, but the Circumstances of things are such at present that I would not have him depend on its being immediately attended to.   I will however do all in my power to serve him.

Our Friend Mʳ Lovell[1] is at last exchangd.   We receivd a Letter from him two or three days ago. Probably before this reaches you he will have arrivd at Boston.   Pray remember me to my Daughter, Sister Polly with the rest of my Family & Friends, and be assured that I am most sincerely & affection ately,

Your,

TO MRS. ADAMS.

[MS., Samuel Adams Papers, Lenox Library.]

PHILADELPHIA Novʳ 29 1776

MY DEAR BETSY

I take this Opportunity by Mʳ Chamberlain to acquaint you that I am in good health & Spirits.   This Intelligence, I flatter myself, will not be disagreable to you.   I have not receivd a Line from you since I left Boston which gives me Reason to suspect that your Letters may have fallen into wrong hands.

Traveling, it seems, is of late become somewhat dan gerous ; should this be intercepted and be seen by the two Brothers,[2] they will have an opportunity of know ing that I am still most firmly attachd to the best Cause that virtuous Men contend for, and that I am animated with the full Perswasion that righteous Heaven will support the Americans if they persevere in their manly Struggles for their Liberty.   I have no

---

[1] Cf. page 248.

[2] Presumably Admiral Howe and General Howe.

Reason to suspect the Virtue of the Generality of my Countrymen. There are indeed Poltrons & Trayters everywhere. I do not therefore think it strange that some such Characters are to be found in this City, but the Indignation of the People kindles at the expected approach of the Enemies Army, and every proper Measure is taking to meet them on the Road and stop their wild Career.——I am told that Lord Howe has lately issued a Proclamation offering a general Pardon with the Exception of only four Persons viz Dr Franklin Coll Richard Henry Lee Mr John Adams & my self. I am not certain of the Truth of this Report. If it be a Fact I am greatly obligd to his Lordship for the flat tering opinion he has given me of my self as being a Person obnoxious to those who are desolating a once happy Country for the sake of extinguishing the re maining Lamp of Liberty, and for the singular Honor he does me in ranking me with Men so eminently patriotick.

I hope you will write to me by every opportunity. Pay my due Respects to my Family and Friends and be assured that I am most affectionately,

Your,

TO JAMES WARREN.

[MS., Chamberlain Collection, Boston Public Library.]

PHILAD^E Novr 29 1776

My dear Sir/

I inclose a Resolve[1] passd in Congress and at-

---

[1] A marginal postscript, in the autograph of Adams, reads : "Pray deliver the inclosd, if your Leisure will admit with your own hand."

tested by the Secretary which I doubt not the Hon^{bl}
House of Representatives will duly regard. Indeed
I am in hopes your Committee for providing Cloathing &^{c} for the Army have already in a great Measure
answerd the Request. You will have heard of the
Scituation of the Armies before this will reach you. A
Part of the Enemy have got on this Side of Hudsons River, but I dare say you will have a good Ac
count of them. I am more chagrind at the Disgrace
than the Loss we have met with by the Surrender of
Forts Washington & Lee. They should not have
cost the Enemy less than thousands of their Troops.
After all, what have the mighty Victors gaind? a
few Miles of Ground at the Expence of many Mil
lions of their Treasure & the Effusion of much of
their Blood. But we must stop their Career. This
I am satisfied can & will be done. Mr Gerry writes
to you by this opportunity—therefore I need not add
more than that I am very affectionately,

                                        Yours,

                         ———————

                    TO JAMES WARREN.

[W. V. Wells, *Life of Samuel Adams*, vol. ii., pp. 452-454; an incom-
                         plete text.]

              [PHILADELPHIA, December 4, 1776.]

It affords me singular pleasure to be informed that
our General Assembly is now sitting in Boston. I
have been of opinion that the public business could
be done with more despatch there than elsewhere.
" You have appointed a committee of war," with very
extensive powers, "and appropriated to their disposi-

tion two hundred thousand pounds to purchase every thing necessary to carry on the war with vigor next year." I heartily rejoice to hear this. I hope the committee are men of business, and will make a good use of the powers and moneys they are intrusted with. Let me tell you, that every nerve must be strained to resist the British tyrant, who, in despair of availing himself of his own troops which lately he so much prided himself in, is now summoning the powers of earth and hell to subjugate America. The lamp of liberty burns there and there only. He sees it, and is impatient even to madness to extinguish it. It is our duty, at all hazards, to prevent it.

But I am sensible I need not write you in this style. You and the rest of my countrymen have done, and I have no doubt will continue to do, your duty in defence of a cause so interesting to mankind. It is with inexpressible pleasure that I reflect that the mercenary forces of the tyrant have for two years in vain attempted to penetrate the Eastern Colonies; there our enemies themselves, and those who hate us, acknowledge that the rights of man have been de fended with bravery. And did not South Carolina nobly withstand the efforts of tyranny? She did. Virginia, too, and North Carolina, have in their turn acted with a spirit becoming the character of Ameri cans. But what will be said of Pennsylvania and the Jerseys? Have they not disgraced themselves by standing idle spectators while the enemy overran a great part of their country? They have seen our army unfortunately separated by the river, retreating to Newark, to Elizabethtown, Woodbridge, Brunswick, and Princeton.   The enemy's army were, by the last account, within sixty miles of this city.   If they were as near Boston, would not our countrymen cut them all to pieces or take them prisoners?   But by the unaccountable stupor which seems to have pervaded these States, the enemy have gained a triumph which they did not themselves expect.   A triumph, indeed!   Without a victory!   Without one laurel to boast of!   For Bunker's Hill they fought and bled. They sacrificed their bravest officers, and we wished them twenty such victories.   But the people of the Jerseys have suffered them to run through their country without the risk of even a private soldier!   They expended their ammunition at trees and bushes as they marched!   But I hear the sound of the drum.   The people of Pennsylvania say of themselves, that they are slow in determining, but vigorous in executing.   I hope that we shall find both parts of this prediction to be just.   They say, We are now determined, and promise to bring General Howe to a hearty repentance for venturing so near them.   I have the pleasure to tell you that, within a few days past, they have made a spirited appearance.   In spite of Quakers, Proprietarians, timid Whigs, Tories, *petit-maitres*, and trimmers, there is a sufficient number of them in arms resolved to defend their country.   Many of them are now on the march.   Heaven grant they may be honorable instruments to retrieve the reputation of their countrymen and reduce Britain to a contemptible figure at the end of this campaign.

I am glad to hear our harbor looks so brilliant.   *I hope it is fortified against every attempt of the enemy next spring.*

In your letters, you ask me two important ques
tions. I dare not repeat them. With regard to the
last, you will understand me when I tell you, let not
your mind be troubled about it.   '

TO MRS. ADAMS.

[MS., Samuel Adams Papers, Lenox Library.]

PHILADELPHIA Dec' 9 1776

MY DEAR BETSY

My last by M' Pliarne I hope you will have receivd
before this reaches you. I am still in good Health
and Spirits, although the Enemy is within Forty Miles
of this City. I do not regret the Part I have taken in
a Cause so just and interresting to Mankind. I must
confess it chagrins me greatly to find it so illy sup
ported by the People of Pennsylvania and the Jerseys.
They seem to me to be determind to give it up—but
I trust that my dear New England will maintain it at
the Expence of every thing dear to them in this Life
——they know how to prize their Liberties. May
Heaven bless them ! It is not yet determind to what
place to adjourn the Congress, if it should be neces
sary to move. Wherever I may be, I shall write to
you by every Opportunity. M' Brown who carries
this Letter will give you a particular Account of the
Circumstances of things here—to him I refer you.
Pray remember me to my Daughter, Sister Polly, the
rest of my Family & Friends. I hope the Life of our
valueable Friend M'' March will yet be spared. She
is indeed a good Woman. Tell my worthy Neighbor
M' Preston, that I rejoyce to hear of his honorable
Appointment. I hope & believe he will use his office

well.   I wish to have a Letter from you.   You can
not imagine how highly I prize such a Favor.   My
daily Prayer is for your Safety, & Happiness in this
Life & a better.   Adieu, my dear.   You cannot doubt
the sincere & most cordial Affection of,

Your,

Decr 11

Since writing the above I have receivd your Letter
of the 9th of Nov^r, for which I am much obligd to you.
If this City should be *surrenderd*, I should by no
means despair of our Cause.   It is a righteous Cause
and I am fully perswaded righteous Heaven will suc
ceed it.   Congress will adjourn to Baltimore in Mary
land, about 120 Miles from this place, when Necessity
requires it and not before.   It is agreed to appoint a
Day of Prayer, & a Com^e will bring in a Resolution
for that purpose this day.   I wish we were a more
religious People.   That Heaven may bless you here &
hereafter is the most ardent Prayer of, my dear, most
cordially,

Your,

TO GEORGE WASHINGTON.

[MS., Samuel Adams Papers, Lenox Library.]

PHILADELPHIA Dec_r 12 1776

SIR

We are this moment informd by a Gentleman who
is Brother of Coll Griffin, and has lately been at New
York, that a Body of ten thousand of the Enemies
Troops had actually arrivd at Rhode Island.   As Con
gress is now adjournd to Baltimore in Maryland, and

the President and the Board of War are not in Town, we think it our Duty to send you this Intelligence; and as there is no General Officer in that Department, we refer it to your Consideration whether the Service does not absolutely require that one be immediately sent to take the Command of Troops that may be raisd there to repel the Progress of the Enemy.

If Major General Gates or Green,[1] who are greatly belovd in that Part of America with a suitable Num ber of Brigadiers could be spared for this Service, it would be attended with another Advantage, that of facilitating the new Inlistments.

We intreat your Attention to this important Matter, and are with great Respect,

Sir your very humble Servants,[2]

TO MRS. ADAMS.

[MS., Samuel Adams Papers, Lenox Library.]

BALTIMORE IN MARYLAND
Decr 19th 1776

My dear Betsy

The Day before yesterday I arrivd in this Place which is One hundred Miles from Philadelphia. The Congress had resolvd to adjourn here when it should become absolutely necessary and not before. This sudden Removal may perhaps be wonderd at by some of my Friends, but was not without the advice of Generals Putnam & Mifflin, who were at Philadel-

---

[1] The words " or Green " and " with a suitable number of Brigadiers," were added by interlineations in the first draft.

[2] Signed by Adams, Elbridge Gerry, William Ellery, and William Whipple.

phia to take Measures for its Preservation from the Enemy. For my own part, I had been used to Alarms in my own Country, and did not see the Necessity of removing so soon, but I suppose I misjudgd because it was otherwise ruled. It must be confessd that deliberative Bodies should not sit in Places of Confusion. This was heightned by an unaccountable Backwardness in the People of the Jerseys & Pennsylvania to defend their Country and crush their Enemies when I am satisfied it was in their Power to do it. The British as well as Hessian officers have severely chastisd them for their Folly. We are told that such savage Tragedies have been acted by them without Respect to Age or Sex as have equaled the most barbarous Ages & Nations of the World. Sorry I am that the People so long refusd to harken to the repeated Calls of their Country. They have already deeply staind the Honor of America, and they must surely be as unfeeling as Rocks if they do not rise with Indignation and revenge the shocking Injuries done to their Wives and Daughters. Great Britain has taught us what to expect from Submission to its Power. No People ever more tamely surrenderd than of that Part of the Jerseys through which the Enemy marchd. No opposition was made. And yet the grossest Insults have been offerd to them, and the rude Soldiery have been sufferd to perpetrate Deeds more horrid than Murder. If Heaven punishes Communities for their Vices, how sore must be the Punishment of that Community who think the Rights of human Nature not worth struggling for and patiently submit to Tyranny. I will rely upon it that New England will never incur the Curse of Heaven for neglecting to defend her Liberties. I pray God to increase their Virtue and make· them happy in the full and quiet Possession of those Liberties they have ever so highly prizd. *Your* Wellfare, my dear, is ever near my heart. Remember me to my Daughter Sister Polly & the rest of my Family and Friends. I am in high Health & Spirits. Let me hear from you often. Adieu,

Mr. Hancock is just now arrivd with his Family ·—all in good health.

TO JAMES WARREN.

[MS., Samuel Adams Papers, Lenox Library.]

BALTIMORE IN MARYLAND Decr 25 1776

MY DEAR SIR

Although I have been continually writing to you, I have had the Pleasure of receiving only one Letter from you since I left New England. The Congress is here, scituated conveniently enough and doing Busi ness. You will ask me perhaps, How we came here. I confess I did not see the Necessity of removing so soon ; but I must think I misjudgd because it was ruled otherwise, not indeed until the Opinions of Putnam & Mifflin then in Philadelphia, had been taken. The Truth is, the Enemy were within seven· teen Miles of us, and it was apprehended by some that the People of Pennsylvania, influenced by Fear Folly or Treachery, would have given up their Capi tal to appease the Anger of the two Brothers & atone for their Crime in suffering it to remain so long the

Seat of Rebellion. We are now informd that they have at length bestirrd themselves and that hundreds are daily flocking to Gen¹ Washingtons Camp, so that it is hoped if our Army pursues as expeditiously as they have retreated, they will take them all Prisoners before they can reach the Borders of Hudsons River.

We have this day receivd a Letter from General Schuyler, which has occasiond the passing a Resolu tion, forwarded to you, I suppose by this opportunity. The General says he is informd that the Levies are making very tardily. I hope he has been misin- formd. It is certainly of the greatest Importance that New England in a particular Manner should be very active in Preparation to meet the Enemy early in the Spring. The British Tyrant will not quit his darling Plan of subduing that Country. The Intent of the Enemy seems to me to be to attack it on all Sides. Howes Troops have penetrated this way far beyond his Expectations; I flatter myself they will be driven back to New York & winter there. Carleton will, unless prevented by an immediate Exertion of New England, most certainly possess himself of Tyconderoga as soon as Lake Champlain shall be frozen hard enough to transport his Army. Clinton it is said is gone to Rhode Island with 8 or 10 thou sand to make Winter Quarters there. The infamous Behavior of the People of Jersey & Pennsylvania will give fresh Spirits to the British Court and afford them a further Pretence to apply to every Court in Europe where they can have any Prospect of Success. Russia has already been applied to. Their whole Force will be poured into N England for they take

it for granted that having once subdued those stub
born States, the rest will give up without a Struggle.
They will take Occasion from what has happend in
Jersey to inculcate this Opinion.   How necessary is
it then for our Countrymen to strain every Nerve to
defeat their Design.   The Time is short.   Let this
be the only Subject of our Thoughts and Consulta
tion.   Our Affairs in France wear a promising Aspect.
Let us do our Duty and defend the fair Inheritance
which our Fathers have left us—our pious Forefathers
who regarded Posterity & fought and bled that they
might transmit to us the Blessing of Liberty.

When we first heard at Philadelphia of Clintons
having saild to Rhode Island, Mr Gerry and myself
joynd with Coll Whipple of New Hampshire & M^r
Ellery of Rhode Island in a Letter to Genl Washing
ton and proposed to him the sending Gen Gates or
Greene with a suitable number of Brigadiers to take
the Command in the Eastern Departm^t.   [In] his
answer which we receivd in this place he tells us he
has orderd M Genl Spencer & B Genl Arnold to re
pair thither who he hopes may be sufficient to head
the yeomanry of that Country & repel the Enemy
in their attempts to gain possession of that part of
the Continent.   He [adds] that he will if possible
send some other Brigadiers, and says Gen Wooster
is also at hand.

I wrote to you after my Arrival at Philad^e & inclosd
a Resolution of Congress relative to the procuring of
cloathing in N E for the Army.   In another Letter
I gave you a hint which I think of great Importance
if the Measure proposd [be] practicable.   I hope

both these Letters were duly receivd by you. You
cannot, my dear Sir, do me a greater Kindness than
by writing to me. I suffer much thro want of Intelli
gence from N E; I pray you therefore let your
Letters to me be very frequent.

I am very cordially your friend,

By a late Letter from London written by a Gent^n
upon whose Intelligence I greatly rely a Treaty is
on foot with Russia to furnish Britain with 20 or
30,000 troops. Levies are making with all possible
Industry in Germany & in Britain & Ireland from
where it is expected that 20,000 will be raisd. It
[is] indeed to be supposd that, as usual, a greater Ap
pearance will be made on paper than they will realize.
But let us consider that they realizd in America
the last year 35,000, and do without doubt . . .
. . . . they lose because they are able to do it,
we may then set down their actual force in America
by May or June next at least 55 and probably 60,000.

We have the pleasure of hearing that a valueable
Prize is arrivd at [Boston]—among the rest of her
Cargo 10,000 Suits of Cloaths! A most fortunate
Prize for us, especially as she is said to be the last of
8 Vessels taken bound to Quebec. However while
we are pleasing ourselves with the Acquisition we
should remember that the Want of those supplys will
be a strong Stimulus to Carleton to make an early &
bold push over the Champlain in hopes of furnishing
himself at Albany; & increases the Necessity of
the Eastern States sending their Troops to Tyconderoga immediately to supply the places of those who

will return home, when the time of their Inlistments shall expire. I have good Information from England that a certain Capt[n] Furze who [was] in Boston the last year & gaind the Confidence & rec[d] the Civilities of the People ; when he returnd gloried in the De ception & carried Intelligence to the British Ministry, particularly of the Fortifications in & about Boston. Some of the People may remember him. How care ful ought we to be lest while we mean only innocent Civility, we expose our Councils & Operations to Spies.

I remain very cordially your friend,

TO MRS. ADAMS.

[MS., Samuel Adams Papers, Lenox Library.]

BALTIMORE IN MARYLAND 26 Dec[r] 1776

MY DEAR BETSY

I have written to you once since I arrivd here, and am determind to omit no opportunity, because I flatter myself you will at all times be gratified in hearing from me. I am at present in good health and am exceedingly happy in an Acquaintance with M[r] Samuel Purviance a Merchant of this Place, with whom I have indeed before corresponded, but I never saw him till I came here. He is a sensible, honest and friendly Man, warmly attachd to the American Cause, and has particularly endeard him self to me by his great Assiduity in procuring Reliefe in this part of the Continent for the Town of Boston at a Time when her Enemies would have starvd her by an oppressive Port bill.

Just now I receivd a Letter from my Son dated the 7th Instant ; he tells me he had very lately heard from his Sister and that she and the rest of my Family were well. I pray God to continue your Health and protect you in these perilous times from every kind of Evil. The Name of the Lord, says the Scripture, is a strong Tower, thither the Righteous flee and are safe. Let us secure his Favor, and he will lead us through the Journey of this Life and at length receive us to a better.

We are now informd that the People of Jersey & Pennsylvania are in Possession of their Understand ing and that they are turning out in great Numbers to the Assistance of General Washington. Had they done this early they would not have so deeply staind the Reputation of America. However I shall hardly think they will do their Duty at last if they suffer the Enemy to return without paying dearly for the bar barous Outrages they have committed in the Country, without Regard to Age or Sex.

Our Affairs in France & Spain wear a pleasing Aspect, but human Affairs are ever uncertain. I have strongly recommended to my Friends in New England to spare no Pains or Cost in preparing to meet the Enemy early in the Spring. We have a righteous Cause, and if we defend it as becomes us, we may expect the Blessing of Heaven.

Remember me to my Daughter, Sister Polly & the rest of my Family & Friends. Adieu, my dear,

TO THE PRESIDENT OF THE COUNCIL OF MASSACHUSETTS.

[MS., Samuel Adams Papers, Lenox Library.]

BALTIMORE Decr 30 1776

SIR

Being a Committee of Congress we are directed to employ some suitable Person to make Application to your Honorable Board for certain Ordnance and other Stores, which have been represented by Gen eral Schuyler as immediately necessary for the Use of the Northern Army. We accordingly send for ward Coll° Stewart, who will lay before the Board such Stores as are wanted ; which we hope may be procurd on just and equitable Terms, and transported with all possible Dispatch to General Schuyler, whose Receipt will be duly acknowledgd by Congress.

We need not urge the great Importance of having our Army in that Quarter well furnishd with every necessary Article, there being not the least Reason to doubt of General Carletons Intentions as early as possible to push his Forces into the Eastern States, or of his Success in such an Attempt unless seasonably prevented.

It is therefore our earnest Request that you would afford Coll Stuart every possible advice & assistance in the Prosecution of this Business, and furnish him with such Money as he may have need of for the purpose in which Case your Draft on the President of the Congress will be duly honord.

We are with the most cordial Esteem
          Sir
                your most obedient
                    & very humble Servants

TO WALTER STEWART.

[MS., Samuel Adams Papers, Lenox Library; a portion is printed in W. V. Wells, *Life of Samuel Adams*, vol. ii., pp. 450, 451.]

BALTIMORE DEC^r 30 1776

SIR

We are a Committee of Congress[1] authorizd and directed to appoint some suitable Person to apply to Mr Livingston Owner of a Furnace in the State of New York, and to Governor Trumbull who has the Direction of the Furnace in the State of Connecticutt also to the Council of the State of Massachusetts Bay, to procure such Cannon and Ordnance Stores, as General Schuyler has represented to be immediately necessary for the use of the Army in the Northern Department.

We know of no one in whom we can more chearfully confide, for the Performance of this important Business than your self; and therefore we request you to under take it, as Major General Gates has assured us, that it is not inconsistent with the General Service, or the Duty of that Station which you hold under his im mediate Command.

You have herewith a List of the Ordnance and Ordnance Stores that are wanted; and you will be pleasd to make your first Application to Mr Living ston for such of the Cannon and Stores as he can furnish. You will then apply to Governor Trumbull, to be furnishd by him with the Remainder, to be sent to General Schuyler as early as possible this Winter.

For the Ordnance Stores we depend chiefly upon

---

[1] The members of the committee were Adams, Lee, Harrison, Whipple and Hayward.

the Massachusetts Bay; and desire you to make Appli
cation to the Council of that State; although we would
by no means restrain you in Endeavors to procure them
in New York Connecticutt or elsewhere.

We doubt not but you will provide these Necessa
ries with all possible Dispatch, and at reasonable Rates;
and we desire you to give Notice to General Schuyler
and to us of the Success you may meet with in your
several Applications.

We would inform you that Congress has contracted
for Cannon to be cast in this State at the Rate of Thirty
Six pounds ten shillings p Ton.   And the highest price
that has been given in Pennsylvania is Forty Pounds.
We desire and expect you will purchase them at the
lowest Rate you can.   The Proof of the Cannon must
be according to the Woolwich Practice.

TO JAMES WARREN.

[MS., Samuel Adams Papers, Lenox Library.]

BALTIMORE Dec' 31. 1776

My dear Sir/

I am determind to omit nö Opportunity of writing
to you, although I of late very seldom receive a Favor
from you.   Your second Letter I receivd a few days
ago inclosing Copies of Papers from Spain.   I am
much obligd to you for them.   Our Affairs in Europe
look well, and additional Measures are taking here to
establish them in that Part of the World on a solid
Foundation.   I assure you Business has been done

since we came to this Place more to my Satisfaction
than any or every thing done before, excepting the
Declaration of Independence which should have been
made immediately after the 19th of April 75. *Our
ministers abroad* are directed to assure *foreign Courts*
that notwithstanding the artful & insidious Represen
tations of the Emissaries of the British Court to the
Contrary, the Congress and People of America are
determind to maintain their Independence at all
Events. This was done before the late Success in
the Jerseys, of which you will have doubtless had In
telligence before this Letter reaches you. I now think
that Britain will soon make a most contemptible
Figure in America & Europe—but we must still make
our utmost Exertions. Pray let the Levies required
of our State be raisd with all possible Expedition. By
this Conveyance you will have a Resolution giving
large Powers to General Washington for a limited
Season. It became in my opinion necessary. The
Hint I gave you some time ago, I still think very im
portant. General Gates arrivd here yesterday. I have
conversd with him upon it. He told me he had conceivd the Idea before and wishes the Measure may [be]
tryed. It requires Secrecy and Dispatch. L⁺ Coll
Steward will set off tomorrow with Directions to pro
ceed as far as Boston to purchase Ordnance & other
Stores if they cannot be procured elsewhere. He is
General Gates Aid de Camp & is very clev[er.] I
wish you would take Notice of him.

But I am now called off. Adieu my Friend,

TO ARTHUR LEE.

[R. H. Lee, *Life of Arthur Lee*, vol. ii., pp. 225, 226; a draft is in the
Samuel Adams Papers, Lenox Library.]

BALTIMORE IN MARYLAND, Jan. 2d, 1777.

MY DEAR SIR,—It has been altogether from a re
gard to your safety that I have restrained myself from
continuing on my part that correspondence which you
was obliging enough to indulge for several years.   I
know very well that your avowal of and warm attach
ment to the cause of justice and truth, have rendered
you exceedingly obnoxious to the malice of the British
king and his ministers ; and that a letter written by a
zealous asserter of that cause addressed to you while
you was in their power, would have brought upon you
the resentment of that most cruel and vindictive court.
But I cannot omit this opportunity of writing to you
after so long a silence, to assure you that I am most
heartily engaged according to my small ability, in sup
porting the rights of America and of mankind.

In my last letter to you near two years ago, I ven
tured to give you my opinion that if the British troops
then in Boston, should attempt to march out in an
hostile manner, it would most surely effect a total and
perpetual separation of the two countries.   This they
did in a very short time ; and the great event has since
taken place, sooner indeed than I expected it would,
though not so soon, in my opinion, as in justice it
might, and in sound policy, it ought.   But there is a
timidity in our nature which prevents our taking a
decisive part in the critical time, and very few have
fortitude enough to tell a tyrant they are determined

to be free. Our delay has been dangerous to us, yet it has been attended with great advantage. It has af forded to the world a proof, that oppressed and insulted as we were, we are very willing to give Britain an op portunity of seeing herself, and of correcting her own errors. We are now struggling in the sharp conflict; confiding that righteous heaven will not look with an indifferent eye upon a cause so manifestly just, and so interesting to mankind.

You are now called to act in a still more enlarged sphere. Go on, my friend, to exert yourself in the cause of liberty and virtue. You have already the applause of virtuous men, and may be assured of the smiles of heaven.

Your brother, Mr. R. H. Lee, will give you a par ticular account of our affairs in America; nothing therefore remains for me to add, but that I am your very affectionate friend,

---

TO JAMES WARREN.

[MS., Samuel Adams Papers, Lenox Library.]

BALTIMORE Jany 8th 1777

My DEAR SIR

I have several times referrd you to a Hint which I gave you not long ago, and which I have not thought prudent to repeat lest by an Accident my Letters should be intercepted. I have still the same opinion of the Importance of the Affair, but having spent this Evening with General Gates and conversd with him upon that and other Matters, we have concluded upon

a more sure Way of effecting it than the Way I proposd to you. I wish therefore if you have already
communicated it to any one of our Friends, that you
would injoyn them to close Secrecy, and that it may
be even forgot till the Event of it shall be known to
the World.

I am much pleasd to find that the New England
Troops have so great a Share in the Honor of the
late Action in the Jerseys. General Gates speaks
very highly of the Militia you sent him last Fall. He
applauds greatly their Zeal for the Cause and par
ticularly their Readiness to tarry in the Service after
the Expiration of the Term of their Inlistments in
November, and tells me he gave them an honorable
Discharge. I have not the Pleasure of knowing
General Bricket but he mentions him to me as a
worthy & good officer.

We have further good Accounts from our Army
which are credited although they are not yet authen
ticated. I verily believe that the Incursions of the
Enemy into the Jerseys will be in the Event much to
our Advantage, and that this Campaign will end
gloriously on our side ; I never will be sanguine in
my Expectation for I know the Events of War are
uncertain, but there seems to be an enterprizing Spirit
in our Army which I have long wishd to see and
without which we may not expect to do great Things.
The same enterprizing Spirit also takes place here.
We have done things which I would not have flatterd
my self with the least hope of doing a Month ago.
This Express will carry to the Council a Resolution
which I presume will of course be communicated to

you.   In my next I will give you a very particular & good reason why it is not communicated *to you* in this Letter.   We understand that by the Enemies Treat ment of General Lee there appears to be a Design to consider him as a deserter & take away his Life. Congress have directed General Washington to ac quaint Howe that if this is his Intention five of the Hessian field officers now in our hands together with Lt Col^l Campbell shall be detained & sacrificd as an Atonement for his Blood should the Matter be carried to that Extremity ; and this Resolution will most undoubtedly in my opinion be executed in full tale.

A dieu,

TO JOHN ADAMS.

[John Adams, *Works*, vol. ix., pp. 448–450.]

BALTIMORE, 9 January, 1777.

I have every day for a month past been anxiously expecting the pleasure of seeing you here, but now begin to suspect you do not intend to give us your assistance in person.   I shall therefore do all that lies in my power to engage your epistolary aid.   You will by every opportunity receive my letters, and, I dare say, you will be so civil as to answer at least some of them.

I have given our friend Warren, in one of my let ters to him, the best reason I could for the sudden removal of Congress to this place.   Possibly he may have communicated it to you.   I confess it was not

agreeable to my mind; but I have since altered my
opinion, because we have done more important busi
ness in three weeks than we had done, and I believe
should have done, at Philadelphia, in six months.
As you are a member of Congress, you have a right
to know all that has been done; but I dare not com
mit it to paper at a time when the safe carriage of
letters is become so precarious. One thing I am
very solicitous to inform you, because I know it will
give you great satisfaction. If you recollect our conversation at New Haven, I fancy you will understand
me when I tell you, that to *one place* we have added
four, and increased the number of persons from *three*
to six. I hate this dark, mysterious manner of writing,
but necessity requires it.

You have heard of the captivity of General Lee.
Congress have directed General Washington to offer
six Hessian field-officers in exchange for him. It is
suspected that the enemy choose to consider him as
a deserter, bring him to trial in a court-martial, and
take his life. Assurances are ordered to be given to
General Howe, that five of those officers, together
with Lieutenant-Colonel Campbell, will be detained,
and all of them receive the same measure that shall
be meted to him. This resolution will most certainly
be executed.

We have this day passed a recommendation to the
Council of Massachusetts Bay of a very important
nature. It will be sent by this express to the Council,
to whom I refer you for a perusal of it.

Our affairs in France and Spain wear a promising
aspect, and we have taken measures to put them on a

respectable footing in other parts of Europe ; and I flatter myself too much if we do not succeed.

The progress of the enemy through the Jerseys has chagrined me beyond measure ; but I think we shall reap the advantage in the end. We have already beat a part of their army at Trenton, and the inclosed paper will give you a farther account which we credit, though not yet authenticated. The late behavior of the people of Jersey was owing to some of their lead ing men, who, instead of directing and animating, most shamefully deserted them. When they found a leader in the brave Colonel Ford, they followed him with alacrity. They have been treated with savage barbarity by the Hessians, but I believe more so by Britons. After they have been most inhumanly used in their persons, without regard to sex or age, and plundered of all they had, without the least compen sation, Lord Howe and his brother (now Sir William, knight of the Bath) have condescended to offer them protections for the free enjoyment of their effects.

You have seen the power with which General Washington is vested for a limited time. Congress is very attentive to the northern army, and care is taken effectually to supply it with every thing neces sary this winter for the next campaign. General Gates is here. How shall we make him the head of that army ?

We are about establishing boards of war, ordnance, navy, and treasury, with a chamber of commerce, each of them to consist of gentlemen who are not mem bers of Congress. By these means, I hope, our business will be done more systematically, speedily, and effectually.

Great and heavy complaints have been made of abuse in the Director-General's department in both our armies ; some, I suppose, without grounds, others with too much reason. I have no doubt but as soon as a committee reports, which is expected this day, both Morgan and Stringer will be removed, as I think they ought.[1]

To the eighty-eight battalions ordered to be raised, sixteen are to be added, which, with six to be raised out of the continent at large, will make one hundred and ten, besides three thousand horse, three regiments of artillery, and a company of engineers. We may expect fifty or sixty thousand of the enemy in June next. Their design will still be to subdue the obstinate States of New England. It was the intention that Carleton should winter in Albany, Howe in New York, and Clinton at Rhode Island, that, with re-enforcements in the spring, they might be ready to attack New England on all sides. I hope every possible method will be used to quicken the new levies, and that the fortifications in the harbor of Boston will be in complete readiness. Much will depend upon our diligence this winter.

The attention of Congress is also turned to the southward. Forts Pitt and Randolph are to be garrisoned, and provisions laid up for two thousand men, six months. By the last accounts from South Carolina, we are informed that late arrivals have supplied them with every thing necessary for their defence.

---

[1] Dr. John Morgan, director general, and Dr. Samuel Stringer, director of hospitals in the northern department, were removed from office January 9 by the Continental Congress.

I have written in great haste, and have time only to add, that I am, with sincere regards to your lady and family, very cordially your friend,

P. S.   Dr. Morgan and Dr. Stringer are dismissed without any reason assigned, which Congress could of right do, as they held their places during pleasure. The true reason, as I take it, was the general dis gust, and the danger of the loss of an army arising therefrom.

TO JAMES WARREN.

[MS., Samuel Adams Papers, Lenox Library.]

BALTIMORE Jany 16 1777

My dear Sir/
We receivd by Mr Williams a Letter from the Council of Massachusetts Bay, requesting a Sum of Money for Payment of Bounties to the Troops to be raisd in that State. Accordingly three hundred thousand Dollars are orderd for that Purpose, which will be forwarded to the Paymaster as soon as it can conveniently be done.

I observe that our Assembly have made it neces sary, that three of their Delegates should be present and concurring in Sentiment before the Voice of our State can be taken on any Question in Congress.   I could have wishd it had been otherwise.   Only three of your Delegates are now present.   So it may hap-pen at other times.   One of them may be sick ; he may be on a Committee, or necessarily absent on publick Business ; in which Case our State will not be effectually represented. While I am writing at the Table, Mr Gerry is necessarily employd on the Business of the Publick at home, and the two present cannot give the Sense of the State upon a Matter now before Congress. Were all the three present, one Dissentient might controul the other two so far as to oblige them to be silent when the Question is called for. Indeed the Assembly have increasd the Number of Delegates to Seven. But I submit the Matter, as it becomes me, to my Superiors.

Major Hawley and my other patriotick Fellow Laborers, Are they alive and in Health? I have not receivd a Line from any of them excepting my worthy Friend Mr Nathl Appleton, whose Letter I will ac knowledge to him by the first opportunity. My Friends surely cannot think I can go through the arduous Business assignd to me here without their Advice and Assistance. I do not know whether you ever intend to write to me again. Assure the Major from me, that a few more of his "*broken Hints*" will be of eminent Service to me.[1]

You cannot imagine how much I am pleasd with the Spirit our Assembly have discoverd. They seem to have put every County into Motion. This fore-bodes in my Mind that something great will be done. I have not, since this Contest began, had so happy Feelings as I now have. I begin to anticipate the Establishment of Peace on such Terms as independent States ought to demand ; and I am even now contem plating by what Means the Virtue of my Country men may be secured for Ages yet to come. Virtue,

---

[1] *Cf.*, page 52.

which is the Soul of a republican Government. But
future Events, I have learnd by Experience, are un
certain ; and some unlucky Circumstance may before
long take Place, which may prove sadly mortifying
to me. But no such Circumstance can deprive me
of the Pleasure I enjoy, in seeing at a Distance,
the rising Glories of this new World. Adieu my
Friend. Believe me to be unfeignedly yours,

TO MRS. ADAMS.

[MS., Samuel Adams Papers, Lenox Library.]

BALTIMORE Jan 29th 1777.

My dear Betsy

Yesterday I had the Pleasure of receiving two Letters
from you by the same hand, dated the 9th and 22d of
December. And just now a Letter is deliverd to me
from my Friend Mr Bradford, dated the 13th of this
Month, wherein I am informd that you was then in
good Health and Spirits. If you had not told me that
you had written to me Six Letters since I left Boston,
I should have suspected that you did not keep a good
Look out for Expresses which come this Way. I have
now receivd only four of them. The others may pos
sibly have fallen into the Hands of the Lords *Protectors*
of America. There is one Way in which you may
probably make up the Loss to me, and that is by writ
ing oftener. I assure you, it would not be troublesome
to me to receive half a Dozen Letters from you at one
Time.

You tell me you was greatly alarmd to hear that
General Howe's Army was on the March to Philadel-

phia. I have long known you to be possessd of much
Fortitude of Mind. But you are a Woman, and one
must expect you will now and then discover Timidity
so natural to your Sex. I thank you, my Dear, most
cordially for the Warmth of Affection which you ex
press on this Occasion, for your Anxiety for my Safety
and your Prayers to God for my Protection. The Man
who is conscientiously doing his Duty will ever be pro
tected by that Righteous and all powerful Being, and
when he has finishd his Work he will receive an ample
Reward. I am not more convincd of any thing than
that it is my Duty, to oppose to the utmost of my
Ability the Designs of those who would enslave my
Country ; and with Gods Assistance I am resolvd to
oppose them till their Designs are defeated or I am
called to quit the Stage of Life.

I am glad to hear that the Winter has been in a
remarkable Degree so favorable in New England, be
cause it must have lessend the . . . . been increasd
. . . . the Poor, is in Holy Writ coupled with him who
oppresses them. Be you warm and be you cloathd,
without administering the necessary Means, is but cold
Consolation to the miserable. I am glad you have
given Shelter to Mrs A. who had not where to lay her
Head. She deservd your Notice, and she has more
than rewarded you for it in being, as you say she is,
grateful. Whenever you see a poor Person grateful,
you may depend upon it, if he were rich he would be
charitable. We are not however, to seek Rewards in
this Life, for Deeds of Charity, but rather imitate the
all merciful Being, of whom, if I mistake not, it is said
in Scripture, that he doth Good to the Evil and

unthankful. There is indeed no such Thing as dis-interrested Benevolence among Men. Self Love and social, as Pope tells us, is the same. The truly char itable Man partakes of the Feelings of the wretched wherever he sees the Object, and he relieves himself from Misery by relieving others.

I am greatly grievd for the Loss we have met with in the Death of Mʳ Checkley. From the Account you give me of the Nature & Extent of his Disorder, I conclude he must have died before this Time. He was indeed a valueable Relation and Friend. Have you lately heard from your Brother at Sᵗ Eustatia?

We have no News here. The Events which take place in the Jerseys must be known in Boston before you can be informd of them from this Place. There is a Report that a Party of the Jersey Militia fell in with a larger Party of the Enemy, killed about twenty and took a greater Number Prisoners besides fifty three Waggons and Provisions. This is believd. It is also said that General Heath has taken Fort Washington. If it be so, we shall soon have the News confirmd. . .

. . .

TO JAMES WARREN.

[MS., Samuel Adams Papers, Lenox Library.]

BALTIMORE Feb. 1, 1777.

MY DEAR SIR/

The Proceedings of the Committees of the four New England States have been read in Congress and are now under the Consideration of a Committee of the whole. They are much applauded as being salutary and wise. I had heard that one of your Delegates

at that Convention had written a long Letter to his
Friend and Confident here, and hearing it whisperd
that the Massachusetts State disapprovd of the Proceedings, I was led to ask the Gentleman who had
receivd the Letter concerning it. He confirmd it
and said that not only the Trade but the landed Gen
tlemen in the House of Representatives were san
guine against it. I beg'd him to let me see his Letter
but he refusd in a kind of Pet, telling me it was a
private Letter, & leaving me to conjecture whether I
had really been impertinent in asking a Sight of his
Letter or whether the Contents of it were such as it
was not proper for me to see. You will easily conceive what a Scituation a Man must be in here, who
having receivd no Intelligence of the Sentiments of
his Constituents himself is obligd in vain to ask
of another upon what Principles they have disapprovd
of a Measure if in truth they did disapprove of it, of
which he is called to give his own opinion. You
may see, my Friend, from this Instance, the Ne
cessity of your writing to me oftener. When I was
told upon the forementiond occasion, that I should
be intitled to see the Letters of another whenever I
should be disposd to show those which I receive my
self, I could have truly said that I had scarcely receivd
any. Two only *from you* in the Space of near four
Months. But I have no Claim to your Favors,
however much I value them, unless perhaps upon the
Score of my having neglected not a single Opportunity
of writing to you. Your omitting even to acknow
ledge the Receipt of my Letters, I might indeed con
strue as a silent Hint that they were displeasing to you,

but I will not believe this till I have it under your own hand.   While I am writing your very agreable Letter is brought to me by Mr Lovell.   You therein speak, as you ever have done, the Language of my Soul. Mr Adams tells me you are President of the Board of War ; I am therefore inducd to recall what I have just now said which you may construe as an implied Censure for your not having written to me oftener. I am sure you must have a great Deal of Business in your hands.   I am not however sorry to hear it, pro vided your Health is not injurd by it.   I pray God to preserve the Health of your Body and the Vigor of your Mind.   We must chearfully deny our selves domestick Happiness and the sweet Tranquility of private Life when our Country demands our Services. Give me Leave to hint to you my Opinion that it would be a Saving to our State in the Way of Sup ply if the Board of War would consign the Cargos wch they order here to a Merchant of good Character rather than to the Master of the Vessell—possibly there may be Exceptions, But I have Reason to think a Cargo which arrivd about a fortnight ago consisting chiefly as I am told of Rum & Sugars was sold at least 30 p C^t under what it w^d have fetched if it had been under the Direction of a Person ac quainted in the place, and Flour is purchasing by the Person who bought the Cargo at an unlimitted Price. I am perswaded that if you had by a Previous Letter directed a Cargo to be procured here you might have had it 20 p Cent cheaper.   If the Board should be of my Mind, I know of no Gentlemen whom I would recommend more chearfully than Mess Samuel &

Robert Purvyance—they are Merchants of good
Character, honest & discrete Men, and warmly attachd to our all important Cause. But I get out of
my Line when I touch upon Commerce, it is a Sub
ject I never understood. Adieu my dear Friend.
Believe me to be yours,

P. S. I forgot to tell you that, a fair occasion
offering, I moved in Congress that the eldest Son of
our deceasd friend Gen¹ Warren mᵗ be adopted by
the Continent & educated at the publick Expence.
The Motion was pleasing to all and a Comᵉ is ap
pointed to prepare a Resolve. Monuments are also
proposd in Memory of him & Gen¹ Mercer whose
youngest Son is also to be adopted & educated. But
these things I would not have yet made publick.

TO SAMUEL COOPER.

[MS., Samuel Adams Papers, Lenox Library.]

BALTIMORE Feb 4ₜₕ 1777

MY DEAR SIR

I send you the inclosd Speech for your Amusement.
One or two Remarks you will observe are made upon
it. There is Room for many more. I wish some in
genious Pen might be employd. The Contest with
America, it seems, is now confessd by the British
Monarch to be "arduous." I think he greatly deceives
himself, if he does not expect it will be more so. In
deed he sees it ; for we must, says he, "*at all Events*
prepare for another Campaign." "If their Treason is
sufferd to take Root, much Mischief will grow out

of it—to the present System of *all* Europe." Here we have the Authority of a King's (not a very wise one I confess) to affirm, that the War between Britain and the united States of America will affect the Ballance of Power in Europe. Will not the different Powers take different Sides to adjust the Ballance to their different Interests? "I am using my *utmost* Endeavors to conciliate the unhappy Differences between two Neighboring Powers." If he is still *using* his Endeavors, it seems, the Differences are not yet made up.—"I continue to receive *Assurances* of Amity from the several Courts in Europe"—But he adds "It is expedient we should be in a respectable State of *Defence* at home." If he has such Assurances of the Continuance of Amity in Europe, why is it so expedient at this time to be in a respectable State of Defence at home? Surely he cannot think the *American* Navy yet so formidable, as to demand this Caution. Or is he at length become wise enough to attend to a good old Maxim, *In Peace prepare for War.*—By his prefixing a "*Notwithstanding*" to his "fair Prospect," and his being manifestly hard pressd with "the present Scituation of Affairs" in America, I am led to conclude, that he looks upon his "Assurances of *Amity*" as the mere Compliments of a Court; and that he strongly apprehends, the Quarrel he has plungd himself into with America hath excited a Curiosity and a Watchfulness in some of the Powers of Europe, which will produce a contrary Effect. I am with very great Esteem,

Your assured Friend
and humble Servant,

TO JAMES WARREN.

[MS., Samuel Adams Papers, Lenox Library.]

BALTIMORE Feb 10, 1777

My dear Sir

I beg Leave to inclose my Account of Expences from the 26th of April 1775 to the 27 of Augt 1776 amounting to. . . .

I intended to have laid it before the House of Rep resentatives when I was last in New England, but the sudden Adjournment of the General Assembly in September last, and my Hurry in preparing for my Journey hither after its sitting again in October pre vented my doing it.

When I sat off from Lexington after the memora ble Battle there, I had with me only the Cloaths on my back, which were very much worn, those which I had provided for my self being then in Boston, and it was out of my Power at that time to recover them. I was therefore under a Necessity, of being at an ex traordinary Expense, to appear with any kind of De cency for Cloathing & Linnen after my Arrival in this City, which I think makes a reasonable Charge of Barrils Leonards and Stilles Bills in my Acco^t.

It may perhaps be necessary to say something of the Charge of Horse hire in the last Article. When I left Watertown in September '75, two Horses were deliverd to me out of the publick Stable for my self & my Servant, by Order of Hon^{bl} Council. They were very poor when I took them and both tired on the Road as you will see in my Account. One of them afterwards died in Philadelphia, which obligd

me to purchase another in that place, and with this
Horse I returnd to Boston last Fall. His being my
own Property, having purchasd him without Charge
to my Constituents, I think gives me a just Right to
make a Charge of Horse Hire, which is left to be
carried out in a reasonable Sum. M^r A says he is
obligd to allow seven pounds 10 s for the Hire of
each of his Horses to Philadelphia.

I shall take it as a favor if you will present the Ac
count to the Hon^bl House, and acquaint the Commit
tee to whom it may be referrd, with the Reasons of
the Charges above mentiond, and make any other
Explanations which you may judge necessary. M^rs A
has the Vouchers, to whom I beg you would apply for
them in Person before you present the Account. I
wish it may be settled as soon as the House can con
veniently attend to it. If an Allowance for my Serv
ices is considerd at the same time, you will please to
be informd that I sat off from Lexington or Worces
ter on the 26th of April '75 and returnd on the 14 of
August following. And again I sat off from Watertown on the 1st of Sept '75 and returnd to Boston on
the 27th of August '76.

I have troubled you with this Epistle of Horse hire
and Shop Goods at a Time when, no Doubt, your
Attention is called to Affairs of the greatest Concern
to our Country. Excuse me, my dear Friend for
once, and be assured that I am your affectionate,

TO WALTER STEWART.

[MS., Samuel Adams Papers, Lenox Library.]

BALTIMORE Feb 12 1777

SIR

I receivd by Mr Babcock, your Letter dated Leba non Jany 23, communicated the same to the Com mittee and afterward laid it before Congress. The Price of the Cannon at Salisbury[1] so much exceeds that at which it is set in a Contract enterd into by Congress with the Owners of a Foundery in this State, that Congress have thought proper not to allow it, but have directed the Committee to request Governor Trumbull to lend them, to be returnd or others in Lieu of them as soon as possible. The Com^e have written accordingly ; and I think it neces sary to give you Notice of the Sense of Congress relating to the Price of Cannon as early as possible, that you may govern yourself thereby in your further Execution of your Commission. I am &c

TO JONATHAN TRUMBULL.[2]

[MS., Samuel Adams Papers, Lenox Library.]

BALTIMORE 12th Feb 1777

SIR/

The Committee on the Affairs in the Northern Department having laid before Congress a Letter receivd from Col^o Stewart who was sent by them agreable to Order of Congress, to procure Cannon, wherein he informs that there is a Quantity of

---

[1] Connecticut.

[2] Governor of Connecticut.

Cannon at Salisbury Foundery which the Governor
& Council of Connecticutt are willing to dispose of to
the Continent, but demand the Price of seventy
Pounds Lawful Money p Ton for 18 & 9 pounders
and Eighty Pounds Lawfull Money pr Ton for 6, 4
& 3 pounders, it is an Order of Congress that the
Committee aforesaid write to Govr Trumbull & inform
him of the Contracts enterd into by Congress, state
to him the Prejudice it will do to those Contracts and
the ill Effects that must ensue to the Continent,
should so high a Price be given for these Cannon,
and request him to lend the Cannon, which are much
wanted for the Defence of Ticonderoga, and assure
him that Congress will return them or others in Lieu
of them as soon as possible.

Your Honor will please to be informd that Congress
have enterd into a Contract with the Owners of a
Foundery in the State of Maryland for 1000 Tons of
Cannon from 32 down to 4 pounders to be deliverd
in such proportion as Congress shall require at £36
10s p Ton accounting Dollars at 7/6.

The Prejudice which will be done to this Contract
if so high a Price should now be given for the Cannon
at Salisbury, must be obvious. It will be an Example
for all others to demand the like Prices; and more
over it may afford a Pretext for those who wish for
Occasions to spread Jealousy and Discord among the
united States, to say, that the State of Connecticutt
have in this Instance taken Advantage of the Ne
cessity of the Continent. As there is no Reason to
entertain so unworthy a Sentiment of that State we
earnestly hope that no Circumstance may take place

which might gratify the Inclinations of our insidi
ous Enemies to do an Injury to our common Cause.
We are with the greatest Respect your honors most
obedient & very hbl Serv^{ts 1}

TO JOHN PITTS.

[MS., Samuel Adams Papers, Lenox Library.]

BALTIMORE Feb 15 1777

MY DEAR SIR

I am favord with yours of the 21 of December for
which I am much obligd to you. I am much concernd
to hear that the Tories in Boston & Massachusetts
Bay have lately grown insolent & that no Measures
are taken to suppress their Insolence. They are the
most virulent, & I am of Opinion, the most danger
ous Enemies of America. They do not indeed openly
appear in Arms, but they do more Mischief secretly.
I am very apprehensive that they greatly operate to
the preventing Inlistments and doing other essential
Injury to our Cause. If they are not properly dealt
with, I am perswaded, the Publick will much regret
the Omission very soon. I do not wish for needless
Severities ; but effectual Measures, and severe ones
if others are insufficient, to prevent their pernicious
Councils & Machinations, I think ought to be taken,
and that without any Delay. It will be Humanity
shown to Millions, who are in more Danger of being
reducd to thraldom & Misery by those Wretches than
by British & Hessian Barbarians.] I cannot conceive
why a Law is not made declaratory of Treason &

---

[1] Signed by Adams, R. H. Lee, Wm. Whipple, and Thomas Hayward.

other Crimes & properly to punish those who are guilty of them.   If to conspire the Death of a King is Treason and worthy of Death, surely a Conspiracy to ruin a State deserves no less a Punishment.   I have Reason to think you have a Number of such Conspirators among you ; and believe me, you will soon repent of it, if you do not speedily take Notice of them.   But let me ask you my Friend, Whether some of the late Addressers, Protesters and Associators, are not seen in the Circles, in the Houses and at the Tables of Whigs?   Is there not Reason to expect that those who exiled themselves thro Fear of the just Vengeance of their Countrymen will be invited by the kind Treatment of those who have equal Reason to dread that Vengeance, to return into the Bosom of their much injurd Country.   But I need add no more.   Believe me to be cordially,

Your Friend,

TO JAMES WARREN.

[MS., Samuel Adams Papers, Lenox Library.]

BALTIMORE Feb 16 1777

MY DEAR SIR

A few days ago a small Expedition was made under the Authority of this State, aided by a Detachment of Continental Regulars to Suppress the Tories in the Counties of Somerset & Worcester on the Eastern Shore of Chessapeak, where they are numerous & have arisen to a great Pitch of Insolence.   We this day heard rumors that one of their Principals, a Doctor Cheyney, is taken & we hope to hear of the Business being effectually done very soon. In my opinion, much more is to be apprehended from the secret Mach ination of these rascally People, than from the open Violence of British & Hessian Soldiers, whose Success has been in a great Measure owing to the Aid they have receivd from them. You know that the Tories in America have always acted upon System. Their Head Quarters used to be in Boston—more lately in Philadelphia. They have continually embarrassd the publick Councils there, and afforded Intelligence Ad vice & Assistance to General Howe. Their Influence is extended thro-out the united States. Boston has its full share of them and yet I do not hear that Meas ures have been taken to suppress them. On the Contrary I am informd that the Citizens are grown so polite as to treat them with Tokens of Civility and respect. Can a Man take fire into his Bosom and not be burnd? Your Massachusetts Tories communicate with the Enemy in Britain as well as New York. They give and receive Intelligences from whence they early form a Judgment of their Measures. I am told they discoverd an Air of insolent Tryumph in their Coun tenances, and saucily enjoyd the Success of Howes Forces in Jersey before it happend. Indeed, my Friend, if Measures are not soon taken, and the most vigorous ones, to root out these pernicious Weeds, it will be in vain for America to persevere in this glorious Struggle for the publick Liberty.

General Howe has declared his Intentions that Gen eral Lee shall be tried by the Laws of *his* Country. So he is considerd as a Deserter from the British Army. You know the Resolution of Congress con-

cerning this Matter.   It is my Opinion that Lt Col^o
Campbell ought immediately to be secured.   He is to
be detaind as one upon whom Retalliation is to be
made.   Would you believe it, that after the shocking
Inhumanity shown to our Countrymen in the Jerseys,
plundering Houses, cruelly beating old Men, ravishing
Maids, murdering Captives in cold Blood & sistemat-
ically starving Multitudes of Prisoners under his own
Eyes in New York this humane General totally disa
vows even his winking at the Tragedy and allows that
a few Instances may have happend which are rather
to be lamented.   ·

Congress is now busy in considering the report of
the joynt Com^tee of the Eastern States.   A curious De
bate arose on this Subject, which I have not time now
to mention.   I will explain it to you in my next.

Adieu my Friend,

TO MRS. ADAMS.

[MS., Samuel Adams Papers, Lenox Library.]

PHILAD^E March 19 1775

MY DEAR BETSY

I wrote to you by the last Post, and am resolvd to
write by every Post as well as other opportunities.
If I have Nothing more to say to you, I flatter my
self you will be pleasd when I have it in my Power
to tell you, as I now do, that I am in good Health and
Spirits.   I must remind you that the last Letter I receivd from you is dated the 26th of January.   I am
in daily Expectation of receiving another.   You do

not conceive with how much Satisfaction I read your Letters. I wish therefore that you would not omit writing to me by the Post if other safe Opportunities do not present.

Yesterday we receivd a very agreeable Letter from Doctor Franklin dated at Nantes (in France) the 8th of December. By this Letter, things appear in a very favorable Light to America in that Kingdom. A general War was thought to be unavoidable. The Differences between Spain & Portugal were not set tled, although the British Monarch (as he tells his Parliament) had been using his Endeavors for that Purpose. The Passengers tell us it is the Determination of the Court of France to prevent the Russian Troops from coming to America, and that General Howe can expect no Reinforcement of foreign Mer cenaries this year. It is however the Wisdom of America to prepare for the most formidable Attacks. I am sorry to tell you that the Vessel which brought us this Intelligence was taken near the Capes of Del aware, having Goods on board belonging to the Con tinent, to what Value is not yet ascertaind. We must expect Misfortunes and bear them. I make no Doubt but this Contest will end in the Establishment of American Freedom & Independence.

I lately received two Letters from my Son. He writes me that he is in good Health. The Affairs of the Department he is in, will soon be settled on a new Plan, when his Friends here say he shall be provided for. I have told him he must expect to derive no Ad vantage in point of Promotion from his Connection with me, for it is well known I have ever been averse to recommending Sons or Cousins. Yet I am far from being indifferent towards him. I feel the affec tion of a Father. It gives me inexpressible Pleas ure to hear him so well spoken of. I hope I am not, indeed I have no Reason to think that I am flatterd and deceivd.

In a former Letter you informd that our valueable Brother Mr Checkley was dangerously ill and his Life despared of. I have heard Nothing of him since, although I have enquired of Persons who came from Providence. My worthy Friend Col^l Henshaw you tell me, still lives, beyond the Expectation of his Phy sician and Friends. I did not promise my self the Pleasure of ever seeing him again in this World when I left Boston. But Mr Checkley was by many years younger, and in high Health when I visited him at Providence.

I have been told that the Law lately made in our State has been attended with ill Consequences, and that the Inhabitants of Boston were in Danger of be ing starvd for Want of the necessary Articles of living from the Country ; but a Letter I have just receivd from a Friend upon whom I greatly rely, assures me that it is likely to answer the good Purposes intended. Pray, my Dear, let me know whether you live accord ing to your own Wishes. I am very sollicitous con- cerning you.—Tell my Daughter and Sister Polly that I daily think of them. Remember me to each of my Family and other Friends. I am

                                        Your affectionate

    After perusing the inclosd, you will seal and send it to Miss Scollay.

TO JOHN SCOLLAY.

[MS., Samuel Adams Papers, Lenox Library.]

PHILAD^E March 20th 1777

My dear Sir/

I am to acknowledge your Favor of the 22^d of Feb. which I receivd a few days ago. The Act for regu lating Prices, you tell me has made a great Convulsion especially in Boston. I am exceedingly sorry to hear that Dissentions should arise in a Community, re- markeable for its publick Spirit, and which has hereto fore by the united Exertions of Individuals repeatedly done essential Services in Support of the Liberties of America. Is it indeed true, my Friend, that "Self Denial is a Virtue rarely to be seen among you"? How great a Change in a few years! The Self De nial of the Citizens of Boston, their Patience and long Suffering under the cruel Oppression of the Port bill was astonishing both to their Friends and their Enemies. Their Firmness and Resolution in that severe Conflict, and the Chearfulness with which they endurd the Loss of all things, rather than the publick Liberty should suffer by their Submission, will be handed down to their Honour in the impartial History. God forbid that they should so soon forget their own generous Feelings for the Publick and for each other, as to set private Interest in Competition with that of the great Community. The Country and the Town, you tell me, mutually complain of each other. I well remember it was the Artifice of our common Enemies to foment such Divisions but by the social Interviews of Committees of Corre spondence and other Means the Affections of the

Town & Country were conciliated. Indeed there is no Time for angry Disputes. While the publick Liberty is in Danger, and every thing that is sacred is threatned, the People should, if ever, be in perfect good humour. At such a Time Citizens should not be over sollicitous concerning their seperate Interests. There should rather be an Emulation to excell each other in their Exertions for the Safety of our Coun try. I confess I am not sufficiently informd to make up a Judgment for myself of the Utility of the Act in every Particular. Perhaps it would have been better if those necessary Articles of Life for the Supply of which you depend upon the Southern Colonies had been put upon a Footing with other imported Ar ticles. As the Price of Flour for Instance is not limitted in these States, I cannot see how it can be fixed at a certain Rate in New England without Danger of injuring the Importer, or altogether pre venting the necessary Supply of Bread. The Com mittees of the middle States I am told are now met, and if they should agree to regulate the Prices of their produce it may put it in the power of our Gen Assembly to fix them at such Rates as to enable the Merchants to supply the Town without Loss to themselves.

I observe what you have written concerning the Supply of the Army with your Mannufacture. Such Matters are out of my Line, but you may assure your self I shall endeavor to promote your Interest as far as it may be in my Power, for I am,

Your unfeigned Friend,

TO MRS. ADAMS.

[MS., Samuel Adams Papers, Lenox Library.]

PHILAD^A April 1st 1777

MY DEAR BETSY

I wrote to you the Week before last by the Post and since by a Mr Vose of Boston. I wish to hear of your having receivd both those Letters, especially the last for a Reason which must be obvious to you if you have seen its Contents.

We have receivd the important Intelligence from New Hampshire of the Arrival of a Vessel from France with near twelve thousand Stands of Arms and a great Quantity of Powder &c. I congratulate my Country on the occasion. By this Vessel I have a Letter from my much esteemed Friend A. L. I will recite to you some Passages in his Letter because I recollect with how much Pleasure you used to read those which I formerly receivd from him, and be cause I think the Spirit with which he writes and the Intelligence contain'd in his Letter, will afford Satisfaction to you and the Circle of our Friends. " It is certain, says he, that the Peace of Europe hangs upon a Cobweb. It is certain that, Portugal & Russia excepted, all Europe wishes us Success. The Ports of France, Spain and the Mediterranean are open to us on the Terms of Neutrality. We have already receivd a Benevolence in this Country, which will enable us to Expedite and augment the Stores necessary for your Defence." The Benevolence he refers to, is a voluntary Loan of a Sum of Money in France, without Interest, and to be paid as soon

as it can conveniently be done after a Peace shall
be establishd.   You may now remember what I
wrote you from Baltimore in December last.   I
think we shall soon reap the happy Fruits of the De
terminations of Congress at that time.   My Friend
tells me " It is with Pleasure he revives a Corre
spondence which the particular Situation of Affairs
has so long interrupted."   His Letter is dated in
Paris the 21st of January.   I had before written to
him on the 2^{d} of the same Month, being then fully
satisfied that mine, if no ill Accident happend, would
find him in that Place.   I then observd to him that
our Country had called him to act in a more en
larged Sphere.   He soon after informs me that he
had "obeyed the Call of Congress into *the immediate
Service* of our Country."   What this Service is our
Friends will conjecture.   You may assure them that
Matters merely commercial are not in the Line of *his*
Genius.   In my Letter, I remark to him that our
Country is now enduring the sharp Conflict, con
fiding that righteous Heaven will never look with an
indifferent Eye upon a Cause so manifestly just, and
so interresting to Mankind.   In his Letter, he tells
me with the Spirit of Prediction " When with Roman
Fortitude & Magnanimity we refuse to treat with
Hannibal at our Gates, he looks forward to Roman
Greatness."   I am perswaded that these united States
will never treat with any Power which will not acknowledge their Independence.   The Inhabitants of
Boston, who have heretofore acted so disinterrested
and patriotick a Part will Surely persevere in supporting this all important Cause.   America has already

the Applause of the virtuous and the brave. If we are not wanting to ourselves, we may be assured of the Smiles of Heaven. However ready some of the Powers of Europe may be to aid us in this glorious Struggle, it will certainly in the End be best for us, if we can save ourselves by our own Exertions. Our Sufferings will indeed be greater if we are left to our selves, but the more dearly we purchase our Liberties, the more we shall prize them and the longer we shall preserve them.

Yesterday an unhappy Man was executed here for attempting to entice some of the Pilots to enter into the Service of Lord Howe. He was first examined by the Board of War, and afterwards tried by a Court Martial and condemned. The Pilots pretended to him that they were in earnest till the Bargain was made and he had given them the Bribe. They then seizd him and had him committed to Goal. Before his Execution the whole Proceedings of the Court were laid before Congress and the Judgment was approvd of. The Evidence against him was full and clear, but not more so than his own Confession. He said that he had been at New York about a Month before he was detected, and that Mr Galloway, a Man of Fortune & a noted Tory in this State, who last Winter went over to the Enemy, was his Adviser there. No Doubt there were others here who secretly abetted & supported him. Some ordinary Persons, I am told have disappeard since this Mans Detection.

It has been reported here these few days past that Lord Howe is gone to England, and it is thought by some to be probable upon this Circumstance that a new Proclamation has made its Appearance signd William Howe only.

I am informd that General Carleton and his Brother have been very ill used and are greatly disgusted with the British Court. That Lord George Sackvill and all the Scotch hate them, and they him. You remember the old Proverb.

I am afraid, my dear, I have tired your Patience with a Letter altogether upon political Matters. I have only time to tell you that I remain in good Health & Spirits—Believe me

Your affectionate

April 2ᵈ
Your Kind Letter of the 19ᵗʰ of March is just come to my hand—-

TO NATHANAEL GREENE.[1]

[MS., Samuel Adams Papers, Lenox Library.]

PHILADᴱ May 12 1777

MY DEAR SIR

Amidst your Hurry of Business and my own, I can not help withdrawing myself for a Moment to throw on paper a single Sentiment for your Consideration. Europe and America seem to be applauding our Imitation of the Fabian Method of carrying on this War without considering as I conceive the widely different Circumstances of the Carthaginian & the British Generals. It will recur to your Memory that the Faction

---

[1] Addressed to General Greene at Morristown, New Jersey.

of Hanno in Carthage prevented Hannibals receiving
the Supplys from them which he had a Right to ex
pect and his Necessities requird. This left him to
the Resources of his own Mind, and obligd him to
depend upon such Supplys as he could procure from
the Italians. Under such a Circumstance, it was the
Wisdom of Fabius to put himself in the State of De
fence but by no means of Inactivity—by keeping a
watchful Eye upon Hannibal and cutting off his for-
raging & other Parties by frequent Skirmishes he had
the strongest Reason to promise himself the Ruin of
his Army without any Necessity of risqueing his own
by a general Engagement. But General Howe (who
by the way I am not about to compare to Hannibal as
a Soldier) has at all times the best Assurances of Sup
plies from Britain. There is no Faction there to dis
appoint him and the British Navy is powerful enough
to protect Transports & provision Vessels coming to
him. Hannibal despaird of Reinforcements from Car
thage, but Howe has the fullest Assurances of early
reinforcements from Britain & cannot fail of receiving
them, unless a general War has taken place which I
think is at least problematical. They are expected
every Day. Would Fabius, if he were his Enemy, pur
sue the Method he took with the Carthaginian General?
Would he not rather attend to the present Circum
stances, and by destroying the Army in Brunswick
prevent as much as possible the Enemy increasing in
Strength even if reinforcements should arrive or puting a total End to the Campaign if they should not.
I am sensible our own Circumstances have been such,
thro' the Winter past, as to make it impracticable to

attempt any thing, but I hope we are or shall be very soon in a Condition to take a decisive part, and I do not entertain any Doubt but we shall see such an enterprizing Spirit as will confound our Enemies and give Assurances to the Friends of Liberty & Mankind that we still retain a just Sense of our own Dignity and the Dignity of our Cause and are resolvd by God's Assistance to support it at all Hazzards.

I am, &c

TO MRS. ADAMS.

[MS., Samuel Adams Papers, Lenox Library.]

PHILAD^E JUNE 17, 1777

My dear Betsy

I am disappointed in not receiving a Letter from you by yesterdays Post. The Fears you expressd in your last of the Arrival of Burgoin gave me Uneasiness. We receivd Advice from our Friends in France which gave us some Reason to apprehend the Intention of the Enemy was to attack Boston, and we thought it necessary to give timely Notice of it. I hope the People there will always be so much on their Guard as to prepare for the worst, but I think you will not be in Danger this Summer. This City has been given out as their Object. Last Saturday General Howe with the main Body of his Army marchd from Brunswick to Somerset Court House about 8 Miles on the Road to Cariel's Ferry with an Intention as it was thought to cross the Delaware there, but Genl Sullivan with about three thousand Regulars and Militia got Possession of the post there. The

Jersey Militia are coming out with great Spirit and I think the progress of the Enemy in that way is effect ually stopped—Col¹ Whipple will set off tomorrow for Boston & Portsmouth.   If I can possibly get time I will write by him.   I am now in great Haste.   I hope you duly receivd my last inclosing one to Henry Gardner Esq.,¹ and that the Matter therein mentioned is settled to your Advantage.   Give my Love to my Daughter Sister Polly &ᶜ.   Write to me by every Post.   Adieu my dear & believe me to be most affectionately,

Your,

TO JAMES WARREN.

[MS., Samuel Adams Papers, Lenox Library.]

PHILADᴬ June 18 1777

My dear Sir/

This Letter will be deliverd to you by my worthy Friend Colᵒ Whipple a Delegate of the State of New Hampshire.   He is a Gentleman of Candor, and wishes he could have the opportunity of conversing freely with some one of Influence in the Massa chusetts Bay upon Matters concerning that State particularly.   To whom could I recommend him on this Occasion with more Propriety than to your self. He will be able to give you such Information of Per sons and Things as one would not chuse to throw on Paper in this precarious Time when an Accident might turn the Intelligence into a wrong Channel.

I observe by the Boston Papers last brought to us,

---

¹ Treasurer of Massachusetts.

that you are again placed in the Chair of the House of Representatives, with which I am well pleasd. Mr Paine Speaker pro Temp. Mr Hancock first Member of the Boston Seat and Mr T. Cushing a Councellor *at large*—I have the Honor of knowing but few of the Members of the House. I hope my Countrymen have been wise in their Elections and I pray God to bless their Endeavors for the establish ment of publick Liberty Virtue & Happiness.

You will hear before this will reach you of the Motions of the Enemy. It has been the general Opinion for many Months past that this City is the Object. Should they gain this Point what will it avail them unless they beat our Army. This I am fully perswaded they will not do. My Wish is that our Army may beat them, because it would put a glorious End to the present Campaign & very prob ably the War. I confess I have always been so very wrong headed as not to be over well pleasd with what is called the Fabian War in America. I con ceive a great Difference between the Situation of the Carthaginian & the British Generals. But I have no Judgment in military Affairs, and therefore will leave the Subject to be discussd, as it certainly will be, by those who are Masters of it. I can not conclude this Epistle without thanking you for your Care in carry ing a Matter in which I was interrested through the General Assemby of which I have been informd by our Friend M^r ——.

I wish to hear from you. Adieu my Friend,

TO JAMES WARREN.

[MS., Samuel Adams Papers, Lenox Library.]

PHILAD^A^ June 23 1777

DEAR SIR

I wrote to you a few days ago by Col° Whipple with whom I hope you will have free Conversation. As he must have been not far from the Spot, he can give you a more particular Acco^t^ than has yet been handed to us, of the late Scituation & Movements of the two Armies. The main Body of our Army was encampd at Middle Brook, and a considerable Force consisting of Continental Troops and Militia lay at a place called Sourland Hills within 6 Miles of the Enemy who were posted at Somersett Court House 9 miles on this Side of Brunswick. The Right of the Enemy was at Brunswick & their Left at Somersett. They were well fortified on the Right and had the Raritan River in front and Millstone on the left. In this Situation General W. tho't an Attack upon them would be attended with bad Consequences. His Design was to collect all the forces that c^d^ possibly be drawn from other Quarters so as to reduce the Se curity of his Army to the greatest Certainty & to be in a Condition to embrace any fair opp^ty^ that m^t^ offer to make an Attack on advantageous terms. In the mean time by light bodies of Militia seconded & encouragd by a few Continental Troops to harrass & diminish their Numbers by continual Skirmishes. But the Enemy made a sudden Retreat to Brunswick and from thence with great Precipitation tow^ds^ Amboy All the Continental Troops at Peeks Kill except the number necessary for the Security of the Post were orderd to hasten on to the Army in Jersey & a part of them had joynd. I am not disposd to ascribe great military Skill to Gen¹ Howe, but if he designd to draw the whole of our Forces from the East to the West Side of Hudsons River, in order to gain advantage by suddenly crossing the River with his own Army I cannot but hope they will be cut off & his Design frustrated. Great Credit is due to the Jersey Militia who have turnd out with spirit & alacrity. I congratulate you on the Success of our State Vessels of War.

Will you be so kind as to call on M^{rs} A & let her know that you have rec^d this Letter, for she charges me with not writing to my Friends so often as she thinks I ought.

The Watchman tells me 'tis past 12 o'Clock.

Adieu my dear friend.

TO RICHARD HENRY LEE.

[MS., Lee Papers, American Philosophical Society; portions are printed in W. V. Wells, *Life of Samuel Adams*, vol. ii., pp. 470, 471, 475.]

PHILAD^A June 26 1777.

MY DEAR SIR

I intended to have written to you by the last Post, but being under a Necessity of dispatching some Letters to Boston by the Eastern Post which went off the same day I was prevented. When you left this City you may remember the Enemy was at Brunswick and our Army at a place called Middlebrook about 9 Miles North of Brunswick Since which General Howe who

had joyned his Army marchd suddenly from thence
with Design as it was generally believd to make a rapid
Push for Philadelphia, but he disappointed the Hopes
of some and the fears of others by halting at Somerset
Court House about 9 Miles on the Road leading to
Caryels Ferry.   General Sullivan who you know had
been at Princeton made a quick March to cover our
Boats at the Ferry and by retarding Howe's March
to give an opportunity to our Army to come up &
attack them.   But the Enemy continuing at Somerset
Sullivan advancd with a considerable Force—consist
ing of Continental Troops and Militia & posted himself
at a place called Sourland hills within six Miles of
Somerset Court house.   The Enemy were very
strongly posted, their Right at Brunswick & their Left
at Somerset well fortified on the Right and having the
Raritan in front and Millstone on the Left.   In this
Scituation Genl W. did not think it prudent to attack
them as it did not appear to him to be warranted by
a sufficient prospect of Success and he thought it might
be attended with ruinous Consequences.   The Design
then was to reduce the Security of his Army to the
greatest Certainty by collecting all the Forces that
could be drawn from other Quarters, so as to be in a
Condition of embracing any fair opportunity that m^t
offer to make an Attack on Advantageous Terms, and
in the mean time by light Bodies of Militia seconded
& encouragd by a few continental Troops to harrass &
diminish their Numbers by continual Skirmishes—But
the Enemy made an unexpected Retreat to Brunswick,
and afterwards with great Precipitation to Amboy.

June 29 –   - On Wednesday last the Enemy re-

inforcd, as it is said, with Marines, marchd from
Amboy, through a Road between Brunswick and
Elizabeth Town to a place called Westfield about 10
Miles, with Design as it is supposd to cut off our Light
Troops and bring on a General Battle, or to take
Possession of the High Land back of Middlebrook ;
for which last purpose Westfield was the most con
venient Route and it was also a well chosen Spot from
whence to make a safe Retreat in Case he should fail
of gaining his Point.   On this march they fell in with
General Maxwell who thought it prudent to retreat to
our main Army then at Quibbletown from whence Gen¹
W. made a hasty march to his former Station and
frustrated the supposd Design of the Enemy.   I have
given you a very general Narrative of the different
Situation & Movements of the two Armies, without
descending to the particulars, because we have not as
yet an Authentick Account, and one cannot depend
upon the many stories that are told.   I think I may
assure you that our Army is in high Spirits and is daily
growing more respectable in point of Numbers.

We are going on within Doors with Tardiness
enough. A Thousand and [one] little Matters too often
throw out greater ones.   A kind of Fatality still pre
vents our proceeding a Step in the important affair of
Confederation—Yesterday and the day before was
wholly spent in passing Resolutions to gratify N. Y.
or as they say to prevent a civil War between that
State and the Green Mountain Men—A Matter which
it is not worth your while to have explaind to you.
Monsʳ D Coudrayˢ affair is still unsettled.   The four
french Engineers are arrivd.   They are said to be very

clever but disdain to be commanded by Coudray. Mr Com^r D— - continuing to send us french German & Prussian officers with authenticated Conventions and strong recommendations. The military Science, for your Comfort, will make rapid Progress in America. Our Sons and Nephews will be provided for in the Army and a long and moderate War will be their happy Portion. But who my Friend, would not wish for peace. May I live to see the publick Liberty restored and the Safety of our dear Country secured. I should then think I had enjoyd enough and bid this World Adieu.

Your,

TO JAMES WARREN.

[MS., Samuel Adams Papers, Lenox Library.]

PHILAD^E June 30 1777

My dear Friend

I have the Pleasure of receiving your friendly Letter of the 16 Instant, and have little more than time enough barely to acknowledge the favor. There is an unaccountable Uncertainty in the Conduct of the Post office. About a month ago I remonstrated to the Post Master General that the time allowd the Eastern Delegates to answer the Letters they receivd by the post (being on the Monday between 9 & 2) was altogether spent in Congress, and requested that we might have one Evening for the purpose. He granted it and the Post has been since detaind till tuesday Morning, but I am now informd that the former Regulation is revivd, for what Reason I know not, and our Letters must be ready at two o'Clock. I do assure you I should hardly forgive my self, could I reflect upon my having once neglected to write to so valueable a Friend as you.

You wish to hear "how our Confederation goes on." I do not wonder at your Anxiety to have it completed, for it appears to me to be a Matter of very great Importance. We every now and then take it into Consideration, but such a Variety of Affairs have continually demanded the Attention of Congress that it has been impracticable hitherto to get thro it. There are but two or three things which in my opinion will be the Subjects of much further Debate, and upon these I believe most if not all the Members have already made up their Minds. One is what Share of Votes each of the States, which differ so much in Wealth & Numbers, shall have in determining all Questions. Much has been said upon this weighty Question upon the decision of which depends the Union of the States and the ˛Security of the Liberty of the whole. Perhaps it would be more easy for a disinterrested Foreigner to see, than for the united States to fix upon, the Principles upon which this Question ought in Equity to be decided. The Sentiments in Congress are not various, but as you will easily conceive opposite. The Question was very largely debated a few days ago, and I am apt to think it will tomorrow be determind that each State shall have one Vote, but that certain great & very interresting Questions, shall have the concurrent Votes of nine States for a Decision. Whether this Composition will go near towards the Preservation of a due Ballance I wish *you* would consider, for if your Life & Health is spared to your Country, you will have a great Share in the Deter mination of it hereafter. You have later Advices from abroad than we. Our last Intelligence I gave you pretty minutely in a Letter which I sent & suppose was deliverd to you by Capt Collins.

I find by the News papers that the Genl Assembly under the Denomination of a Convention are form ing a new Constitution.[1] This is a momentous Busi ness, I pray God to direct you. Shall I be favord with your own & others Sentiments upon it. I am greatly afflicted to hear that angry Disputes have arisen among my dear Countrymen, at a time es pecially when perfect good Humour should subsist and every Heart and Tongue & Hand should be united in promoting the Establishment of publick Liberty & securing the future Safety & Happiness of our Country. I am sure you will cultivate Harmony among those who Love the Country in Sincerity. With regard to *others* I will say in the apostolick Language " I would they were all cut off" (banishd at least) "that trouble you."

Will it too much infringe upon your precious time to acquaint M^{rs} A that I am in good health & Spirits, and have not opportunity to write to her by this post. I am with the most friendly regards to your Lady & Family very affectionately your Friend,

---

[1] Columbia University *Studies in History, Economics, and Public Law*, vol. vii., pp. 194–226.

TO ARTHUR LEE.

[MS., Samuel Adams Papers, Lenox Library.]

PHILAD^E July 4 1777

MY DEAR FRIEND

I did myself the Honor to write to you on the 2^d of Jany last since which your favor of the 21st of the same month from Paris came to my Hand. You have supposd that this Campaign would put General Howe, after the Junction with Burgoyne in Posses sion of the States of New York, New Jersey Penn sylvania & the Delaware with Rhode Island as his Center of Attack upon the States of New England; you have even considerd such a situation of things as almost certain. But I have now the Satisfaction of informing you that General Howe has found it neces sary to withdraw all his Troops from New Jersey, and I am of Opinion that it is impracticable for him to distribute his Troops among the States you have mentiond in sufficient Numbers to keep possession of them and afford enough to attack the New England States with the least Prospect of subduing them. I have thought that the Impression which the Enemy made the last Winter on the State of New Jersey was owing to favorable Circumstances which then took place, and was not in pursuance of the original Plan. The Time for which our Troops were inlisted had ex pired—our Army was reducd to a mere handful and General Howe had flatterd himself that the middle States were so generally disaffected to our Cause as to render their total Submission practicable & easy. He therefore made a vigorous push in the Depth of

Winter as far as Trenton upon Delaware, and there
cantond his Troops with a Design probably of avail
ing himself of this City early in the Spring before we
should be able to collect a force sufficient to prevent
it. But General Washington, having gaind a signal
Advantage by an Attack as you have heard obligd
him to retreat and make his remaining Winter Quar
ters in Brunswick, since which the Vigilance & Activ
ity of the people of Jersey who by frequent Skirmishes
have lessend his Army, has given him reason to alter
his opinion of their Disposition & his removing from
thence has I think afforded sufficient Proof that he has
not been able by Arts or Arms to conquer even one
of our smallest States. What his next Step will be is
uncertain, perhaps he may embark his Troops for
Philadelphia, or more probably he may attempt a Junc
tion with Burgoyne. If the first, has he to expect
more Laurels or better Success than he gaind in Jer
sey? Or, if the latter should be his Choice judge
what must be his Prospect. Burgoyne who it is said
cannot muster more than 7 or 8 thousand will be opposd by our Northern Army & I hope overwhelmd be
fore they can reach Albany. Howe will be followd
close by the Army under the immediate Command of
G W, at present more than equal it in number, in
high Spirits, full of the Idea of Victory and daily in
creasing. Under these unpromising Circumstances
should he even complete a Junction, he will then have
to begin an attempt of the most arduous Business of
conquering the whole Army of the united States to
gether with the numerous, hardy & stubborn Militia
of New England. These are my Views of the present

State of our military affairs, and I am perswaded,
when I reflect on the Spirit & Valor discoverd in my
Countrymen of Georgia So & No Carolina Virginia
& Jersey to say nothing of Lexington & Bunker Hill
in my own dear native State, Great Britain will ever
show her self feeble in her Efforts to conquer America.
I beg you to write to me full as often as you may find
Leisure, and for my own part I feel a Disposition al
most to persecute you with my Letters but I must
conclude with congratulating you on this first Anni
versary of American Independence, and assuring you
that I am unfeignedly and very affectionately,

Your Friend,

<hr/>

TO SAMUEL HEWES.

[MS., Samuel Adams Papers, Lenox Library.]

PHILADELA July 7 1777

MY DEAR SIR/

I intreat you to ascribe my not having yet acknowledgd the Receipt of your favor[1] to the true
Cause, a perpetual Hurry of affairs. I have not been
unmindful of its Contents. Major Ward, as you
have heard, is appointed Commissary General of
Musters with the Rank and Pay of a Colonel. I have
long known him a Man of Sense and a zealous and
steady Patriot, in Times less promising than the pres
ent ; and the Part he took on the ever memorable
19th of April 75, together with the Experience he has
gaind by constant Application ever since in the milita-

: Of March 25, 1777.

ry Line, intitles him to particular Notice. I will bear in my Memory the Hint given in the Close of your Let ter. If at any Time I may have it in my power to render benefit to a Friend by puting him in the Way of serv ing our Country it will afford me double Satisfaction. You will have heard before this reaches you that General Howe has at length drawn all his Forces from the State of Jersey to New York. It is the Business of General Washington to penetrate his fu ture Design. This City has been threatned for some Months past ; if he ever had such an Intention, it is probable he has now laid it aside, and that he will at tempt to force a Junction with Burgoyne, and subdue the Eastern States. [But] why should I hazzard a Conjecture of this kind who profess no Skill in mili tary affairs. I hope my Countrymen are prepared to give the Enemy a proper Reception whenever they may be attackd !

I have written you a friendly Letter though a short one—short for want of time to write more. I have twenty things to say to you but at present must con clude with most respectful Compl^{ts} to your Lady Family & Connections very cordially your friend,

TO JOHN PITTS.

[MS., Samuel Adams Papers, Lenox Library.]

PHILAD^F July 8 1777

MY DEAR SIR

I do not recollect to have receivd a Letter from [you] of a later Date than the 25 of Decr last, although

I have been since writing to you as often as I co^d find Leisure. I do not know that I have by any thing I have written given you just Cause of offence. If you think otherwise pray let me know it, and I will make as full Atonement as I am able, for I do assure you I wish to continue a friendly epistolary Correspondence with you. Be so kind as to write me by the very next Post and assure yourself that I am unfeignedly and most cordially,

Y^r Friend,

TO RICHARD HENRY LEE.

[MS., Emmet Collection, Lenox Library.]

Philad^e July 15 1777

My dear Friend

I wrote to you a Fortnight ago in so great Haste that I had not time to transcribe or correct it and relied on your Candor to overlook the slovenly Dress in which it was sent to you. You have since heard that our Friends in Jersey have at length got rid of as vindictive and cruel an Enemy as ever invaded any Country. It was the opinion of General Gates that Howes advancing to Somerset Court House was a Feint to cover the Retreat of his Battering Train, ordinary Stores and heavy Baggage to Amboy. I confess I can not help yet feeling myself chagrind, that in more . . . . diminish his paltry Army in that State. If their Militia, among whom so great an Animation prevaild, had been let loose upon the Enemy, who knows but that they w^d have destroyd their Army, or at least, so far have weakend it as to have put a glorious End to this Campaign, and perhaps the War? I will acknowledge that my Temper is rather sanguine. I am apt to be displeasd when I think our Progress in War and in Politicks is Slow. I wish to see more of an enterprizing Spirit in the Senate and the Field, without which, I fear our Country will not speedily enjoy the Fruits of the present Conflict—an establishd Independence and Peace. I cannot applaud the Prudence of the Step, when the People of Jersey were collected, and in spired with Confidence in themselves & each other, to dismiss them as not being immediately wanted, that they might go home in good Humour and be willing to turn out again in any *other* Emergency. I possess not the least Degree of Knowledge in military Matters, & therefore hazzard no opinion. I recol· lect however that Shakespear tells us, there is a Tide in human Affairs, an Opportunity which wise Men carefully watch for and improve, and I will never forget because it exactly coincides with my religious opinion and I think is warranted by holy writ, that " God helps those who help themselves."

We have letters from General Schuyler in the Northern Department giving us an Account of the untoward Situation of our Affairs in that Quarter & I confess it is no more than I expected, when he was again intrusted with the Command there. You re member it was urged by some that as he had a large Interest and powerful Connections in that Part of the Country, no one could so readily avail himself of Supplys for an Army there, than he. A most sub stantial Reason, I think, why he should have been appointed a Quartermaster or a Commissary. But it seems to have been the prevailing Motive to appoint him to the Chief Command! You have his Account in the inclosed Newspaper, which leaves us to *guess* what is become of the *Garrison*. It is indeed droll enough to see a General not knowing where to find the main Body of his Army. Gates is the Man of my Choice. He is *honest* and *true*, & has the Art of *gaining the Love of his Soldiers* principally because he is *always present* with them in *Fatigue* & *Danger*. But Gates has been disgusted! We are however waiting to be relievd from this disagreeable State of uncertainty, by a particular Account of Facts from some Person who *was near* the Army who trusts not to *Memory* altogether, lest some Circumstances may be *omitted* while others are *misapprehended*.

I rejoyce in the Honors your Country has done you. Pray hasten your Journey hither.

Your very affectionate,

TO SAMUEL COOPER.

[MS., Samuel Adams Papers, Lenox Library.]

PHILADᴱ July 15 1777

MY DEAR SIR

Before this reaches you, it is probable you will have heard of the untoward Turn our Affairs have taken at the Northward. I confess it is not more than I expected when Genˡ Schuʳ was again intrusted with the Command there. But it was thought by some Gentlemen that as he had a great Interest &

large Connections in that Part of the Country, he could more readily avail himself of Supplys for an Army there as well as Reinforcements if wanted upon an Emergency, than any other Man. You have the Account in the inclosed Paper, which leaves us to guess what is become of the Garrison. There is something droll enough in a Generals not knowing where to find the main Body of his Army. Gates is the Man I should have chosen. He is honest and true, & has the Art of gaining the Love of his Soldiers, principally because he is always present and shares with them in Fatigue & Danger. We are hourly ex pecting to be relievd from a disagreable State of Uncertainty by a particular Relation of Facts. This Account, as you are told, is related upon *Memory*, & therefore some Circumstances may be *omitted*, others *misapprehended*. But the Post is just going, & I have time only to acknowledge the Receipt of your favor of the 12 of June & beg you would write to me often.

I am affectionately,

Your friend,

TO RICHARD HENRY LEE.

[MS., Samuel Adams Papers, Lenox Library ; the text, dated July 12, 1777, is in W. V. Wells, *Life of Samuel Adams*, vol. ii., pp. 484-486.]

PHILAD^A July 22 1777

MY DEAR SIR

Your very acceptable Letter of the 12th came to my hand yesterday. The Confederation, is most certainly an important Object, and ought to be attended to

& finishd speedily.   I moved the other Day and urgd
that it might then be brought on ; but your Colleague
Col° H opposed and prevented it, Virginia not being
represented.   It is put off till you shall arrive ; you
see therefore the Necessity of your hastening to
Congress.

We have still further & still confused Accounts from
the Northward.   Schuylers Letters are rueful indeed !
even to a great Degree, and with such an awkward
Mixture as would excite one to laugh in the Midst of
Calamity.   He seems to contemplate his own Happi
ness in not having had much or indeed any Hand in
the unhappy Disaster.   He throws Blame on St Clare
in his Letter of July 9th.   " What adds to my Distress
is, that a Report prevails that I had given orders for
the Evacuation of Tyconderoga, whereas not the most
distant Hint of any such Intention can be drawn from
any of my Letters to General Sinclare or any other
Person whatever."   He adds " What could induce the
General Officers to a Step that has ruind our Affairs
in that Quarter, God only knows."   And indeed Sin-
clares own Letter of the 30th of June dated at Ty. would
induce one to be of the same Opinion, for he there
says " My People are in the best Disposition possible
and I have no Doubt about giving a good Account of
the Enemy should they think proper to attack us."
Other Parts of his Letter are written in the same spir
ited Stile.   The General Officers blame N E for not
furnishing their Quota of Troops.   It is natural for
Parties to shift the Fault fro mone to the other; and your
Friend General Steven, who seems desirous of clearing
his Countryman from all Blame, in a Letter to your

Brother says " Eight thousand Men were thought adequate to the Purpose. They (N E) furnishd about three thousand—for Want of the Quota the Place is lost & they stand answerable for the Con sequences." The General forgets that five of the ten Regiments orderd from Mass. Bay were counter manded and are now at Peeks Kill. I will give you an Abstract of the Forces at Ty & Mount Indepen dence the 25th of June taken from the Muster-master General Col⁰ Varicks Return.

Fit for Duty of the 9 Continental Regi ments Commissiond & Non commis- siond & Staff Officers included	2738
Col⁰ Wells' & Leonard's Regiments of Militia [their time expired the 6th of July]	637
Col⁰ Long's Regimᵗ of Militia [engagd to 1ˢᵗ of Augᵗ]	199
Major Stephens' Corps of Artillery	151
5 Companies of Artificers	178
Whitcombs Aldrichs & Lees Rangers	70
	3973
Men at Out Posts not included in the Above	218
Sick in Camp and Barracks	342
	4533

Besides a Number of Recruits belonging to the Continental Regiments arrivd at Ty. between the 18th & 29th of June, that are not included in the above Ab stract. General Schuyler in his Letter of the 9th of

July says, " I am informd *from undoubted Authority* that the Garrison was reinforced with twelve Hundred Men *at least,* two days before the Evacuation." When the Commander in chiefe writes in so positive Terms, one would presume upon his certain knowledge of Facts ; *but as he was not present with his Army,* let us suppose (though it does not seem probable by the general gloomy Cast of his Letters) that he has over rated the Numbers, and set down 967 and it would complete the Number of 5500. Deduct the sick 342. and I am willing also to deduct the two "licen tious and disorderly" Regiments from Massachusetts who left Sinclare, though he acknowledges they kept with him two days upon the March, and there re-maind near five thousand. Mentioning this yester day in a publick Assembly, I was referrd to the Gen erals Information to his Council of War, who says " the whole of our Force consisted of two thousand & Eighty nine effective Rank & file." But allowing this to be the Case, Is an Army the worse for having more than one half of its Combatants Officers ?

Notwithstanding Nothing is said of it in the publick Letters Gen¹ Sinclair writes to his private Friend that the Enemy came up with the Rear of the retreating Army, & a hot Engagement ensued. Other Accounts say that many were killed on both sides, that our Troops beat off the Enemy & that Col° Francis of the Massachusetts & some of his officers were among the slain.

I shall not write you any more Letters for I hope to see you soon.

Adieu my Friend,

TO PAUL REVERE.

[MS., Samuel Adams Papers, Lenox Library.]

PHILADᴱ July 28 1777

My dear Sir

I receivd your favor of the 26ᵗʰ of June and also one from Colᵒ Crafts of the same Date. I wrote to him by the Return of the Post & desired him to com·municate the Contents to you. I conversd with Mʳ J A upon the Subject of your Letter, and we ven-turd, both of us, to step out of the Line of strict order in a Debate in Congress the other day, to bring your Regiment of Artillery into View. It oc-casiond a Conversation in the House in which we had a Opportunity of acquainting the Members of the long Standing of that Regiment & the Seniority of its Officers. But still it was considerd as a Regi-ment raisd by a State & not by the Continent. And though we caused the Merit of it to be well under stood & it was acknowledgd in the House, the Dif ficulty of altering the Regulation you refer to appeard so evidently in the Minds of the Gentlemen, that we waved making any Motion at that time, because we apprehended that the Issue would be unfavorable. Indeed I am of Opinion that Congress will not be in duced to make the Alteration you wish for, until it shall become a Continental Regiment. In that Case, I am apt to think there would be no Difficulty with Regard to the Seniority of other Regiments which have been raisd since, over yours. But till that is done, it is feared that an Alteration in this Instance would cause Discontent in other States, where it is

said there are Instances similar. A Regiment of
Artillery raisd in this State under Command of Col°
Procter was lately taken into Continental Service
and the Commissions were dated at the time they
were raisd. It was upon this Occasion that Col°
Crafts Regiment was mentiond; and I suppose that
Regiment w^d be admitted on the same terms. But I
think I foresee an insuperable Obstacle in that Case.
If any thing can be done consistently with the gen
eral Service, to show Honor, but especially to do
Justice to the Regiment of Artillery in Boston, I
shall not fail to push it as far as I may have Influ
ence. My fellow Citizens well know that I have
never been indifferent *to them.* I am thought here
in a great Degree partial in their Favour. I have in
particular a Predilection for that Regiment. But my
Friend, let me intreat you and the Gentlemen of
your Core, above all other feelings to cherish those
of the virtuous Citizen. I will allow that the Ambition of the Soldier is laudable. At such a Crisis as
this it is necessary. But may it not be indulgd to
Excess? This War we hope will be of short Dura
tion. We are contending, not for Glory, but for
Liberty Safety & Happiness of our Country. The
Soldier should not lose the Sentiments of the Patriot;
and the Pride of Military Rank as well as civil Pro
motion should forever give Way to the publick Good.
Be assured that I am very cordially,

Your Friend,

TO JAMES WARREN.

[MS., Samuel Adams Papers, Lenox Library.]

PHILAD^E July 31 1777

My dear Sir

It is a long time since I had the pleasure of a Letter from you. I have not heard your opinion of the Evacuation of Tyconderoga. You are doubtless chagrind as much as I am. It is ascribd to different Causes. Congress is determined that the true Reasons shall be enquird into, and the Conduct of the General Officers. Sch—rs friends are endeavoring to clear him from all Blame, because, say they, *he was not there.* This is true, and as it was well known, that he had never been used to keep himself near his Army, perhaps it may be pertinently asked, Why *He* was pitchd upon to take the Command. *Your* Dele gates, I can assure you, were utterly against it. And Notwithstanding it was publishd in some of the Boston News papers, said to be warranted by a Letter from this City, that Sch^r had the entire Confidence of Congress, there were five only of 11 States present, in favor of it. The paper I think was of the 5 of June. I wish I could know who gave the Letter to the Printer. In order, I suppose, to give Credit to that Letter, there was another publication in the papers here, informing the World, that when he set off for the Northern Department he was accompanied by —— and several other Members of C— —, which I take for granted is true. These are trifling political Manœuvres similar to those which we have seen practicd in the Mass Bay when a prop was wanted for a

sinking Character. You may think them not worth
your Notice. Excuse my troubling you with them.
Cunning Politicians often make use of the Names of
Persons, & sometimes of the Persons themselves who
have not the least Suspicion of it, to serve their own
Purposes. When I mentiond 5 out of 11 I sh^d have
explaind my self. There were 5 for the measure 4
against it & 2 divided. Had not the state of Rhode
Island been at that Juncture accidentally unrepre
sented there w^d have been an equal Division, which
w^d have prevented the Measure. The most important
Events sometimes depend upon small Circumstances.
Some Gent^n of the State of N Y are exceedingly
attachd to Genl Sch^r. They represent him as Instar
Omnium in the Northern Departm^t. But after all
that has been said, I conceive of him, as I have for a
long time, excellently well qualified for [a] Com
missary or Quartermaster. The N E Delegates were
(perhaps one excepted) to a Man against his having
the Command of that Army. But [of] this I will
write particularly in another Letter.

I am not willing to prejudge ; but I must say, it is
difficult to reconcile the sudden Evacuation of the
Fortress with the previous flattering Letters of Gen
eral St Clair. In one of his Letters written but a few
days before, he says, " My People are in the best Dis
position possible, and I have no Doubt about giving
a good Account of the Enemy if they shall think
proper to attack us." He has been esteemd here a
good Officer, & in his Letter he bespeaks the Candor
of the publick till he can be heard. Pains will be

taken to lay the Blame upon the N E States, for not furnishing a sufficient Quota of Men. I wish there-fore you w^d procure for me an authentick Acco^t of the Number of Men, both regular & Militia, sent to the Northward from our State, and how they were cloathd and armd. You may remember that Congress recom mended it to the Eastern States, some time, I think in Decr last, to send a Reinforcem^t of 4500 Militia to Ty. to remain there till they co^d be replaced by Con tinental Troops then raising. I have never been in-formd of the Effect of that Recommendation ; or if I have been informd I do not recollect it. Pray put it in our Power to state Facts precisely so far as they regard our State. It is agreed on all sides that a Fault lies somewhere. I hope the Truth will be thoroughly investigated, and, to use the homely Proverb, the Saddle laid on the right Horse.

We are looking every hour for the Arrival of the Enemy in this River. 255 sail were seen on Wed-nesday last steering from the Hook S. E. Seventy sail were seen from the shore near Egg Harbour & about 15 or 20 Leagues from these Capes on Saturday steering the same Course—the Wind ag^t them. They co^d not come here at a better time. G Washington is drawing his Troops into this Neighborhood. Some of them are arrivd. But as the Enemy has the Ad vantage of us by Sea, it s too easy for them to oblige us to harrass our Men by long & fruitless Marches, and I sh^d not wonder to hear that they have tackd about & gone Eastward. I hope my Countrymen are prepared. *Let brotherly Love continue.*

Adieu,

TO JAMES WARREN.

[MS., Samuel Adams Papers, Lenox Library.]

PHILAD Aug⟨t⟩ 1—77

D⟨R⟩ S⟨R⟩

I wrote to you on the 30th Ult° by M⟨r⟩ Bruce who did not leave the City on that Day as I expected. His Stay gives me an Opp⟨ty⟩ of acquainting you that an Express who left the Capes yesterday informs us that the enemies ships all went out to Sea in the morning steering E N E supposd to be going to Hudsons River Rh Island or Boston. M⟨r⟩ B will give you as particular an Acc⟨t⟩ as I can. I therefore refer you to him. This is what I expected. I trust you are upon your Guard. Con. has orderd an Enquiry be made into the reasons . . . . that Sch⟨r⟩ S⟨t⟩ Clair . . . . repair to Head Q⟨rs⟩ & that G W order such Gen⟨l⟩ officer as he shall think proper immediately to repair to the N⟨n⟩ Departm⟨t⟩ to relieve Sch⟨r⟩ in his Command there. A Com⟨e⟩ is appointed to digest & rep⟨t⟩ the Mode of con ducting the Enquiry.

It appears to me difficult to account for the Evacua tion of these posts even upon the principle of Cowardice. The whole Conduct seems to carry the evident Marks of Deliberation & Design.

If we are vigilant active spirited & decisive, I yet flatter my self, notwithstanding the present vexatious Situation of our Aff⟨rs⟩ at the northw⟨d⟩ we shall humble our Enemies this Campaign. I am truly mortified at their leaving this place because I think we were fully prepared for it, & I believe the Cowardly Rascals knew it. May Heaven prosper our Righteous Cause. Adieu,

TO MRS. ADAMS.

[MS., Samuel Adams Papers, Lenox Library.]

PHILAD. 2ᵈ Augᵗ 1777[1]

My dear Betsy

Mʳ Bruces tarrying in this City longer than I ex
pected, affords me an Opportunity of giving you a
second short Letter by him. The Enemies Fleet
have left these Capes & it is supposd they are gone
either to N York or N England. Secure a Place in
the Country to which you may Retreat in case there
shᵈ be a Necessity for it. Preserve your usual Steadi
ness of Mind. Take the Advice of those who are
your and my Friends with Regard to removing. I
hope there will be no Necessity for it. I am truly
sorry the . . . . have not made this City their Ob
ject, as they . . . . long threatend. I think we were
fully prepared to receive them. Perhaps Providence
designs that N England shall have the Honor of giv
ing them the decisive Blow. May Heaven prosper
our righteous Cause, in such Way and by such Instru
ments as to his infinite Wisdom shall seem meet.
I am in good Health and Spirits.

Adieu my dear,

---

[1] For a letter on this date by Adams to Washington, see W. V. Wells,
Life of Samuel Adams, vol. ii., p. 487; *cf.* Sparks, *Writings of Washington*,
vol. v., p. 14; Ford, *Writings of Washington*, vol. vi., p. 4.

TO SAMUEL FREEMAN.

[MS., Samuel Adams Papers, Lenox Library.]

[August 5, 1777]

Dᴿ Sɪʀ

I have had the pleasure of receiving several Letters from you, and I thank you for the Intelligence therein communicated to me. I beg you will continue your favors although it may not be in my Power to ballance the Account.

Our Affairs are now in a critical Situation. There is strong Reason however to Promise ourselves by the Assistance of Heaven a favorable Issue. Men of Virtue throughout Europe heartily wish well to our Cause. They look upon it, as indeed it is, the Cause of Mankind. Liberty seems to be expelled from every other part of the Globe & the Prospect of our affording an Asylum for its Friends in this new World, gives them universal Joy. France & Spain are in reality though not yet openly yielding us Aid. Nevertheless, it is my Opinion, that it would be more for the future Safety as well as the Honor of the united States of America, if they would establish their Liberty & Independence, with as little foreign Aid as possible. If we can struggle through our Difficulties & establish our selves alone we shall value our Liberties so dearly bought, the more, and be the less obligd & consequently the more independent on others. Much depends upon the Efforts of this year. Let us therefore lay aside the Consideration of every Subject, which may tend to a Disunion. The Reasons of the late Conduct of our General Officers at Ty, must endure a strict Scrutiny. Congress have orderd an Enquiry & for this purpose Generals Schuyler & St. Clair are orderd to Head Quarters. Gates immediately takes the Command of the Northern Army. He gains the Esteem of the Soldiers and his Success in restoring the Army there the last year from a State of Confusion & Sickness to Health & good order, affords a flatter ing Prospect. In my opinion he is an honest & able Officer. Bad as our Affairs in that Quarter appear to be, they are not ruinous. Reinforcem^ts of regular Troops are already gone from Peeks Kill, and I hope the brave N E Militia will joyn in sufficient Numbers, to damp the Spirits of Burgoin. One grand Effort now may put an End to this Conflict.

I am &^c

TO JOHN LANGDON.[1]

[MS., Samuel Adams Papers, Lenox Library.]

PHILAD^E August 7, 1777

MY DEAR SIR/

Major Bass will be kind enough to deliver to you this Letter. He brought me a very friendly Message from you, for which I return you my hearty Thanks. If I had Inclination or Leisure to write a Letter of Compliment, I am sure you would not be pleasd with it. The Times are very serious; our Affairs are in a critical Situation. The Enemy, after long promising a Visit to this City, made an Appearance last Week near the Capes of Delaware. But they have not been seen these six days past. The Hounds are in fault

---

[1] Of Portsmouth, New Hampshire; member of the Continental Congress.

VOL. IV.—26,

and have lost Scent of them. We shall hear where they engage, I dare say, before long. It belongs to the military Gentlemen to frustrate their Design. I think they could not have come here in a better time, because we were well prepared for them. General Washington had drawn his Forces into the Neighbor hood of this Place, and I verily believe, the people here, divided and distracted as they are about their internal Government, would have joynd in sufficient Numbers to have given a good Account of them.

The shameful Defeat of our Forces at Ticonderoga is not more distressing to us than it is vexatious. A thorough Scrutiny into the Causes of it must and will be made. For this Purpose Schuyler and St Clair are orderd to Head Quarters. I confess I cannot at pres ent account for it even upon the Principle of Cowardice. There seems to me to be the evident Marks of Design. Bad as our Affairs are in that Quarter they are not desperate. Gates is gone to take the Command.. He is an honest and able officer; always belovd by his Soldiers because he always shares with them in Fatigue and Danger. This has not been said of his immediate Predecessor. I hope the N England States will once more make a generous Exertion, and if they do I am deceivd if Burgoyns Prosperity does not soon prove his Ruin.

Our Intelligence from Europe is very flattering to us. The virtuous and sensible there universally wish well to our Cause. They say we are fighting for the Liberty and Happiness of Mankind. We are at least, contending for the Liberty & Happiness of our own

Country and Posterity. It is a glorious Contest. We shall succeed if we are virtuous. I am infinitely more apprehensive of the Contagion of Vice than the Power of all other Enemies. It is the Disgrace of human Nature that in most Countries the People are so de-bauchd, as to be utterly unable to defend or enjoy their Liberty.

Pay my respects to Co° Whipple. He promisd to write to me. I hope he will soon have Leisure to fulfill his promise. A Letter from you would oblige me much. Adieu.

TO MRS. ADAMS.

[MS., Samuel Adams Papers, Lenox Library.]

PHILADᴬ Augₜ 8 1777

MY DEAR BETSY

I have lately written to you by every Opportunity and am determined to omit none for the future, till I shall have the Pleasure of seeing you, which I intend some time in the Fall. We have heard Nothing of the Enemies Fleet since this Day Week. General Gates is gone to take the Command of the Northern Army in the Room of Schuyler . . . Gates has al-ways been belovd by his Soldiers & I hope will restore our Affairs there; for although they are in a Situation bad enough I do not think them desperate. He is empowerd to call on the N England Militia, who I hope will once more make a generous Effort. If they do, I am mistaken if Burgoyns present Success does not [prove his ruin.] A Change of Officers, I dare

say, will give new Spirits [to] the Men. But I forget
that I am writing [to] a female upon the Subject of
War. I know your whole Soul is engagd in the
great Cause. May Heaven prosper it! Adieu my
dear,

My Respects to my
Family & Friends.

TO ROGER SHERMAN.

[MS., Library of Massachusetts Historical Society ; a draft is in the Lenox
Library.]

PHILAD^A Augt 11. 1777

DEAR SIR/
    I duly receivd your obliging Letter of the 11th of
July. I thank you for the favor, and beg you to con
tinue to write to me as often as your Leisure will
admit of it. The Rumour you mention'd has since
appeard to be a serious Fact. We have lost Ti[c]on-
deroga, and as far as I can yet judge, shamefully : I
was going to add, vilainously ; for indeed I cannot
account for it, but upon the worst of Principles. The
whole appears to me to carry the evident Marks of
Design. But I hope & believe it will undergo the
strictest Scrutiny. The People at large ought not,
they will not be satisfied, until a thorough Inquiry is
made into the Causes of an Event in which their
Honor and Safety is so deeply interested. The only
Letter receivd by Congress from St Clair, you have
seen publishd under their Sanction. Schuyler has
written a Series of weak & contemptible *Things* in a

Stile of Despondence which alone, I think, is suffi
cient for the Removal of him from that Command ;
for if his Pen expresses the true Feelings of his
Heart, it cannot be expected that the bravest Vet
erans would fight under such a General, admitting
they had no Suspicion of Treachery. In a Letter
dated the 4th Instant at Still Water, he writes in a
Tone of perfect Despair. He seems to have no Con
fidence in his Troops, nor the States from whence
Reinforcements are to be drawn. A third Part of
his Continental Troops, he tells us, consists " of Boys
Negroes & aged Men not fit for the Field or any
other Service." " A very great Part of the Army
naked—without Blanketts—ill armed and very de
ficient in Accoutrements : without a Prospect of Reliefe." " Many, too Many of the Officers wo^d be a
Disgrace to the most contemptible Troops that ever
was collected." The Exertions of others of them of
a different Character " counteracted by the worthless."
" Genl Burgoyne is bending his Course this Way.
He will probably be here in Eight Days, and unless
we are well reinforced " (which he does not expect)
" as much farther as he pleases to go."- —Was ever
any poor General more mortified ! But he has by this
Time receivd his Quietus. Gates takes the Command
there, agreeably to what you tell me is the Wish of
the People ; and I trust our Affairs in that Quarter
will soon wear a more promising Aspect.

The Enemies Ships, upwards of 200 sail, after
having been out of Sight six Days, were discoverd on
Thursday last, off Sinapuxint 15 Leagues from the

Capes of Delaware Steering towards Chesapeake Bay.

Your Friends here are well, except Col° Williams, who has been confined a few days, but is growing better. I have a thousand things to say to you, but must defer it to other Opportunities, & conclude in Haste, with friendly Regards to your Family, very affectionately yours,

---

TO JAMES WARREN.

[MS., Samuel Adams Papers, Lenox Library.]

PHIL^A Augt 12 1777

My dear Sir

The inclosd is an attested Copy of Genl Schuylers Letter to the President of the Congress. It needs no Comment. How far the Massachusetts state de serves the Strictures therein made, you can tell. I send it to you for the Perusal of the Members of your Hon^bl House. If they have sent into the Army, Boys Negroes & Men too aged to be fit for any Ser vice they will lay their Hands upon their Mouths. If not, I hope some decent but keen Pen will vindicate them from that & other Aspersions. This, like all his other Letters, is written in such a desponding Stile, that it is no Wonder if Soldiers decline fight ing under him, though they may be under no Ap prehension of Treachery. But he has by this time receivd his Quietus, at least till he can give a good Account of his Conduct. Gates has gone to take the Command, and our Affairs in that Quarter, I dare say will soon wear another Face.

The Enemies Fleet have been again seen 200 sail off Sinipunxint 15 Leagues South of the Capes of Delaware. I think I have now a just Demand upon you for a Letter. I shall be disappointed if I do not receive one by the next Post. Adieu my Friend.

TO WILLIAM HEATH.[1]

[MS., Library of Massachusetts Historical Society; the text has recently been printed in *Collections* of Massachusetts Historical Society, 7th ser., vol. iv., p. 140.]

PHILAD^E Augt 13th 1777

My dear Sir,

The Surrender of Tyconderoga has deeply wounded our Cause. The Grounds of it must be thoroughly inquired into. The People at large have a Right to demand it. They do demand it and Congress have orderd an Inquiry to be made. This Matter must be conducted with Impartiality. The Troops orderd for the Defence of that Post were chiefly from New England. It is said there was a great Deficiency in Numbers—and General Schuyler tells us that a third Part of the Army there were Boys Negroes and aged Men not fit for the Field or indeed any other Service, that a great Part of them were naked, without Blanketts, ill armed & very deficient in Accoutre ments. Such is the Picture he draws. I wish to know as soon as possible, how many Men actually marchd for that place from N E, & particularly from Massachusetts Bay. What Quantity of Cloathing was sent for them & under whose Care; and how

---

[1] Major General in the continental army.

they were furnishd with Arms & Accoutrements.   In
short I am desirous of being informd by you as mi
nutely as possible, of the part taken by Muster Mas
ters Quartermasters Cloathiers & their Agents and all
other Persons employed in making and providing for
the Army in the Northern Department, as far as it
has properly fallen under your Notice & Direction.
Excuse me for giving you this Trouble & be assured
that I am very cordially,

your Friend,

TO MRS. ADAMS.

[MS., Samuel Adams Papers, Lenox Library.]

PHILAD^E Augt 19 1777

MY DEAR BETSY

I was favord with yours of the 2^d of this Month by
yesterdays Post.   I am much obligd to you for writing
to me so often, and hope you will not omit any future
opportunity.   [One] or another of my Boston Friends
write to me by every Post, [so] that I think I
should be informd if any extraordinary Accident
should happen to my Family, but I am never so
well satisfied as when I receive one from you.   I am
in continual Anxiety for your Safety, but am happy
in committing you to the Protection of all gracious
Heaven.   May He be your Refuge in every Time of
Distress!   I had before heard that the Enemies Fleet
was seen off Cape Ann.   We had an Account of it
[by] an Express from General Heath, who con
tradicted it the [same] Day by another Express.

Indeed I did not give Credit to . . . . News for the British Ships were seen off the Maryland Shore on the first of August, the very day on which they were reported to have been seen off Cape Ann. Having the Command of the Sea, they have it in their Power to give frequent Alarms to our Seaport Towns. We have not heard of them since, and it is the opinion of some that they are gone to South Carolina, but as it is altogether uncertain where they will go, it is prudent to be ready to receive them in every Place. It is a Question with me whether they have any Plan upon which they can depend themselves. I pray God that [their] Councils may be confounded.

I earnestly hope with you, my Dear, that our . . . . Life is not always to live at this Distance from each [other] but that we shall see the happy Day when Tyranny [shall] be subdued and the Lib erty of our Country shall be settled upon a permanent Foundation. If this is not to be accomplishd in our Day, May we hereafter meet our virtuous Friends in that blessd Region, where the wicked shall cease from troubling.

My Love to my dear Daughter, Sister Polly & the rest of my Family & Friends. Tell my Servants I thank them for their kind Remembrance of me. I am, my dear,   ever yours,

I have sent the Letter to
Capt M. inclosd in one
to D^r F.

TO HENRY BROMFIELD.

[*Publications* of Colonial Society of Massachusetts, vol. vi., pp. 78, 79.]

Philadᴬ Sept 2, 1777.

My dear Sir

I am requested by a Member of Congress from South Carolina for whom I have a particular Regard, to introduce his Friend Mʳ Henry Crouch to some of my Boston Friends. He is a Merchant of Charlestown and will set off on a Visit your Way tomorrow. I take the Liberty of addressing a Letter to you by him. Your friendly Notice of him will greatly oblige me.

I heartily congratulate you on the happy Change of our Affairs at the Northward. The Feelings of a Man of Burgoyne's Vanity must be sorely touched by this Disappointment.

Howe's Army remains near where they first landed and is supposed to be ten thousand fit for Duty. Washington's Army exceeds that Number, is in health & high Spirits, and the Militia have joynd in great Numbers, well equip'd and ambitious to emulate the Valor of their Eastern Brethren. Our light Troops are continually harrassing the Enemy. The Day before yesterday they attack'd their out Posts & drove them in, killing & wounding a small Number. By the last Account we had taken about seventy Prisoners without any Loss on our side. Our Affairs are at this Moment very serious and critical. We are contending for the Rights of our Country and Man kind—May the Confidence of America be placed in the God of Armies! Please to pay my due Respects to my old Friend Mr Phillips & his Family and be assured that I am very cordially

Yours,

TO MRS. ADAMS.

[MS., Samuel Adams Papers, Lenox Library.]

PHILAD^A Sept 17, 1777

MY DEAR BETSY

Your kind Letter of the 29th of August is now before me. You therein take a very proper Notice of the signal Success of our Affairs at the Northward. I hope my Countrymen are duly sensible of the obli gation they are under to Him from whose Hand, as you justly observe, our Victory came. We had a Letter from General Gates yesterday, from which we every hour expect another great Event from that Quarter. The two Armies this way had an obsti nate Engagement last Thursday. The Enemy have gaind a Patch of Ground but from all Accounts they have purchasd it as dearly as Bunkers Hill. Two or three more such Victories would totally ruin their Army. Matters seem to be drawing to a Crisis. The Enemy have had enough to do to dress their wounded and bury their dead. Howe still remains near the Field of Battle. Genl Washington retreated with his Army over the River Schuilkill through this city as far as . . . . and we are every day expecting an other battle. May Heaven favor our righteous

Cause and grant us compleat Victory.   Both the Armies are about 26 miles from this City.

I am pleasd to hear that Col⁰ Crafts invited Mʳ Thacher to preach a Sermon to his Regiment.   He discoverd the true Spirit of a New England officer. I dare say it was an animating Discourse.   Religion has been & I hope will continue to be the ornament of N. England.   While they place their Confidence in Go they will not fail to be an happy People.

I am exceedingly rejoycd to hear that Miss Hatch is in hopes of recovering her Health.

Remember me, my dear, to my Family and Friends. I am in good Health & Spirits and remain with the warmest Affection

Your,

TO ARTHUR LEE.

[R. H. Lee, *Life of Arthur Lee*, vol. ii., pp. 228, 229.]

PHILADELPHIA, Oct. 26th, 1777.

My DEAR SIR,—Your several letters, with their en closures, came to my hand.   And although I have not hitherto acknowledged to you the receipt of them, I assure you I have been and am still improving the intelligence you have given me to the best of my pow ers, for the advantage of this country.   From our for mer correspondence you have known my sentiments. I have not altered them in a single point, either with regard to the great cause we are engaged in, or to you, who have been an early, vigilant, and active supporter of it.   While you honour me with your confidential letters, I feel and will freely express to you my obligation. To have answered them severally, would have led me to subjects of great delicacy ; and the miscar riage of my letters might have proved detrimental to our important affairs. It was needless for me to run the risk for the sake of writing ; for I presume you have been made fully acquainted with the state of our public affairs by the committee. And as I have con stantly communicated to your brother R. H. the contents of your letters to me, it was sufficient on that score for him only to write, *for he thinks as I do.*

The Marquis de la Fayette, who does me the honour to take this letter, is this moment going ; which leaves me time only to add, that I am and will be your friend, because I know you love our country and mankind.

I beg you to write to me by every opportunity.

Adieu, my dear sir,

TO HORATIO GATES.

[MS., Samuel Adams Papers, Lenox Library.]

[1777]

SIR

I have had the Honor of laying before the Council Board of this State your Letter of the 19th of October, inclosing Copy of a Convention by which the British Lt Genl Burgoyne surrendered himself & his whole Army on the 17 of the same Month into your Hands. The repeated Instances of the Success of the Ameri can Army in the Northern Department reflect the highest Honor on yourself & the gallant officers & Soldiers under *your* Command. The Board congrat-

ulate you on this great Occasion ; and while the Merit
of your signal Services remains recorded in the faithful
Breasts of your Countrymen, the warmest Gratitude
is due to the God of Armies, who has vouchsafed
in so distinguished a Manner to favor the Cause of
America & of Mankind.

I have the Honor to be
in the Name of the Council Board,
Sir &c

RESOLUTION OF THE CONTINENTAL CONGRESS.

[NOVEMBER 1, 1777.]

[MS., Papers of the Continental Congress.   Reports of Committees.
No. 24, p. 431.]

Forasmuch as it is the indispensible Duty of all
Men, to adore the superintending Providence of Al
mighty God :—To acknowledge with Gratitude their
Obligation to Him for Benefits receivd, and to im
plore such further Blessings as they stand in Need
of :—And, it having pleased Him in his abundant
Mercy, not only to continue to us the innumerable
Bounties of His common Providence ; but also to
smile upon us in the Prosecution of a just and neces
sary War for the Defence and Establishment of our
unalienable Rights and Liberties. Particularly in
that He hath been pleased, in so great a Measure
to prosper the Means used for the Support of our
Troops, and to crown our Arms with most signal
Success.

It is therefore recommended to the Legislative or
Executive Powers of these United States, to set

apart Thursday the Eighteenth Day of December, next, for solemn Thanksgiving and Praise. That at one Time, and with one Voice, the good People may express the grateful Feelings of their Hearts, and consecrate themselves to the Service of their divine Benefactor. And, that together with their sincere Acknowledgments and Offerings, they may joyn the penitent Confession of their manifold Sins, whereby they had forfeited every Favor ; and their humble & earnest Supplication that it may please God through the Merits of Jesus Christ mercifully to forgive and blot them out of Remembrance. That it may please Him, graciously to afford His Blessing on the Gov ernments of these States respectively, and prosper the publick Council of the whole. To inspire our Commanders both by Land and Sea, & all under them with that Wisdom and Fortitude which may render them fit Instruments, under the Providence of Almighty God, to secure for these United States, the greatest of all human Blessings, *Independence* and *Peace*. That it may please Him, to prosper the Trade and Manufactures of the People, and the Labor of the Husbandman, that our Land may yet yield its Increase. To take Schools and Seminaries of Education, so necessary for cultivating the Prin ciples of true Liberty, Virtue, & Piety, under His nurturing Hand ; and to prosper the Means of Relig ion for the Promotion and Enlargement of that King dom which consisteth "in *Righteousness Peace and Joy in the Holy Ghost.*"

And it is further recommended, that servile Labor, and such Recreation as, though at other times inno-

cent, may be unbecoming the Purpose of this Ap
pointment, may be omitted on so solemn an occasion.

[TO JOHN ADAMS.]

[MS., Samuel Adams Papers, Lenox Library.]

BOSTON Decr 8 1777

MY DEAR SIR

I heartily thank you for your two favors of the 12th
& 18th of Novem^r, the former of which gave me a piece
of Intelligence which I thought proper to give the
Publick through the News paper.

Unluckily for me, on my Arrival here, I found the
General Assembly sitting, and consequently I am
plungd in publick Business sooner than I could wish
to have been. Among other things I have the Satisfaction of informing you of your Reelection as a
Member of Congress. Your old Colleagues are all
again chosen. I honestly told some of our Countrymen that I thought it incumbent on them thorowly
to acquaint themselves with the Character and Con
duct of those who represent them at the Distance of
four hundred Miles ; but I fear they are too unsuspect
ing. What do frequent Elections avail, without that
Spirit of Jealousy & Strict Inquiry which alone can
render such Elections any Security to the People?
But surely the more implicit the Confidence of the
Publick is, the more circumspect ought those to be,
who are entrusted with publick Affairs.

M^r —— came to this Town with great Pomp, and
was receivd by the military and naval Gentlemen, as

I am informd, with equal Ceremony. His Colleagues arrivd in the Dusk of the Evening and without Obser vation. He is the most happy who has the greatest Share of the Affections of his Fellow Citizens, with out which, the Ears of a sincere Patriot are ever deaf to the *Roaring of Cannon and the Charms of Musick.* I have not seen nor heard of any Dangers on the Road that should require Guards to protect one. It is pretty enough in the Eyes of some Men, to see the honest Country Folks gapeing & star ing at a Troop of Light Horse. But it is well if it is not some times attended with such Effects as one would not so much wish for, to excite the Con tempt of the Multitude, when the Fit of gazing is over, instead of the much longd for Hosannas.

I have not been long enough in Town to be able to give you a full Account of the Affairs of this State. The Assembly are interresting themselves as much as possible for the Supply of our Army—a small parcel of Cloathing is ready to be sent, which is intended for the Troops of this State. It is proposd that they shall purchase them at the first Cost and Charges, but not yet determined. The late Commissary Gen eral Col° Trumbull came to Town a few days ago. I have not yet seen him. Your Affairs in that Depart ment suffer for want of a Commissary of Issues in the Eastern District to receive the provisions in Col° Trumbull's Hands. The two Houses have requested him to deliver to Mr Colt who is also here, 12000 bushells of Salt belonging to the Continent in this State, and have authorizd a good Man to furnish him with Waggons, & to impress them if they cannot be

otherwise procured.   I fear if the Commissaries De
partment is not soon alterd, a dangerous Convulsion
will take place.   Pray attend to this.

I had the pleasure of waiting on your Lady yester
day.   She & her little Flock, or as I might better
express it, her great Flock of little Folks are in good
Health, as I suppose she will inform you in a Letter
which I hope to inclose in this.

Be so kind as to pay my warm Respects to M^r
Gerry and Dana General Roberdeau the two Col^o
Lees and many others, not forgetting the Connecticutt Gentlemen and all who may enquire after me.
Among these I flatter myself I shall not be forgotten
by the worthy Ladies in the Generals Family.   Pray
make my very respectful Compliments together
with those of my Spouse to them, and assure them
that I have a most grateful Remembrance of the
many Civilities I receivd from them.   May Heaven
bless them and the little Folks under their Charge.

THE COUNCIL OF MASSACHUSETTS TO HENRY LAURENS.[1]

[MS., Massachusetts Archives.]

STATE OF MASS. BAY COUNCIL CHAMBER Decr 1777

SIR

I have the Honor to acquaint you that your Letter
of the 28th of Novr inclosing Articles of Confederation
and diverse Resolutions of Congress have been laid
before the General Assembly of this State.   But the
Assembly having previously requested the Coun-

---

[1]President of the Continental Congress. .

cil to order an Adjournment, and many of the
Members having returnd to their respective Homes,
the Council have adjournd the Assembly to a short
Day when it is expected there will be a full Meeting ;
and the important matters above mentiond will be
taken under due consideration.

I am in the Name of the Council—

Sir

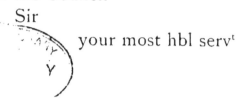   your most hbl serv[t]

END OF VOLUME III.

Made in the USA
Las Vegas, NV
13 November 2021